EVIDENCE FOR HOPE

Human Rights and Crimes against Humanity

ERIC D. WEITZ, *SERIES EDITOR*

A list of titles in this series appears at the back of the book.

Evidence for Hope

MAKING HUMAN RIGHTS WORK IN THE 21ST CENTURY

Kathryn Sikkink

PRINCETON UNIVERSITY PRESS
PRINCETON & OXFORD

Copyright © 2017 by Princeton University Press

Published by Princeton University Press,
41 William Street, Princeton, New Jersey 08540

In the United Kingdom: Princeton University Press,
6 Oxford Street, Woodstock, Oxfordshire OX20 1TR

press.princeton.edu

Cover design by Jennifer Heuer

All Rights Reserved

First paperback printing, 2019

Paper ISBN 978-0-691-19271-0

Cloth ISBN 978-0-691-17062-6
Library of Congress Control Number: 2017941736

British Library Cataloging-in-Publication Data is available

This book has been composed in Miller

Printed on acid-free paper. ∞

Printed in the United States of America

To the memory of Albert O. Hirschman and to my lifelong mentors/friends, all of whom modeled different ways to be a committed and rigorous scholar:

Raymond Duvall, Elizabeth Jelin,
Robert Keohane, John Ruggie, and David Weissbrodt

CONTENTS

PART I

Introduction
and
Overview

CHAPTER ONE

Introduction

ANGER, HOPE, AND THE BELIEF YOU
CAN MAKE A DIFFERENCE

DO HUMAN RIGHTS WORK? That is, have human rights law, institutions, and activism produced positive change in the world? And, if so, how do they work and under what conditions? How can we learn from past successes and failures to make human rights work better in the future?

These questions have provoked vigorous debates among scholars and practitioners. In particular, there is a recent increase of pessimism about the legitimacy and effectiveness of human rights law, institutions, and movements. This pessimism comes from governments and scholars, and, more importantly, from many within human rights movements.[1]

Some of the pessimists are, understandably, activists at the front lines of the most difficult human rights challenges today. Heba Morayef, an Egyptian human rights advocate, told me at a conference that she "has lost hope." In the last five years, she has moved from a "dream moment" during the Arab Spring uprising to sometimes being "too scared to tell people" what work she does. She has been working for many years on human rights in Egypt with Human Rights Watch and later as associate director of the Egyptian Initiative for Personal Rights in Cairo, a group at the forefront of advocacy for freedom of belief and expression, as well as freedom from gender-based discrimination.[2]

As a young woman, Morayef knew she wanted to work on some kind of political reform. She liked the human rights law class she took at the university because it "combined an activist agenda with something that was tangible." After graduating, she saw "there was a small group of human rights organizations in Cairo that were unafraid and so I found myself there." Morayef started her career as a human rights defender under the authoritarian government of Hosni Mubarak, mainly working to get prisoners out of jail or to stop torture. She said, "I wasn't scared as a human rights defender under Mubarak, but you didn't feel terribly effective in the big picture. . . . We didn't expect any big changes, so all you could do was to work on the little corners, but these little corners were at the heart of the police state, of course. So it was subversive per se."

Morayef's sense of effectiveness began to change after the Arab Spring uprising in Egypt in 2011:

> The only frustration I felt was that I couldn't clone myself because there was so much to do. We were being invited to government meetings by parliamentarians, who were saying, "Give me a law on police reform or tell me what I need to do to stop journalists from being locked up." . . . There wasn't enough time to be doing everything, and we were a really small community. We were very fashionable. That's silly, but what I mean is—young people were coming to us as volunteers, rich businessmen wanted to support our work, and there were lots of citizen initiatives popping up at the grassroots level in different cities around the country that had a rights discourse.[3]

Then came elections that brought to power the deeply conservative Muslim Brotherhood party under the leadership of Mohammed Morsi. But Morayef says that she still wasn't pessimistic about the big picture because "We felt we could fight them and we were not without power."

All of that changed after 2013 when a military coup against President Morsi brought the Egyptian Arab Spring to an end. The new president of the military-civilian regime cracked down, not only on Morsi's Muslim Brotherhood, but also on the media, NGOs, and anyone who voiced criticism. On August 14, 2013, one month after Morsi had been removed from office, police violently attacked camps of his supporters who were protesting the coup in two squares in

Cairo. "That day," Morayef said, "was really the loss of hope. Because, if you can kill 1,000 people in one day, there is not much you won't do. Up to that moment, things weren't looking good, but I didn't feel so hopeless about Egypt's future in my lifetime in the way I did after the massacre." The massacre ushered in a chilling atmosphere for human rights work. "We are now called foreign agents and spies. I had a couple of talk show hosts mentioning me as a spy, and got lots of Twitter hate," Morayef explained. After the coup in 2013, Morayef said, "it is the worst moment Egypt has seen in my lifetime, in terms of the number of people killed through the use of lethal force by the police, numbers of political prisoners, mass trials, mass death penalty sentences, and extrajudicial executions."

By 2017, Morayef had moved to Tunisia to head Amnesty International there, directing its research work on North Africa. When asked if she expected to see change in her lifetime, Morayef replied, "The thing about change is that change can be good or bad. I have no sense that I will see change in the good sense, meaning fewer human rights violations, more political space, less fear. . . . I don't believe that the darkness of this moment will last forever, but it will take a long time to rewind."[4]

Across the world in Mexico, in a very different political situation, long-time human rights activist and scholar Sergio Aguayo appeared to echo some of Morayef's words. Although Mexico has had a competitive electoral democracy since 2000, repression has worsened in recent years. When Aguayo first started working on human rights in Mexico in the early 1980s, he said, "there was hope. We were part of an adventure. . . . We were an alternative to revolutionary violence. We knew we perhaps were not going to be at the vanguard of change, but we nevertheless knew we were the protectors of the victims of political violence." But now, he said, "Hope has gone away." He pointed to the dramatic increase in disappearances and deaths at the hands of those in various levels of the government, organized crime groups, and companies. Mexico's government had created human rights institutions, but these institutions failed to protect human rights. New "pretender" human rights NGOs had sprung up, who "corrupted the concept of NGOs and human rights." Individuals in the human rights movement with contacts abroad were being attacked and discredited as antinational or corrupt. "And you don't even know if it is the government, a local boss, or organized crime groups that are attacking you," said Aguayo.[5]

Egypt and Mexico are not the only countries where human rights activists on the front lines are under attack. Many governments— China, Russia, Ethiopia, Israel, and India, to name a few—have sought to crack down on human rights NGOs by blocking their access to foreign funds or by forcing them to register as foreign agents.[6] From 1993 to 2012, thirty-nine countries enacted restrictive laws on the foreign funding of civil society organizations.[7] These restrictions were part of a larger plan whereby governments discredit and delegitimize human rights organizations, attacking them as antinational because they receive foreign funds or portraying their ideas as foreign. In some cases, such as India, the very same governments that welcome foreign capital view foreign support for human rights and justice issues from a nationalistic lens.[8] Efforts to weaken human rights activism suggest that governments perceive organizations that promote human rights to be effective. Why else devote considerable energy to regulating, silencing, and delegitimizing them? Still, evidence of their apparent effectiveness provides little comfort to targeted activists.

Meanwhile, in the United States, President Donald Trump campaigned on an open promise to "bring back a hell of a lot worse than waterboarding."[9] Immediately after taking office, the Trump administration issued an executive order banning people from seven Muslim countries from entering the United States. Leaders of repressive states were among the first foreign dignitaries to visit President Trump, while at the same time Secretary of State Rex Tillerson argued for more separation of US values and its foreign policies, acts widely interpreted as signaling a desertion of US human rights policies.[10] Given these political developments, it is no surprise that human rights activists in the United States feel discouraged and hopeless as well. I have never been so worried about how US politics could negatively influence human rights at home and around the world.

I write this book for people like Heba Morayef and Sergio Aguayo, people on the front lines of human rights work who say that they have lost hope. I also write for human rights advocates and the general public in the United States who share my concerns about the impact of US policy on human rights in this country and abroad. I write because I believe that the longer history of human rights has a more positive message that could help sustain them in the context of their current struggles.

Pessimism about human rights progress is widespread. Whether on the news, in the academy, or when one talks to a member of the general public, the standard view is that all types of human rights abuses in the world are getting worse. At the World Humanitarian Summit in May 2016, UN Secretary General Ban Ki-moon said, "We have reached a level of human suffering without parallel since the founding of the United Nations," seventy years ago.[11] He had in mind the global refugee crisis, but he was making a claim about human suffering in general. In light of the devastating news coming from Syria, South Sudan, Burundi, and other human rights hot spots around the world, it is not surprising that Ban Ki-moon was concerned.

Most people around the world would agree with Ban Ki-moon's conclusion about the state of human rights in the world. A 2015 survey of 18,000 people in seventeen countries asked, "All things considered, do you think the world is getting better or worse, or neither better nor worse?" In only two countries—China and Indonesia—did a majority of people think the world is either getting better or staying about the same. In the fifteen other countries, very low percentages of people thought the world was getting better—in the United States only six percent and in Germany only four percent.[12]

Some academics critique human rights law, institutions, and movements for this perceived lack of progress. A number of new books, blogs, and op-eds bear titles like *The Endtimes of Human Rights*, *The Twilight of Human Rights Law*, or "Welcome to the Post-Human Rights World."[13] According to Eric Posner, author of *The Twilight of Human Rights Law*, "Countries solemnly intone their commitment to human rights, and they ratify endless international treaties and conventions designed to signal that commitment. At the same time, there has been no marked decrease in human rights violations."[14] Elsewhere he writes, "The law doesn't do much; we should face that fact and move on."[15] Posner is a realist legal scholar with little sympathy for human rights law; still, scholars who are more invested in human rights also express negative opinions.[16]

When the Human Rights section of the International Studies Association was planning for its annual meeting in 2016, the chair proposed an all-day session around the theme of "What is wrong with Human Rights?" The email invitation said, "Together we ask: 'what's wrong with rights?' and what can we learn from these encounters?"[17] The International Studies Association is the major professional association for International Relations scholars and its Human Rights section draws those with a special dedication to this topic; if the most committed academics want us only to focus on "What is wrong with Human Rights," what do the real critics say?

It is entirely appropriate that human rights should be under constant review and debate. The concept of human rights has become one of the dominant moral and political discourses in the world today.[18] It is one of the ways that we discuss our values and our beliefs. As an increasingly influential set of norms, laws, and institutions as well as a powerful global movement, human rights should be subject to inquiry and critique.[19] Genuine human rights crises around the world, such as those in Syria or the attacks by ISIS on the Yazidi people in Iraq, demand our attention and concern. The purpose of this book is not to deflect criticism or to diminish concern with human rights crises, but to clarify some of the terms of the debate, the types of comparisons being used, and the kinds of evidence that would be more or less persuasive in supporting and evaluating claims.

I will address two main types of criticism and pessimism involving the *legitimacy* and the *effectiveness* of human rights law, institutions, and movements. By legitimacy, I mean a generalized perception that a movement or institution is desirable, appropriate, and authentic.[20] Those who critique human rights institutions believe they are less desirable, appropriate, or authentic than others they can imagine. Effectiveness, on the other hand, involves whether human rights work produces positive change in the world. Legitimacy and effectiveness are linked; for example, the effectiveness of an institution can affect whether it is seen as desirable.

Four main types of actors with quite different positions and rationales articulate these critiques. The first are the governments with poor human rights records that criticize human rights because they don't want to bind their own hands or be held accountable for human rights violations. The second are members of the general public who fear that the world is on fire and that human rights isn't doing enough to help, an opinion that is at times also held by policymakers. The third includes various academics from different disciplines and viewpoints, ranging from realists to critical theorists. The fourth includes human rights activists, especially from the Global South, who worry about lack of progress and lack of consultation in the human rights world. They resent the high-handedness of some large human rights NGOs based in the Global North and the indifference and privilege of some staff in human rights institutions. Each of the four critiques is separate in theory, but sometimes they are blurred together in practice. For example, repressive governments may find it useful to deflect criticism of their own human rights practices by echoing academic criticisms saying that human rights concerns originated in the Global North and are imposed upon the Global South as a form of cultural or political imperialism. Venezuelan president Nicolás Maduro claimed at the UN in 2015 that Venezuela faced "imperialist attacks" and ongoing harassment through the "manipulation of human rights by the West."[21] As we shall see in chapters 3 and 4, however, Venezuela has advocated historically for the international protection and promotion of human rights and democracy.

If I am more hopeful than others, it may be because I have seen dramatic improvements in some human rights in my lifetime, such as greater equality and opportunities for women and sexual minorities. When she was young, my mother, Arlene Sikkink, was told that if she wanted to work, there were three careers she could aspire to: nurse, secretary, or teacher. Because she liked science, she chose to be a nurse. My mother then brought up my two sisters and me to believe that we could be whatever we wanted to be. However, when I got to graduate school in political science at Columbia University in 1981, I discovered that there were no full-time women professors in my department. Given this context, I was not certain that I could become a professional political scientist, much less a tenured one.[22] While women still have a way to go in my profession, I have seen impressive progress in my lifetime, and I believe that I owe a debt to the feminist movement and its demands for women's rights and equality, for opening space for women in academia. My situation is not unique; as we shall see in chapter 6, women throughout the world have seen significant progress in levels of education, including university education, and increasing numbers of women around the world are taking academic jobs, although there is variation among countries.[23]

Change is happening not only in the United States and Western Europe. When I lived in Uruguay in the late 1970s, friends I now know are gay or lesbian could not tell their closest friends or family members about their sexual identity. In 2013, the Uruguayan Congress legalized same-sex marriage, becoming the second country in Latin America and the thirteenth country in the world to recognize marriage equality.[24] Although Uruguay is in the vanguard, changes there do reflect broader global trends, where LGBT rights have shifted from a completely taboo topic to a matter of increasing acceptance and debate.

Sometimes we hear about human rights crises, but not about progress. We learn about the failure of the Arab Spring in Egypt or Syria, but not about a more successful outcome in Tunisia, which in 2016 started the public hearings in its Truth and Dignity Commission.[25] We learn about the breakdown of democracy in Burundi, but not about the struggle for democracy in Gambia, where people voted in late 2016 to oust a strongman who had been president for twenty-two years. Where we find human rights progress, as in these cases, we see that it has been the result of countless struggles over decades.

Let me distinguish my arguments from other recent contributions to the debate over global pessimism and optimism. Some chalk up progress to the global spread of "the march of reason, triggered in the West by the Enlightenment."[26] Others make a related but contrary claim: since human rights came only from the United States and Western Europe, and these regions are on the decline, it is now the "endtimes" of human rights.[27] My approach focuses instead on the impact of a long series of human rights struggles, often led by oppressed people, inspired by human rights ideas, and targeting powerful institutions and practices, including colonialism and deep exclusion and repression. Governments in the United States and Europe sometimes supported these struggles and sometimes blocked or hindered them, but governments were rarely the main protagonists. These human rights struggles did not occur only in what we now call the Global North, the powerful countries of Western Europe and North America. Latin American jurists, diplomats, and activists were ardent advocates for the international protection of human rights in the 1940s, when they urged the Great Powers to include human rights language in the UN Charter. Post-colonial states in Africa and elsewhere led the way to a stronger international human rights regime in the 1960s, when they mobilized against apartheid and racial discrimination and built the first strong international human rights institutions.[28] In short, all of human rights history is a "contentious" history.[29]

Human rights struggles led to concrete laws and institutions that have altered the fabric of the world we live in. Today, human rights norms have become deeply institutionalized in international and domestic law and institutions, including institutions in the developing world, making possible their continuity despite the realignment of global power relations. Understanding the diverse origins and deep institutionalization of human rights lets us envision a different future for human rights law and practice from what pessimistic literature predicts.

I will also argue that some of those critiquing human rights are vague about their comparisons and careless in their use of history and evidence. To engage in a more productive debate, the nature of the critique, definitions of terms, and methods being used all need to be clarified. Employing primarily empirical comparisons with careful use of human rights data can generate persuasive evidence for the effectiveness of some human rights law and activism. When we examine the human rights situation carefully in this manner, we find that blanket statements—like Ban Ki-moon's that there is more suffering in the world today than at any point since the founding of the UN or Eric Posner's that there have been no improvements in human rights—are as inaccurate as they are unhelpful. The human rights situation in the world is characterized by some areas of retrogression and worsening, such as the situations in Syria, Egypt, Mexico, and the United States, but also by other areas of increasing awareness and improvements, such as current developments in gender equality, the rights of sexual minorities, and the rights of people with disabilities. Although human rights change takes a long time and its progress ebbs and flows, we do not see wholesale abandonment of human rights ideas or loss of confidence in the institutions designed to advance and protect these rights.

Unless scholars and activists are able to distinguish areas of improvement from areas of worsening, we cannot take the next step to evaluate what works. We need to ask not only, "What is wrong with human rights?" but also, "What is right with human rights?" The former South African judge and former UN High Commissioner for Human Rights, Navi Pillay, said:

> It is very interesting for academics to take a challenging view as long as they don't knock everything down. . . . Every new system that is started gets its fair share of criticism. I welcome criticism, but I would also welcome academics telling us then what to do, what is missing, rather than taking up the view that everything is useless, everything falls into a black hole, don't even try to change the world.[30]

In order for academics to give these kinds of answers to people like Navi Pillay, we must make a much more careful and in-depth examination of what has been effective and ineffective in promoting human rights.

The Legitimacy of Human Rights Law, Institutions, and Movements

One of the main ways that governments and scholars attack the legitimacy of human rights law, institutions, and movements is to portray them as foreign or antinational. As we saw in the case of Heba Morayef, repressive governments portray human rights activists as motivated by foreign ideas, perhaps even as foreign agents. But repressive governments are not the only ones to call into question the legitimacy of human rights ideas and human rights activism. A somewhat different critique comes from within academia.[31] Stephen Hopgood, for example, says that the human rights movement "risks rendering itself politically irrelevant outside Geneva, London, New York, and a few other middle-class enclaves globally. Here the usefulness of human rights as ethical ideas and practical politics reaches its end."[32] Hopgood's prediction for the future of human rights is based on a particular understanding of the history of human rights. He says, "It is only as a by-product of American power and money that human rights have been globalized."[33]

These issues are debated seriously within human rights movements. In both the Global North and the Global South there are divided opinions on the origins and the legitimacy of human rights. Paulo Sérgio Pinheiro, a long-time Brazilian human rights advocate who has worked at the highest levels of the UN human rights institutions, claims, "Nobody spouts that nonsense anymore about human rights being imposed by the imperialism of the North."[34] Fellow Brazilian Raquel Rolnik, however, argues that human rights are locked into liberal thought and into "the model of private property in the capitalist system."[35]

In order to address these debates about legitimacy, I will draw on a wide variety of sources, from historical archives and new historical research to survey data. I will argue that excellent recent historical research and other empirical sources like surveys show that human rights law has origins in the Global South as well as in the Global North and that many people around the world have high levels of trust in human rights organizations. Countries in the Global South, especially in Latin America and Africa, have created regional institutions to protect and promote human rights while also enforcing these rights through national court decisions. The Inter-American Commission on Human Rights and the Inter-American Court of Human Rights have produced some of the most far-reaching decisions on human rights issues, including indigenous rights. National courts in Brazil, South Africa, and India have made innovative decisions about enforcing difficult economic rights such as the right to water, food, health, and shelter. These more diverse origins as well as the broad institutionalization of human rights in the Global South imply that human rights has greater legitimacy than the critics suggest.

The Effectiveness of Human Rights Law, Institutions, and Movements

My more hopeful assessment is based not on wishful thinking, but on an effort to understand more comprehensively the strengths and weaknesses of human rights data. When we go carefully, issue by issue, and consider the quality of the data and trends over time, as I do in chapter 5, we see that there are some human rights issues that have experienced worsening—such as the absolute number of refugees and migrants displaced by war, or economic inequality among individuals. But there are many other instances where the situation is improving, including a decline in genocide and politicide in the world, the declining number of battle deaths as well as the number of civilians killed in war, a declining use of the death penalty, and dramatic improvements in equality for women.

The empirical research I discuss is not unified or simple. In order to understand it, we will need to delve into some endemic problems with human rights documentation and data.[36] Basically, we need to understand the tangled debate over what kinds of yardsticks to use when measuring effectiveness as well as the tension between ideal and empirical reasoning. Reliable information about human rights violations has always been difficult to secure and will continue to be so in the future. I will also summarize recent work from a variety of scholars on this issue of human rights effectiveness over time. This research led me to have a "bias for hope" for human rights progress based not on simple optimism, but on reasoned evaluation of evidence.[37]

But if human rights law, institutions, and movements have been effective, why do so many people believe that human rights violations in the world are getting worse rather than better? Why do many people today think that there is more torture, rape, and repression in the world than ever before? The short answer is that we think the world is worse off because we care more and know more about human rights than ever before. The human rights movement has succeeded in drawing attention to an increasingly wide range of rights violations around the world. Inadvertently, as the reports accumulate and are taken up by the media, they may also convince people that human rights movements are not making any progress at curbing such violations.

Ethics and Human Rights

Later in the book I will call upon other authors to be more transparent about their ethical stance, so I first need to be clear about my own. It is difficult for social scientists to talk about ethics; we fear that if we take an explicit ethical stance on an issue, it calls into question our objectivity and thus undermines the credibility of our research.[38] When I went to graduate school in 1981, human rights policy and activism were not considered serious topics for scholarly social science research. They were topics for lawyers and for activists, but not for political scientists, who were supposed to talk about how the world really is, not how it should be. When I started researching human rights in the early 1990s, I thought the choice of topic alone was such a normative signal that I needed to spend the rest of my time demonstrating that I was being rigorous in my theory and method.[39]

I have been influenced by the ideas of the late economist and philosopher Albert Hirschman and I will refer to his arguments throughout this book. Hirschman called for a different kind of social science:

> ... a moral-social science where moral considerations are not repressed or kept apart, but are systematically commingled with analytic argument ... where the transition from preaching to proving and back again is performed frequently and with ease; and where moral considerations need no longer be smuggled in surreptitiously, nor expressed unconsciously, but are displayed openly and disarmingly.[40]

I believe that human rights, as defined in current human rights law, provides a morally defensible starting place for talking about progressive change in the world. There is nothing original about this position. Philosophers like Amartya Sen, Martha Nussbaum, Mathias Risse, John Tasioulas, and Charles Beitz have used the fulfillment of rights as a basis for normative theorizing.[41] Like the practical philosophers of human rights, I start with existing human rights principles embodied in international human rights law, especially the International Covenant on Civil and Political Rights (ICCPR) and the International Covenant on Economic, Social and Cultural Rights (ICESCR).[42]

International human rights law now represents an "overlapping international political consensus."[43] To say there is an overlapping consensus does not mean there is no conflict. There are still lots of disagreements about human rights in the world, but there is also considerable consensus and support. Starting with existing international norms drafted through exhaustive debate and consultation among many states has the virtue of being less ethnocentric than having the analyst substitute her own normative criteria. Examined closely, the process of drafting and implementing human rights law also provides a model for deliberative, nonviolent, and noncoercive processes of global governance and change that could be useful for other issue areas. But exactly because it is deliberative and noncoercive, human rights change has been and will be slow.

My concern with the effectiveness of human rights in the second half of this book may make me appear to be a consequentialist—that is, someone who judges the morality of an action solely by its consequences. I am not a consequentialist; I believe in the intrinsic value of human rights norms, regardless of the consequences. But I also want to ask about effects or consequences of human rights. The topic of consequences is too important to be left solely to the consequentialists. Discerning and evaluating consequences is an inherently comparative and empirical enterprise, and thus empirically grounded scholars can make an important contribution.[44]

I will also argue that human rights law does not mention, and certainly does not require, the use of military means to promote human rights. Social science suggests that military intervention is as likely to worsen human rights as to protect them.[45] The UN Charter (not human rights law per se) permits the Security Council to use military means to address issues of international peace and security. I do not oppose Security Council action to protect human rights, but my ethical commitments are to a deliberative, nonviolent, and noncoercive approach to human rights that characterizes much of the history of human rights law and institutions. When states are called upon or pressured to comply with human rights treaties they have helped draft and have consented to through legal ratification, it does not constitute coercion; rather, it holds states accountable to their own commitments.

Overview of the Book

This book is more like an à la carte menu from which to choose than it is a full course meal that you have to eat your way through from first course to last. As such, I encourage readers to delve into the chapters that most interest them and to feel free to jump around if they so desire. After the introduction (chapters 1 and 2), the second part of the book (chapters 3 and 4) addresses questions about the legitimacy of human rights and the processes of human rights change based on historical research. Part III (chapters 5 and 6) addresses questions about the effectiveness of human rights, and deals more with data and social science. So, if you are interested mainly in the issue of the effectiveness of human rights law, institutions, and movements, you could skip to chapter 5, where I address the effectiveness issue most directly. If your interest was piqued by the subtitle promising suggestions for making human rights work in the twenty-first century, you may wish to move directly to chapters 6 and 7, which provide evidence-based policy recommendations for human rights grounded in social science literature, as well as summarize the main conclusions of the book.

In chapter 2, immediately following this introduction, I outline a number of my disagreements with academic human rights critics and pessimists about both effectiveness and legitimacy. This is the most abstract chapter in the book and may bore a more policy-oriented audience; such readers should feel free to skip the chapter and move ahead. In chapter 2, I tackle one of the biggest sources of disagreements around human rights effectiveness—methods of measurement. How can we better explain change, if we cannot first agree on whether change has occurred? Both scholars and practitioners tend to use two different types of comparisons to conceptualize effectiveness: comparison to the ideal and empirical comparisons.[46] Depending on the choice of metric, one can arrive at very different conclusions about legitimacy, effectiveness, or the progress of human rights. If I compare the International Criminal Court (ICC), for example, to my ideal of justice, I reach a different evaluation than if I compare the world today, with an ICC, to the world before 1998, when such a court did not exist. Both evaluations are valid and can lead to useful conclusions, but scholars need to be more explicit about their chosen metrics to help us interpret their claims. Because of the problems with comparisons to the ideal, I prefer systematic comparative empirical research as a basis for my evaluation of progress.

Histories of human rights have much to tell us about what led to change and why. In chapter 3, I provide a detailed discussion of the early history of the international protection of human rights in the 1940s, which reveals how human rights ideas and law came from far more diverse sources than the powerful countries in the Global North. Though I focus especially on protagonism from Latin America, I also point to early protagonists from other regions, such as diplomats from India. I argue that these more diverse origins mean that human rights are more legitimate than critics claim.

Chapter 4 takes up the long, painful, and contingent struggle for human rights during the Cold War. It reminds us that human rights change is never easy or fast. This history can perhaps provide some solace for activists like Heba Morayef, to whom change seems elusive. The story of human rights during the Cold War also reveals flaws in both domestic and international policy. During the Cold War, both the revolutionary left and the anticommunist right devalued liberal democracy and human rights.[47] The US government, rather than leading human rights efforts, supported coups against elected leftists and embraced anticommunist authoritarian regimes.

In chapter 5, I turn to the issue of effectiveness, beginning the chapter with a battery of charts and tables exploring trends on different human rights issues over time. Later in the chapter I try to explain why people feel pessimistic about human rights, in spite of the ample evidence of progress, by exploring a series of cognitive heuristics and biases that may contribute to negativism. Some characteristics of the human rights movement itself have exacerbated the sense of negativity. Information politics, for example, is the main tactic of the human rights movement—the gathering and distribution of politically usable information. Activists grab attention with dramatic denunciation of severe abuses. In order to sustain attention, funding, and support, they need to heighten awareness of terrible things happening in the world. Activists sometimes fear that if they stress progress or success, they will breed complacency or indifference to ongoing abuses. But this tendency toward negativity may also create the impression that the human rights movement has not been effective.

In chapter 6, I provide policy recommendations for making human rights work in the future, grounded in a review of social science research. Not only has this research started to reveal that human rights activism and law have often been effective, but it has also identified some of the conditions under which human rights can function most effectively. An ability to identify failure and pinpoint its causes is essential to improving future human rights policy. But it is equally important to have the ability to identify what policies and practices have contributed to improvement, as well as how those experiences can be expanded. I suggest six policy tools that have been and should be used to address human rights violations: 1) diminish war and seek nonviolent solutions to conflict; 2) promote democracy and enhance the quality of existing democracies; 3) guard against dehumanizing and exclusionary ideologies and practices, whether about race, religion, gender, class, or any other status; 4) encourage states to ratify existing human rights treaties, and to work to enforce human rights law and norms through nonviolent means; 5) end impunity by supporting domestic and international accountability that can deter future crimes; and 6) support, expand, and protect domestic and transnational mobilization on behalf of human rights. Some states, international organizations, and human rights organizations are already working to advance some of these policy options, such as ending impunity and enforcing human rights law. Other parts of this policy agenda are receiving less attention, such as the need to diminish war and to guard against dehumanizing and exclusionary ideologies.

Finally, in chapter 7, I conclude by summarizing the main arguments and policy implications of the book.

Conclusions

This book maps out a pragmatic and hopeful response to the pessimism and critiques concerning the legitimacy and effectiveness of human rights, grounded in historical and social science research and guided by a philosophy that Hirschman called "possibilism."[48] The stakes in this human rights debate are high. Where it has occurred, human rights progress has been the result of activism and struggle, and such progress is not at all inevitable, but rather contingent on continued commitment and effort. This is what Albert Hirschman meant by possibilism, an idea that grew out of his work in development economics in the 1960s. He proposed possibilism as an alternative to the tendency of governing elites to proclaim that all previous efforts had been complete failures. He called upon policymakers to highlight instead "those measures which might have been conducive to development and progress."[49] Hirschman wanted to draw attention to what was possible rather than what was probable, and to stress the importance of "widening the limits of what could be perceived as possible."[50] This is exactly what the human rights movement has done, repeatedly. By widening the limits of the possible, the human rights movement has sometimes changed what is probable. I have been inspired by Hirschman and, in this book, I aim to tell not a triumphalist history but a possibilist one.

Hirschman argued that processes of change are gradual, disorderly, and a result of a unique constellation of disparate events, including the activism of individuals he called "reformmongers" and whom others have called "norm entrepreneurs." In the history of human rights, norm entrepreneurs both within the state and outside of it have moved ahead human rights agendas. Without the belief and the untiring activity of such reformmongers, change won't occur. If people around the world come to believe that their efforts on behalf of human rights are suspect or even counterproductive and retreat to inactivity, human rights progress could indeed stall or move backward. Hope sustains human rights work. But while hope is necessary, it is certainly not sufficient. Reasoned, well-informed, patient hope is the goal. My purpose is not to cheerlead for the human rights movement, but rather to provide it with the best advice about what works and what doesn't and to explain how and why change takes so long. This book is about what has happened in the past and what is possible in the future, with continued commitment, struggle, and fortuitous circumstances.

Hirschman would be the first to warn us against overconfidence in the "solvability" of all problems and in the ability of certain paradigms to provide an easy or simple solution.[51] Hirschman was particularly attentive to the counterintuitive and to unintended consequences, both positive and negative. But he would also warn us against what he called "fracasomania," or a "failure complex."[52] He found that perceived failure was often the result of idealism, especially of the radical left, which pointed to the difference between "real" and apparent change. Modern human rights writers seem at times to have a failure complex when comparing results to their (often implicit) ideals of "real" change. For these reasons, I try to embrace Hirschman's idea of *A Bias for Hope,* where hope is not wishful thinking, but instead is founded on data and research.

I aim to show how broader historical work and more careful and explicit conceptual and methodological assumptions can lead to a new assessment about the positive impact of human rights law and activism, what I call evidence for hope. My husband Douglas Johnson, a longtime human rights organizer and the current head of the Carr Center for Human Rights Policy at the Harvard Kennedy School, likes to quote Saul Alinsky about the dynamics for creating social change. Alinsky said that you need to have anger, hope, and the belief that you can make a difference. Some see anger as the primordial emotion of justice. But although anger stimulates action, it also burns out quickly and can lead to apathy. Anger is not sufficient to maintain motivation over time; you also need to have hope and to believe that you can make a difference. In order to know that you can make a difference, you need to have and celebrate small victories that will sustain the work for larger ones.[53] It is this delicate balance of anger, hope, and belief that you can make a difference that is at play here. I would suggest that it is the gap between our ideals and our current practice that gives us the anger we need to fight for change, but it is our knowledge of how far we have come that gives us hope. Finally, it is not just knowing that we *can* make a difference but also knowing more specifically *how* we have made a difference that gives us the energy to keep working. By focusing exclusively on the gap between our ideals and our practice, organizers and scholars may have tipped the balance toward pessimism and despair. The challenge we face now is to use our research to sustain hope and action without complacency or indifference.

Response to the Critics

HOW TO EVALUATE THE LEGITIMACY AND
EFFECTIVENESS OF HUMAN RIGHTS

A RESEARCHER WITH Amnesty International (AI) Netherlands, Doutje Lettinga's job involves discerning human rights trends around the world. When asked how she first got interested in this type of work, she said she "always knew" that she wanted to do human rights work. Though she grew up in "a very Western European context," from an early age she became interested in human rights issues in the non-Western world, such as the history of slavery and of colonial wars, because so little attention was paid to it in her formal education. Despite her long-standing interest in and promotion of human rights, Lettinga gets discouraged because "there is this whole impressive machinery of human rights, but it is still not effective enough because human rights atrocities are still going on."[1]

Together with her colleague Lars van Troost, Lettinga has produced a bridge between the world of human rights activism and the world of academic human rights. In the last three years, van Troost and Lettinga have organized and edited two volumes for AI Netherlands which brought together human rights activists and some of the primary academic critics of human rights. The first volume, entitled *Debating the Endtimes of Human Rights*, leads with an essay by Stephen Hopgood called "The Endtime of Human Rights," based on his book by the same name.[2] Samuel Moyn's essay, "Human Rights in the Age of Inequality," begins the second volume, *Can*

Human Rights Bring Social Justice?: Twelve Essays.[3] In producing these volumes, AI and the collaborators involved show how closely some parts of the human rights movement follow and are affected by academic debates. AI took the critiques very seriously and wanted to provide a platform to share and debate them.

Not at all the caricature of the smug human rights activist, Lettinga is reflective, concerned with the legitimacy and effectiveness of her work, and willing to engage in self-criticism. In the introduction to the *Social Justice* volume, Lettinga and van Troost encourage an honest evaluation of human rights as a tool and as a concept.

> The Occupy movement, the Greek and Spanish Indignados—what did human rights have to offer to their resistance to austerity measures in times of economic stagnation? The Arab uprisings—what did human rights have to offer those calling for "bread, freedom, social justice, and dignity," apart from defending the public space for peaceful protest and political dissent? A lot, according to some; almost nothing, according to others.[4]

In a blog post connected to her book, Lettinga wrote:

> ... in their legalized form, human rights are modest in their goals, seeking to ensure minimum essential levels of protection for the most marginalized—they do not really seek a fundamental redistribution of wealth, resources and power. Samuel Moyn therefore calls human rights "a powerless companion in the age of neoliberalism." ... Moyn questions their effectiveness to deliver substantive socio-economic equality. Perhaps Moyn is right too.[5]

When I read Lettinga and van Troost, or indeed when I recall any of the human rights activists I have interviewed for this book—people like Heba Morayef, Sergio Aguayo, Lucia Nader, César Rodríguez-Garavito, and Navi Pillay—I think about how different they are from the type of human rights professionals David Kennedy describes in his essay, "The International Human Rights Regime: Still Part of the Problem." Kennedy faults human rights for idolatry, which "rules in the name of unambiguous virtue." He says human rights "overestimates the singularity of its vision and refuses to place the costs of its rulership centre-stage where they can be assessed and either refuted or taken into account."[6]

Lettinga and van Troost place the possible costs of human rights center-stage to be assessed and taken into account. Indeed, I wonder if they are too willing to question and underestimate themselves and their work in their attempts to take into account all the criticisms of their enterprise. Lettinga and van Troost are not idolatrous, as Kennedy would call them; rather, they are idealists and part of being an idealist is to hold one's own practice up to the highest ideals.

In their contribution to the volume on social justice, Lettinga and van Troost approvingly cite a 2013 speech by Patrick Corrigan of AI United Kingdom:

> This is our message—we want a world without war, without repression, without environmental degradation. We want a world without poverty, without hunger, without the inequality which divides us. The G8 leaders say they want free trade. We say we want fair trade and free speech. The G8 leaders say they want globalisation of business. We say we want to globalise peace and globalise justice. They say they want to tinker with the tax havens. We say we want a world where no longer will 800 million people go to bed hungry every night and where [no longer] every 5 seconds a child dies from extreme poverty.[7]

This speech captures the power and eloquence of some human rights activism, as well as the dilemma faced by a movement devoted to such high ideals that it finds it hard to recognize improvement until 800 million people no longer go to bed hungry.

In this book I address critiques from four different groups: repressive governments, the general public, human rights activists, and academics. This chapter focuses on the academic critics of human rights. It does so in part for reasons Lettinga and van Troost made clear—the critics' voices are heard loud and clear in human rights movements, affecting activists' sense of self-worth and the directions for future work.

Before I begin my discussion of the critiques offered against human rights movements and policies, I want to be clear that the big issues in the human rights world are not quibbles among human rights scholars, but rather the efforts that powerful governments, including the current US government, are making to roll back the human rights agenda. In the remaining chapters of this book, I focus on the governments that have made the lives of human rights workers in their countries impossible, on what countries have done to violate human rights, and on what activists and governments can do to best promote human rights. Readers who want to proceed immediately to those larger issues are welcome to skip this chapter, which focuses on academic debates.

The Prevalence of Critique

Human rights scholarship has become a large interdisciplinary field, with many debates both among human rights scholars and between scholars and practitioners. Many of these debates are about the legitimacy and effectiveness of human rights laws, institutions, and movements. As a survey of the literature on the human rights crisis makes clear, critiques vary and come from such diverse sources as authoritarian governments, post-colonial and post-modern scholars, conservative legal scholars and think tanks, as well as from within the human rights movement itself. In organizing and unpacking this critique, I am indebted to the survey of the literature organized by César Rodríguez-Garavito, from the human rights organization Dejusticia, and his Human Rights Lab at the University of los Andes in Bogotá, Colombia, although I have organized my categories and responses somewhat differently.[8] Among other things, the Human Rights Lab report confirmed the impression that motivated this book—there is no shortage of critiques of human rights; we are literally awash in them.

I have a number of disagreements with the academic critics of human rights that I will address in this chapter, and for which I will provide more support in the remaining chapters of the book. In particular, I will argue that human rights ideas and institutions have far more diverse origins than critics claim. The human rights movement, with its associated activists, ideals, and goals, is not primarily a product of the Global North. Wide historical research, including but not limited to my own research on Latin America, has made it clear that voices and actors from the Global South were deeply involved in demanding the international protection of human rights and in building the institutions that started to make enforcement of these rights possible. Research that I will review in chapters 3 and 4 documents the emergence of discourses and institutions for the international protection of human rights in the 1940s, not the 1970s as Samuel Moyn has argued. Tracing the origins of human rights to the 1940s is significant in showing the broader origins of the human rights movement as well as its longer institutionalization. In the last sixty years, human rights advocates have embedded their ideas in laws and institutions, often working together effectively with these institutions. As a result of its diverse origins and lengthier institutionalization, the human rights movement and its associated institutions are not experiencing an endtimes, twilight, or death as various critics have claimed. The struggles for human rights are as essential today as they have been in the past.

Finally, I will demonstrate that human rights law, institutions, and movements have been far more effective than they are often given credit for. The differences in my evaluations of effectiveness with respect to those of critics have to do with a variety of factors, discussed more at length in chapter 5. The most important aspect of my disagreements with critics has to do with issues of comparison, especially with what I call "comparison to the ideal," which I discuss in this chapter.

Legitimacy and Human Rights

Martha Finnemore reminds us that legitimacy is, "by its nature, a social and relational concept." In other words, even powerful actors cannot create legitimacy by themselves; it can only be given by others, including by peers or "by those upon whom power is exercised."[9] Another author, Juan Linz, says legitimacy "is the belief that, in spite of shortcomings and failures, the existing political institutions are better than others that could be established, and that they therefore can demand obedience."[10]

Understanding legitimacy in this way helps us talk about human rights laws and institutions. Linz reminds us that, while legitimacy is a matter of comparison, it is not necessarily comparison to the ideal. We may have disagreements with human rights institutions like the ICC, for example, and feel that they have shortcomings and failures, but we still believe that such institutions should be obeyed.

For Linz, an institution is not illegitimate just because we can imagine a preferable ideal, but rather it gains its legitimacy, at least in part, because we see it as better than other institutions that could, in reality, be established. Linz goes on to say that intellectuals play a major role in "formulating, elaborating, and transmitting" ideas about legitimacy.[11] I agree with Linz about the influence of intellectuals on perceptions of the legitimacy of human rights law and institutions and, for that reason, I am particularly attentive to their perspectives in this volume.

This stress on legitimacy as beliefs about institutions and whether they deserve obedience, however, is less relevant for human rights *movements* since we don't expect the movements themselves to be obeyed. A better definition of legitimacy as regards movements and nongovernmental *organizations* (NGOs) is that it involves generalized perceptions that the actions of an entity are desirable or appropriate.[12] Thus legitimacy becomes a kind of comparison people make, with the key question being—legitimate compared to what? Just as with effectiveness, organizations can be more or less legitimate compared to an ideal, or they can be compared to actually existing rules and organizations. For example, we might have an ideal of a human rights organization that is funded completely by small donations from local people and compare existing organizations and their funding to that ideal. Alternatively, we could compare actual organizations to other existing organizations, in which case we can ask how legitimate human rights organizations in a given country are compared, for example, to churches or other NGOs in that country.

We can also compare the legitimacy of current human rights discourses with that of other existing political ideas and discourses. This is the kind of comparison that Brazilian scholar and human rights advocate Paulo Sérgio Pinheiro is doing when he says, "I do believe that there is no other language, no other set of principles that allow, given our universal diversity, the respect for a few fundamental standards for human beings to live with dignity and respect. Until now, no other reference has been found."[13] Pinheiro compares human rights ideas to other existing alternatives to determine legitimacy, not to ideals we can imagine but have not yet found in the world. He suggests that, when scholars discuss alternatives to human rights, they should spell them out so that the reader can evaluate those alternatives as well.

One of the biggest challenges to the legitimacy of human rights movements and law is the argument that human rights ideas originated in the Global North and are imposed coercively on the Global South. When looking at the question of who sets the global human rights agenda, scholars such as Hopgood and Kennedy argue that attention to human rights issues was generated by powerful Western states—hence the "tainted origins" of human rights, to use Kennedy's terminology.[14] This argument is not new, but has been reinforced in some recent books.[15] Moyn, for example, has argued that debates over human rights emerged in the 1970s rather than in the 1940s, and he associates such debates with US President Jimmy Carter.[16] Because of the gap between the Universal Declaration of Human Rights (UDHR) of 1948 and the powerful human rights social movements that emerged in the 1970s, Moyn writes off the importance of the 1940s, 1950s, and the 1960s.[17] He calls the UN human rights regime "dead on arrival" and he says that the Inter-American system proved to be "the beneficiary not the cause of the transformation in the direction of human rights."[18] There are many problems with this viewpoint, as chapters 3 and 4 will demonstrate. In particular, Moyn does not understand what grassroots activists learned in the 1970s—that the UN and Organization of American States (OAS) human rights treaties and institutions set up in response to the human rights commitments in their charters were crucial resources for later mobilization.

Moyn's flawed history of human rights also has the effect of giving the United States and Jimmy Carter more credit for the birth of the international protection of human rights than they deserve. Moyn mistakenly interprets human rights policy in the Americas as mainly about Carter, instead of as an encounter between Latin American activists and the new human rights concerns in the US Congress and the Carter administration. The important human rights policies of the Carter administration helped *activate and eventually consolidate*, but did not initiate, the institutional developments that had been underway in the Americas for thirty years. To credit Carter with the change ignores these intellectual and institutional developments. Likewise, Moyn is only able to say that human rights emerged in the 1970s by dismissing any link between the human rights movement and the processes of decolonization that occurred in the 1960s. Moyn claims that decolonization was about sovereignty and *not* about rights; as we shall see in chapter 4, however, the best historians of decolonization and human rights say decolonization was about *both* sovereignty and human rights.[19]

David Kennedy makes a related argument. He says that human rights as a "text"—the UDHR—emerged after World War II but that, "as a form of governance, a profession, a movement, a universal ideological practice, human rights was launched much later, in the late 1970s and early 1980s, just as the pendulum swung for a generation toward Thatcher, Reagan, and the politics of neo-liberalism."[20] But, as we will see in chapters 3 and 4, human rights in the 1940s, 1950s, and 1960s was far more than a text. It was a set of interconnected struggles—for the institutionalization of human rights in the UN, for decolonization, against apartheid, and against foreign military coups. Moreover, these struggles were often led by countries of the Global South against the powerful countries of the Global North. While these "tainted origins" accounts differ somewhat, each one erases these struggles and suggests that countries in Africa, Latin America, Asia, and the Middle East would not have thought of human rights had it not been for the goading or modeling by states in the North.

The historical origins of the human rights movement are far more complicated and interesting than the accounts of Moyn and Kennedy allow. In reality, for much of the post-World War II period, the United States and the United Kingdom were major obstacles to the advancement of human rights, not its main proponents.[21] At times US foreign policy has supported the international protections of human rights, and at other times it has blocked or undermined them.[22] The political implications of the debate over the origins of the human rights movement are crucial. Understanding this more complicated history is essential in making sense of the present state of human rights and in envisioning the future. Many people despair at this moment as they see countries like the United States and the United Kingdom moving away from their support for human rights. People are right to be worried—the human rights project is more likely to flourish when it has support from powerful states. But powerful countries have never been a constant, or even a primary, source of support for the international protections of human rights. Hopgood says that we are now in the "endtimes of human rights" because he believes that human rights originated with powerful states in the Global North and, since those states are losing power in the new multi-polar world, attention to human rights will subside. However, because the history of the human rights movement is much more diverse than Hopgood presents, its future is likely to be more promising.

The belief that human rights ideas come only from the Global North flattens differences and disagreements about human rights within countries and regions and calls into question the legitimacy and authenticity of human rights activists in the Global South. This historical critique by scholars inadvertently echoes the discourse of many repressive governments in the Global South, who try to discredit their local human rights activists by portraying them as "foreign agents," carrying inappropriate ideas from abroad into national political debates. Resurrecting the human rights contributions of activists and diplomats from the Global South can energize human rights activists as they see themselves as reconnecting to currents and traditions within their own countries, rather than channeling ideas from abroad.

We understand the complex internal debates about politics and human rights in our own country. We can see the difference between the politics of Jimmy Carter, who worked hard to incorporate human rights issues into US foreign policy, and George W. Bush, who permitted torture, kidnapping, and secret detention without publicly advocating these policies. We can recognize the potential for harm in Donald Trump, who publicly announced that he believes "torture works" and said he would use waterboarding and "worse" forms of torture.[23] There are equally complex variations within many countries in the Global South, as they move from one government to another and, particularly, as they move from a democratic government to an authoritarian one. As we heard from Heba Morayef at the opening of this book, in a few short years, she moved from a moment when human rights was on everyone's lips to a time in which she is afraid even to tell people that she does human rights work. Less dramatic but similar divergences affect rights activists in many parts of the Global South, from India to Thailand and Myanmar. Latin American countries at various times in their history have been at the vanguard of the promotion of the idea of international protection of human rights and, at other times, have been the well-deserved targets of the human rights movement. I have written, for example, about Argentina's transition from a "pariah state" to a global protagonist of human rights.[24] Important differences also exist among different regions of the Global South. Latin American and African regional organizations, for instance, have been more supportive of regional norms to promote democracy and rights than have organizations in Asia, where traditional sovereignty norms have held much more firmly.[25] I will document all of these claims in detail in chapters 3 and 4.

Legitimacy and Effectiveness as Matters of Comparison

Any discussion of legitimacy or effectiveness is essentially an exercise in comparison. We can only say that an institution or policy is legitimate or effective compared to something else. Thus, it is essential to start any discussion about legitimacy and effectiveness by calling attention to the central question: Compared to what?

The single biggest unrecognized and unnamed source of disagreement among human rights scholars and within human rights movements is a matter of measurement: the difference between those making empirical comparisons and those making comparisons to an ideal.[26] We can think of these types of comparisons as lenses or yardsticks. A comparison to the ideal involves contrasting what has actually happened with what *should* happen in an ideal world, whereas empirical comparison contrasts what is actually happening to what has happened in the same country in the past or to what is happening in other countries at the same time.

These two yardsticks map along a division common among philosophers: the difference between ideal theory and non-ideal theory. This distinction is the difference between theorizing about the ethical ideal and theorizing about what is possible for governments or individuals to do in a non-ideal world.[27] In the words of my colleague Mathias Risse, "Ideal theory explores what the world would be like if everybody did as they ought to. Non-ideal theory tells us what we ought to do given that others will not do what they ought to do."[28] A number of the scholars I discuss in this chapter are engaged in ideal theory, while I am interested in non-ideal theory. My non-ideal theory makes empirical comparisons, using qualitative and quantitative human rights data. Yet, just as those who use ideal theory can arrive at different conclusions, so too can people using non-ideal theory. The second part of the book will take up these data and empirical issues and survey a large body of existing research on the effectiveness of human rights institutions, advocacy, and policy.

The distinction between ideal and non-ideal theory relates to one that Amartya Sen makes in his book, *The Idea of Justice*, between the optimum approach and the maximum approach to justice.[29] Sen's theory is about the optimum, that is, the best alternative compared to other existing alternatives within the realm of the possible, as opposed to the maximum ideal of justice, which is what perfect justice would look like in an ideal world. My understanding of comparison to the ideal is related to maximalist theories of justice, while empirical comparisons are connected to the optimum approach, or alternatives within the realm of the possible.[30] In this book, I will adapt this to the field of human rights in order to argue for an optimum goal for human rights policy. This approach is consistent with Hirschman's "possibilism"—keeping our focus on alternatives within the realm of the possible, though not necessarily the probable.

Some of the key claims of scholars making comparison to the ideal include that there has been no progress on human rights, that there is more suffering than ever before, that human rights are "minimal" claims, that human rights are "powerless to address inequality," that the "entire enterprise" of states prosecuting their citizens for human rights crimes is "ethically insupportable," and that refugees have never been treated so unfairly. Each of these arguments will be discussed below. Since all these claims are so negative, it may sound odd to the reader that I call them comparison to the ideal, but the question we need to ask of each of these claims is—compared to what?

In *The Twilight of Human Rights*, Eric Posner repeatedly stresses that the continued existence of repression and human rights violations around the world is evidence that human rights law has not worked and should be abandoned. In her reply to Posner's book, a blog post entitled "Twilight or Dark Glasses," Beth Simmons points out that Posner "never really confronts the question: compared to what?"[31] Simmons suggests that the ways in which we conceptualize effectiveness provide lenses through which our conclusions are perceived. Is it the twilight of human rights, as Posner claims, or does his method give him a dark lens through which everything seems grim?

Empirical Comparison vs. Comparison to the Ideal for Measuring Effectiveness

I make empirical comparisons by conceptualizing movement along what I call a "compliance continuum" for human rights (see Fig. 2.1). Starting with a specific type of human rights violation, I look at how the practice has changed over time. I compare, for example, what discrimination against women in the workplace was like fifteen years ago to how it is today. I use the compliance continuum to differentiate visually between the various approaches to measuring improvements or retrogression in human rights practices.[32] One advantage to this method is that empirical comparison can detect both progress and retrogression. Comparison to the ideal cannot.

Scholars are not the only ones who rely on comparison to the ideal; it is also the preferred mode of thinking for human rights activists. In the moving speech from AI member Patrick Corrigan quoted at the beginning of this chapter, we read, "We want a world without poverty, without hunger, without the inequality which divides us . . . We say we want a world where no longer will 800 million people go to bed hungry every night and where [no longer] every 5 seconds a child dies from extreme poverty."[33]

I share Corrigan's sentiment. However, questions remain—if we want that world, how are we to measure if we are getting closer to it? Furthermore, how can we use these measures to learn about what does and does not work to achieve that progress? A detailed look at Corrigan's remarks on hunger demonstrates how empirical measurements can signal effectiveness. The UN Food and Agriculture Organization's (FAO) annual report for 2013, when Corrigan

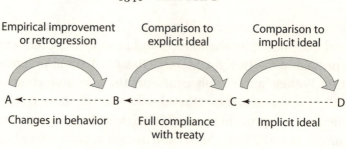

FIG. 2.1. Human rights compliance continuum.

spoke and which seems to be the basis of his statement, lists a number of undernourished people in the world that is very close to Corrigan's figure of 800 million people who go to bed hungry.[34] Using comparison to the ideal (a world without hunger), we are 800 million people short of our goal—a clearly negative result. But, using the same source of data, we can make an empirical comparison from 1990 to 2015, which reveals progress. Between 1990 and 2015 we have witnessed a decline in the absolute number of hungry people in the world, as well as hungry people as a percentage of the total world population. The developing regions, home to the largest percentage of hungry people, saw a forty-two percent reduction in the prevalence of undernourished people between 1990–92 and 2012–14. About one in eight people remained chronically undernourished in these regions in 2012–14, but that is down from one quarter of the population in 1990–92. Some critics will attribute this decrease entirely to China, which has indeed brought down hunger substantially. But it turns out that Latin America is the most successful developing region in decreasing hunger; it witnessed a decrease in the absolute number of hungry people as well as in the prevalence of hunger from fifteen percent to five percent. Sub-Saharan Africa has been the least successful—the prevalence of undernourishment declined ten percent between 1990–92 and 2014–16, though the absolute number of undernourished people increased.[35] The diverging measurements of progress in the case of Sub-Saharan Africa—percentage versus absolute numbers—should also serve as a reminder that empirical comparison is not simple, and should be done with care and precision.

It is striking to say that 800 million people go to bed every night hungry. Rightfully, it makes people angry about injustice. Stating that the number of hungry people is down by forty-two percent since 1990 and then trying to explain the difference between a percentage decline and a decline in absolute numbers might make people's eyes glaze over. But boredom is not the only possible reaction. Demonstrating the effectiveness of past efforts to improve outcomes such as these could also give people hope and a belief that they can make a difference, both of which, as Alinsky reminds us, are essential. When faced with the challenge of worldwide hunger, we can use empirical comparisons to show what has worked and what more needs to be done to eliminate hunger.

The Use of Implicit vs. Explicit Comparison to the Ideal to Evaluate Legitimacy and Effectiveness

Many ideal theorists explicitly state the ideal to which the world is being compared. For example, numerous human rights activists tell us that the ideal to which they aspire is full compliance with the letter of the law. One such law says that women and men shall receive equal pay for equal work, so, using the ideal theory metric, until that is the case, many activists will remain unsatisfied.[36] On the other hand, someone doing an empirical comparison would say that in 1981 US women earned fifty-nine cents for every dollar earned by a man and, in 2015, women earned eighty cents—evidence of human rights progress.[37] As this example shows, the same situation could be called completely unsatisfactory by someone engaged in comparison to the ideal and good progress by someone using empirical comparison.

There is another group of ideal theorists whose grounds for comparison are implicit—they don't tell us the ideal to which they are comparing the existing world and we have to try to find that ideal hidden within their critique. Moyn, for instance, is critical of the existing human rights regime, saying it is "minimalist" and is engaged in "anti-politics," but he never tells us the ideal to which he is comparing human rights.[38] My colleague at Harvard Law School, David Kennedy, is similarly oblique about his comparisons. He critiques human rights for "How narrowly the human rights tradition views human emancipation," but fails to spell out the alternatives.[39] We have a sense of some more capacious understanding of human emancipation, but Kennedy never tells us exactly what the alternative is.

Moyn also critiques human rights because it is "powerless against inequality" and only "created a floor of protection without making a ceiling for inequality."[40] The critique is apparently persuasive, since Lettinga, a smart human rights activist and scholar, believing that Moyn may be right, devoted an entire volume to the critique.[41] But let's think about all the comparisons in Moyn's claims. Human rights are "powerless against inequality" compared to what other existing political platforms or set of ideas? Moyn never tells us. Reading the entirety of his work, the reader does not find a clear idea of what Moyn advocates or believes in. Reading between the lines in *The Last Utopia*, I assumed that Moyn was a disillusioned ex-Marxist; I thought his implicit ideal was some kind of radical revolutionary change. If true, that would have been fine, but I would have liked him to state it so that I didn't have to guess at the alternative to which he was making his comparisons. In conversation, however, he has told me he is a social democrat. This raised more questions for me. If Moyn were comparing human rights to social democratic ideals and policies, wouldn't he know that social democratic ideas, like those embraced in Scandinavia, and human rights ideas do not conflict? Indeed, human rights ideas are often part and parcel of the social democratic agenda.

Another ideal to which Moyn compares human rights is that of "a ceiling for inequality."[42] Lettinga and van Troost find the phrase compelling. They echo it in their chapter of the social justice volume, calling for a vision of justice "where Amnesty would not only plead for a minimal floor of basic rights, but also adhere to the idea that there is a maximum ceiling of inequality that the realization of human rights can afford."[43] It sounds good, but what does it mean? Moyn never gives any real world examples of what such a ceiling would look like, where such ceilings have been advocated or implemented, or their effects. Presumably, the ideal would be something like that proposed by some management experts where the salaries of managers should not be more than, for example, twenty times the salaries of workers. This is an interesting proposal. I would like to know if it is being used as national policy in any countries in the world. I see that NGOs are advocating it in some countries, in Canada for example, as a solution to inequality.[44] Alternatively, a ceiling could refer to health care policies where certain kinds of expensive surgeries are rationed until all people have basic care. But Moyn never provides any details about policies he advocates. He finds human rights policies to be minimal and powerless against an unclear ideal. We need to know more. I don't want to silence debate based on comparison to the ideal, but rather to enhance and deepen our debates by calling on people making these comparisons to acknowledge them and to provide more concrete details about the alternatives they advocate.

Some critical theorists believe that they should never be obliged to provide any alternative proposals. One week after the election of Donald Trump as President of the United States, I was part of a panel discussion on History and Human Rights at the Mahindra Humanities Center at Harvard. The first to speak was Bernard Harcourt, a professor of law and political science at Columbia University. Harcourt said that we are witnessing the "waning or death of human rights discourse in America." He explained that he had "always believed adamantly" that it was not the task of academics who engage in critique to provide anything in the way of concrete proposals for change, or what he called "an alternative political landscape." Harcourt continued, "I have always strenuously resisted the idea that we critical thinkers should be compelled to offer solutions after exercising critique, that we should have to propose a way forward, that we should have to solve the problems, not just identify them." It is sufficient, in his words, to "clear the ground of a harmful illusions" and "nominalist error."[45]

Yet how can we move forward if we only have critique? In this moment, in the United States and in the world, to proclaim the death of human rights and refuse to provide any proposal for what to do is a recipe for inactivity and despair. Despair is certainly what some members of the audience felt that night after listening to Harcourt.

Implicit Comparison to the Ideal Combined with Hidden Causal Statements

Of particular frustration for those of us looking for clear comparisons is that comparison to the ideal is sometimes combined with hidden causal statements. Hidden causal statements take the form of an insider hint that the author, for example, knows the "root causes" of the problem, but then doesn't reveal them. David Kennedy is the master of this. Kennedy wrote that, in human rights work, "We are often troubled when we acknowledge the suffering of others without abandoning our commitment to the system that produces it."[46] To say that a "system" produces suffering is a causal statement. Kennedy suggests that he knows the system that produces suffering but then doesn't tell us what it is. He hints here that it is, perhaps, capitalism, but never clarifies his argument. I believe that when scholars make a causal statement they should make it clearly and then take responsibility for it by providing evidence to support their argument.

Moyn also accompanies his comparison to the ideal with a hidden causal argument, which implies that human rights may have contributed to the rise of market fundamentalism, "or at least the decline of national welfarism," because of the "apparently tight chronological relationship between the twinned rise of human rights and of 'neoliberalism.'"[47] I explore his claim in the next section.

Neoliberalism and Human Rights

The debate over the complicity of human rights with neoliberalism often involves the use of implicit comparison to the ideal with hidden causal statements. The hidden causal statement is the idea that human rights policies somehow lead to or make possible neo-liberal policies. Recently, in some academic and policy circles, and especially in the humanities and in critical legal studies, it has become commonplace to hear people claim that human rights are somehow "complicit" with neo-liberal economic policies.[48] Costas Douzinas, for example, writes that the Western conception of human rights "turned them into the perfect companion of neoliberalism."[49] Mary Nolan argues that human rights and neoliberalism, or market fundamentalism as it is sometimes called, are similar because they both "adhered to methodological individualism," "critiqued the state," and gained prominence in the 1970s. In addition, Nolan writes that both human rights and neoliberalism "valorize a normative individual who is coded as male."[50]

There are many problems with these arguments. Conceptually, the ways in which human rights and neoliberalism focus on the individual are quite different. The human rights movement has treated the individual as a normative and legal matter—that is, human rights ideas stress that the well-being of the individual in the broadest sense should be the main object of our concern and that individual human rights should legally and morally take precedence over other policy matters or concerns. This makes the individual focus of human rights not at all like the methodological individualism of neo-liberal economics, which focuses on the individual as a rational, self-maximizing actor in a model where self-interest provides the motivation for economic production. The human rights agenda, on the other hand, often requires us to limit self-interest to take into account the needs of others. With regard to the human rights movement valorizing an individual who is male, as we will see in chapter 3, human rights activists like Bertha Lutz of Brazil or Hansa Mehta of India, starting as early as 1945, insisted on the recognition of women's rights as part of the human rights agenda. Feminists within the human rights movement made "women's rights are human rights" the catchphrase of the 1993 World Conference on Human Rights; since that time, there is hardly a human rights organization without a program working on women's rights. Moreover, the human rights movement does not attempt to limit the role of the state in the same way as neoliberalism. Human rights organizations "critiqued the state" when the state was abusing the rights of individuals, but more often they called upon the state to take up a more capacious role to further rights, often by protecting civil, political, economic, and social rights. The protection of civil and political rights requires not only that the state stop doing things, like torture, but also that it expand its capacities to do other things: for example, to protect due process by funding and training high-quality public defenders for the poor. In the area of social and economic rights, human rights advocates constantly urge governments to expand educational opportunities, health services, and social security. Neoliberalism, on the other hand, often urges the state to cut back its services.

The hidden causal argument that human rights ideas are somehow complicit with neoliberalism is also highly problematic, not least because it is historically inaccurate. With regard to the temporal claim about simultaneity, the term "neoliberalism" was not used with its current meaning of referring to particular types of liberal market policies until the late 1970s and early 1980s.[51] Only in Moyn's flawed chronology of human rights, which locates the human rights movement's emergence in the 1970s, can human rights and neoliberalism be seen as appearing near the same time. In actuality, the rise of norms, laws, and institutions for the international protection of human rights predates the use of the term neoliberalism by decades. The post–World War II rise of the idea and practice of the international protection of human rights instead coincides with the emergence of the model that John Ruggie called "embedded liberalism," a blend of international multilateralism and domestic interventionism aimed at taming global instability at the same time as it protected domestic constituencies.[52]

When neoliberalism emerged in the late twentieth century, human rights actors in some parts of the world began fighting in opposition to neo-liberal policies, not in complicity with them. Early human rights activists in Latin America, for example, were often protesting human rights violations by authoritarian anti-communist regimes that were simultaneously implementing neo-liberal economic policies. Therefore, those who insinuate that neoliberalism somehow "caused" human rights activism or vice versa are guilty of ahistoricism as well as erroneous causal inferences.

In other parts of the world, human rights organizations arose in struggles not against neoliberalism, but against autocratic communist regimes. The three historical strands that converged in the 1970s to create the modern human rights movement included anti-apartheid activists in Africa, Latin American activists against neo-liberal authoritarian regimes, and activists from the Soviet Union (USSR) and the Eastern bloc against the practices of autocratic communist regimes.[53] Many of the activists from the former USSR initially supported the introduction of market reforms, whereas activists from Latin America and the anti-apartheid struggle were more likely to oppose market fundamentalism. Just because one group of human rights activists from communist countries advocated market reforms does not mean that one can confuse human rights and neoliberalism.

Many human rights activists in the 1970s and 1980s focused on civil and political rights, not because of the influence of neoliberalism as some critics have claimed, but because of the nature of repression during those decades. Throughout Latin America, governments were murdering, disappearing, and imprisoning human rights activists by the thousands. It is not surprising that the human rights groups in those countries first demanded an end to executions, disappearances, and the holding of political prisoners. Across the globe, dissidents in the former Soviet Union and Eastern Europe mainly lacked political rights and civil liberties, not social and economic rights, and so they made civil and political rights the centerpiece of their demands.[54] Finally, the global demand for the end of apartheid aimed at ending harsh legal discrimination and political exclusions. These movements demanded the civil and political rights that were their most pressing concern at the moment, while at the same time believing that economic and social rights were an essential part of the human rights agenda. They realized that gaining, or regaining, civil and political rights would not be the endpoint of their struggles.

Many of the people making the argument about the "striking affinities" of human rights and neoliberalism appear to confuse the term human rights with the human rights policies of the US or UK governments, or the human rights work of a few US-based nongovernmental organizations (NGOs).[55] Just because President George W. Bush sometimes justified the invasion of Iraq in 2003 on human rights grounds does not make him a spokesperson or personification of human rights. If I make any point in this book, it must be that the term human rights or the notion of a human rights movement should never be conflated or confused with the human rights policies of the US or UK governments or even with the practices of powerful and important human rights NGOs based in the United States. Most human rights activists in the world were deeply opposed to the US invasion of Iraq. The fact that a small handful of human rights writers in the United States supported the invasion does not earn it the label of a human rights war rather than a war of aggression.

All of this discredits Moyn's observation about the "twinned rise of human rights and of 'neoliberalism.'" The evidence is simply not there. One big problem with comparison to an implicit ideal and hidden causal arguments is that authors using these techniques free themselves from the obligation of providing evidence or substantiation for their arguments. In the case of Moyn's argument about the relation between human rights and market fundamentalism, he only hints at the causal argument and does not provide evidence beyond a chronological relationship. Moreover, the chronological relationship only exists in Moyn's own idiosyncratic history of human rights, which claims human rights emerged in the 1970s, not the 1940s as will be demonstrated in chapter 3. In his view, market fundamentalism "has massively transformed the world," whereas human rights has been "condemned merely to watch."[56]

Another critic, Eduardo Arenas Catalán, is more forthcoming in his writing on this topic: Human rights must address "the structural sources of exclusion" and these "are connected to one phenomenon: the rise of global capitalism."[57] Here we have an open causal argument, not a hidden one. Catalán clearly believes that, without addressing capitalism, it will be impossible to deal with inequality. But he still doesn't spell out an alternative. Should capitalism be reformed to address exclusion, and, if so, how? Or does he advocate a revolution against capitalism? What type of alternative society does he advocate? As you can see, it is difficult to decide whether we can support a comparison to the ideal if the author doesn't flesh out the comparison more fully.

Hopgood provides another example of implicit comparison to the ideal. He disparages much of what human rights institutions have done without telling the reader what he believes could be a desirable alternative. Throughout his book *The Endtimes of Human Rights*, Hopgood inconsistently hints about what might be a preferable alternative. He praises the contributions of former East Timorese freedom fighters, some religious humanitarian groups, and even the Chinese and Russian governments because at least they are not hypocritical. But all this does not add up to a clear vision of an ideal to which human rights policies or institutions are being compared. Meanwhile, no institution receives more criticism in Hopgood's book than the International Criminal Court (ICC). Hopgood critiques the ICC for many things (including its architecture), but his main point seems to be that because it is "unimaginable" that the ICC will prosecute the head of state of a great power or of a client state of one of the great powers, "there is a clear double standard at work."[58]

Navi Pillay, the South African jurist and former UN High Commissioner for Human Rights, told me that she often meets in South Africa with young students who believe that South Africa should withdraw from the ICC exactly because of these double standards. She said:

> Well, it is a twenty-year-old democracy. It is really a very short time for a complete change. The young people are disillusioned with the slow pace of change. There is huge unemployment. Poor students can't get into the University. . . . When I tell them about human rights, they say—don't talk to us about human rights—go and talk to the US. Why wasn't Bush arrested for the invasion of Iraq? They complain that the outside world is applying double standards. They are not interested in the external point of view because they are so disheartened by their own immediate needs.

Pillay also finds it unacceptable that the United States, China, and Russia have not ratified the Rome Statute. But sometimes, she said, "the criticism made by an academic that nothing is working is taken up by those who have an interest in seeing that they are not held accountable." Pillay said she looks to academics to explain things, "rather than provide fodder to various governments who look at Human Rights negatively because it comes with accountability. So, I've been on the radio explaining that five of the eight African countries under investigation by the ICC invited the ICC to look at the cases. Practitioners and academics have a duty to set out facts like that."[59]

I understand why students in South Africa might see the ICC as deeply, perhaps irredeemably, flawed as it prosecutes crimes against humanity committed in Africa but not those committed by the United States or Israel. But for a scholar of international relations like Hopgood to criticize the ICC as hypocritical or as using double standards because it doesn't prosecute a country that hasn't ratified its Statute or because it permits the Security Council to refer cases, is either disingenuous or highly idealistic. Why? Because he is comparing the behavior of the ICC not to its own Statute or to other courts, but to the ideals that he believes should have been in the treaty. The ICC, like any other international treaty, is based on state consent; that is, it applies only to states that have ratified the Rome Statute. As for the referral of cases by the Security Council, did Hopgood expect that the creation of the ICC would somehow erase all power dynamics in the world and remake the United Nations? He holds the ICC up to his own implicit ideal of international justice and finds it wanting.

In my own work, I prefer empirical comparisons. In an earlier book, *The Justice Cascade*, I presented the results of multiple forms of empirical comparisons about domestic and international prosecutions for human rights violations.[60] First, I looked at the dramatic increase in human rights prosecutions in the current period as compared to the past and argued that these prosecutions are evidence of new legitimacy for the norm that state officials should be held accountable for past crimes. This is a form of empirical comparison over time. I also used a form of cross-national empirical comparison in an article I wrote with Hun Joon Kim in which we compare those countries that have held domestic human rights prosecutions to those that have not. We found that countries with prosecutions have fewer core human rights violations.[61]

My conclusions diverge from those of other authors because of the different methods of comparison we use. For example, Mark Osiel wrote a compelling book in 1997 about the role of trials in helping societies come to grips with atrocities.[62] Today, his disappointment that international criminal law has not met his ideals is palpable. When writing about international criminal law in 2014, Osiel was explicit about his comparison to the ideal:

> We theorists of international law like to pose venturesome, vitalizing questions, sweeping in scope: What would an ideal system of international criminal law look like, for instance, relieved of today's geostrategic constraints? . . . What kind of world would be required for such a program to become possible, even intelligible? How should we imagine the workings of such a hypothetical world?[63]

Osiel is engaged in explicit comparison to the ideal because he tells us his ideal—a system of international criminal law relieved of geopolitical constraints.

Next, Osiel moves on to a more focused question: "What would have to change, in the very near future, for international criminal law to survive at all, in any moderately acceptable form?" Here we run into a problem; he does not tell us what he means by "any moderately acceptable form." While Osiel is explicit and compelling about his desire for human rights practices to fit an ideal, the standards he presents for this ideal are vague at best. Osiel writes:

> Only very rarely, however, will states conscientiously prosecute their own citizens for international crimes, much less the citizens of more powerful states. When states prosecute at all, their case selection will be indefensibly partisan, rendering the entire enterprise ethically insupportable by contemporary standards, higher than ever before.[64]

In this instance, Osiel compares to the ideal while also making an empirical claim—states rarely prosecute their own officials. Our new database on transitional justice mechanisms in the world records over 500 cases of domestic human rights prosecutions in transitional countries, involving over 1100 accused individuals.[65] Many of these prosecutions ended in a guilty verdict, for both low-level and high-ranking individuals. Based on this evidence, I would say Osiel's empirical claim is wrong—it is not rare for states to prosecute their own officials. His comparison to the ideal causes him to understate, and even to ignore, empirical data that reveals the progress made by human rights movements.

Osiel goes on to argue that a criminal prosecution which happens too many years after a crime is committed, such as the trials in Uruguay and Chile in the 2000s for crimes that occurred in the 1970s, "remains deeply at odds with any defensible account of 'the rule of law.'"[66] Again, his comparison is to an ideal future, where state officials would be promptly held accountable, not to a past where no state officials were ever prosecuted. Using an empirical comparison, I would ask—is it more deeply at odds with the rule of law that high levels officials should be prosecuted late than never at all?

Osiel's work reminds us that, even when our yardsticks are explicit, disagreements will be difficult to resolve. Despite our data and our findings, my team will have a hard time ever convincing Mark Osiel of the effectiveness of international criminal law because we rely on empirical comparisons and it is unclear what empirical proof, if any, would satisfy his ideals. My ability to persuade Osiel will depend on what he means by states "conscientiously" prosecuting officials and what he would characterize as "indefensibly partisan" and "ethically insupportable" prosecutions.

I had a similar discussion with Milli Lake, an expert on rape prosecutions in the Democratic Republic of the Congo (DRC). Lake has done painstaking field research on mobile courts in the DRC that tried combatants for sexual violence.[67] She interviewed the prosecutors and discovered that, against great odds, they were prosecuting and convicting soldiers and insurgents for rape. But as she delved more deeply into her interviews, she discovered a more complex story. The soldiers who were convicted and served time in prison were usually outsiders who were turned over to authorities because they had fallen out with those in power in one armed group or another. We discussed whether these trials qualified as what Mark Osiel would call "ethically insupportable." Lake clarified that it appeared the convicted soldiers had committed the rapes for which they were being prosecuted. They had access to trial lawyers and due process of law. The prosecutors themselves were not corrupt or in on the deals—rather, as in any judicial system, they issued indictments and they depended on the police to arrest and deliver suspects to them for trial. If the police were "indefensibly partisan," and it appears they were, and only delivered some suspects for prosecution, did that make the entire enterprise "ethically insupportable"? I didn't think so.

In the past, soldiers were never prosecuted for rape. If some were now being prosecuted in procedurally fair trials (at least with regard to what happens in the mobile court), this is not "ethically insupportable" in my eyes. Not only that, more soldiers were being tried for rape in the DRC than in any other country in Africa. Since the DRC had been seen as having an epidemic of rape, careful legal prosecutions that satisfy some victims' demands for justice and perhaps deter future crime are an improvement. At the same time, I understand why Lake called attention to the unfairness that only some soldiers were delivered to the Courts while others went free. It is hard to say simply that things are getting better with regard to justice for rape in the DRC without also pointing to all the ways in which the trials fall short of our ideals.

My critique of comparison to the ideal is thus complex. To some, perhaps, I appear to be forestalling any critique. But I mainly plead for transparency. Those doing comparison to the ideal, I believe, have the obligation to tell us their method, as is the standard practice for any scholarly work. If I use empirical comparison, I need to state the empirical comparisons I am making, as well as justify why those comparisons are good ones (e.g., why Argentina is being compared to Brazil and not to Mexico, for example, or why transitional countries with trials are being compared to transitional countries without trials). If I am using quantitative methods, I have to explain why I am using one model instead of another. If an author is using comparison to the ideal, the reader should be told the ideal to which reality is being compared and the reasons why the ideal is a plausible comparison. So, if Hopgood's ideal were a form of justice that would require the erasure of all power dynamics, as it seems to be, I would say that this ideal is desirable, but so unlikely that his critique should be taken less seriously.

Even Osiel, the most explicit of the scholars I quote above, does not fulfill my criteria. He tells us that he is engaged in comparison to the ideal, and we know that no such ideal international system of justice exists. But his ideal, "a system of government relieved of geopolitical constraints," like the one that can be discovered in Hopgood's work, seems similarly unattainable.

When yardsticks are not explicit, a disagreement about the effectiveness of human rights law between someone using comparison to the ideal and someone using empirical comparisons can be a dialogue among the deaf. I think of the yardstick used by people engaged in comparison to the ideal as having only negative numbers on it, since all real-world outcomes fall short of the ideal. They, in turn, may think that my empirical comparison yardsticks have only positive numbers when I'm comparing to the past. Yet, as I have studied situations where, compared to the past, the situation is far worse, I believe my yardstick has the ability for both positive and negative evaluation. The use of torture under the Bush administration, for example, is a clear example of an empirical comparison yielding a negative picture.[68] In any case, an essential starting point for trying to sort out disagreements about human rights effectiveness is to try to characterize explicitly what measures scholars and practitioners are using.

I am not saying that researchers should refrain from critiquing human rights work. I believe that such critique is necessary and healthy. Nor should they fail to draw attention to countries in which there is an alarming turn of events for the worse. Furthermore, I am not suggesting that people who are deeply worried about a particular case of severe and worsening human rights violations, such as the current situations in Thailand, Egypt, or the United States, take a more optimistic view. I am talking more generally about the perspective that sees all human rights as worsening without clearly specifying, "compared to what?"

What I am suggesting are simple standards of method and scholarship. Just as with any scholar, we expect human rights critics to be clear about their methods. If they are comparing cases to the ideal, the ideal should be explicit, not implicit. If there are causal statements, these too should be explicit, not hidden. This allows others to evaluate the arguments and the quality of the evidence and judge the work. The problem with many critics is that they take for themselves the luxury of criticism without making their own suppositions sufficiently clear that they too could become objects of critique.

Human Rights Activists and Comparison to the Ideal

As we have seen, human rights activists also frequently use comparison to the ideal, though their comparisons are more likely to be explicit comparisons to the ideal than implicit ones. Activists are most likely to hold up current practice to the ideals contained in human rights treaties, documents which are often drafted to embody our ideals of what humans need to live with dignity. Such texts include aspirations or promises that states endorse, but may not be able to deliver in the short term. This is the distinction between having rights and enjoying rights; human rights treaties proclaim rights that humans "have" by virtue of being human, but that they may not yet enjoy.[69]

When many activists, scholars, and members of the general public think about progress, they correctly point to all the ways in which our practices fall short of the ideals embodied in human rights law. Activists use the gap between the codified rights and actual practice as a tool to mobilize for change. They may worry that if they do not constantly stress the gap, people will become complacent. If activists say things are getting better, will people still want to work for change? Some activists feel that the awareness of the negative is what sustains their energy for the struggle. As one person I interviewed told me, "I thought my energy for doing human rights work for the last twenty years was coming from the same place inside of me where suffering comes from. . . . I was always worried that if I am more comfortable with this, will I still have the energy to fight for human rights on a daily basis?" [70]

Activists also sometimes engage in comparison to an ideal that goes far beyond existing human rights law. In current debates over migration and refugees, many activists point to an ideal that is not embodied in the Refugee Convention. They argue for a radical reconceptualization and redesign of citizenship rules and institutions that are not well defined, but would involve a dramatic change in the current system of states as we know it. The comparison may still be explicit—activists can tell you the kind of world they envision—but it has not yet taken the form of refugee or migrant law.

Comparison to the ideal is an important form of ethical reasoning. We need to hold our practices up to our ideals and measure where they fall short. Such reasoning creates pressure for change and is thus one of the main tools of human rights advocacy. Human rights activists, however, need to be careful that their ideals don't lead them to feel hopeless and to sense that no human rights progress has occurred in the world. Activists would be well advised to engage also in empirical comparisons to help them measure actual human rights change in the world.

Conclusion

As I was completing this manuscript, I read a moving article by Alex de Waal, a human rights activist and scholar with a deep history of research and advocacy in Africa. It was entitled, "Writing Human Rights and Getting it Wrong."[71] His idea that "human rights is an emancipatory practice that must be set by affected people" particularly resonated with me. In fact, part of this book documents that human rights is an emancipatory practice that sometimes has been set by affected people and that this agenda setting has often been ignored or erased by scholars, governments, and even activists.

I likewise agree profoundly with his idea that "human rights should make no distinction between political allies and adversaries: all should be held to the same standard."[72] This has been the bed-

rock of my work and writing, for example, about the need to hold
the United States accountable for human rights violations along
with the rest of the world. This is why I advocate the prosecution of
Bush administration officials for torture and for the illegal invasion
of Iraq.[73] Finally, I find de Waal's call for humility a valid reminder
that there is still much we need to learn about what works and what
doesn't work in the protection of human rights.

But then there is this line: "Human rights advocacy is a critique
of power, not a directive for exercising it."[74] It is one thing to say that
our allies and adversaries should be held to the same standards; it
is quite another to say that human rights can only be a critique,
never a directive. De Waal and I both teach at public policy schools.
At the Harvard Kennedy School, many of our students are international, including an amazing group of mid-career students from
around the world. Some have been human rights advocates or
worked in international organizations or the private sector, but a
good proportion come from government and plan to go back into
government work. Some of them will, in different ways, exercise
power. Do I teach my students only to critique, but never to propose
or support policies? Do I only teach them humility, but not our best
social science about what works and what doesn't work? There are
plenty of people out there saying, without much humility, that
human rights movements and policies don't work (including many
from repressive governments). Are we to be silent in the face of such
critique, or only join our voices to it? De Waal has produced an im-
pressively introspective article, but to propose that human rights
work can only be a critique of power and not a directive for exercising it would leave us quite empty-handed when our students ask—
what should we do?

Sometimes human rights scholars seem to forget the reality of
the world's problems. Reading some of de Waal's earlier work, you
might occasionally think that the ICC is the problem, rather than
the government of Sudan's killing of its citizens and expelling of UN
workers.[75] Similarly, in his book *The Endtimes of Human Rights*,
Hopgood reserves his strongest language of critique for former UN
High Commissioner for Human Rights Mary Robinson, who handed
out badges and advice that he characterizes as "obscene" and "gro-
tesque" at a meeting in East Timor. He sees her actions as illustra-

tive of the paternalistic and hypocritical attitude of human rights institutions, which had failed to prevent human rights violations in East Timor in the first place. He reserves his most venomous statements not for the Indonesian militias who killed people in East Timor, but for Robinson.[76] I'd like to keep my focus on the genuine culprits of human rights violations in the world, and Mary Robinson is among the last people I would mention on that list.

In the grand scheme of things, many of the human rights scholars with whom I have disagreements are allies in the larger cause of enhancing human rights around the world. We may disagree about the history, or the types of rights that should be at the forefront of the struggle, but that does not make us opponents. Alex de Waal has done incredibly important work on Sudan. Stephen Hopgood continues to consult for Amnesty International. Critical theorist Bernard Harcourt is a leading litigator against the death penalty in the United States. I admire their work; I just wish Harcourt could figure out a way to mention his death penalty work as an example of the kind of work people who care about human rights could and should do, rather than insist that critical theorists like himself are under no obligation whatsoever to provide any proposals for action.

I believe we must be prepared to critique *and* to propose. We need to determine what works and what doesn't work, and to propose that we try to stop doing what doesn't work and do more of what does. This book tries to steer such a course. Albert Hirschman offers us some guidance here. He warns against intransigent discourses and asks for a "mature" position, recognizing that there are dangers and risks in both action and inaction. The risks of both should be "canvassed, assessed, and guarded against to the extent possible."[77] But in order to assess the risk of both action and inaction, we need to know exactly what kinds of actions are being recommended. In this sense, we need to move beyond critique. This is one of my tasks, to try to canvass and assess both the risks and benefits of human rights activism, law, and policy. To do so I will survey both the history of human rights and the best social science about its effectiveness. If I have a "bias for hope," it is partly in homage to Hirschman and his wonderful book with that title, but it is also because we hear so much about what is wrong with human rights these days and not enough about what is right.

PART II

The Legitimacy of Human Rights

DIVERSE STRUGGLES

CHAPTER THREE

The Diverse Political Origins of Human Rights

ONE OF MY BRIGHTEST and most idealistic undergraduates was writing a promising paper on violence against women in Ciudad Juárez, Mexico.[1] A key leader in our Human Rights Program, the student's research was connected to a project of activism in Ciudad Juárez itself, where she was working to support a women's shelter. Yet one day she came to my office suddenly unsure of her project. She had been taking a course with one of my critical theorist colleagues and, as a result, wanted to problematize her honors paper topic and change the focus of her activism. Her course had made her concerned that focusing on human rights would be a form of cultural imperialism and she wished to reorient her work to address what she called the root cause of human rights violations in Mexico: the US demand for drugs. After all, she explained, she now understood that human rights discourse, including all her previous research and activism, was insufficient, maybe even counterproductive, in bringing about change.

This was not the first time I had had such a conversation with a student. I had hoped this student's exposure to critical theory would make her a more reflective student and activist, yet I suspected that now it would be easier for her to leave her activism behind rather than risk what she had been taught to see as "othering" poor women in Mexico, instead of working in solidarity with them.

Believing that some context might help, I began by stating that the Mexican Constitution of 1917 was the first constitution in the world, not just in Latin America, to articulate not only civil and political, but also economic and social rights. At the San Francisco Conference in 1945, when the United Nations was created, the Mexican government spoke in favor of a broader system of international protection of human rights. The United States, on the other hand, was reluctant to include any human rights language in the UN Charter until persuaded by NGOs and less powerful states, including Mexico and other countries in Latin America. Given this background, I argued that it did not follow that supporting or researching women's rights in Mexico was cultural imperialism. In fact, one could argue that it was more culturally insensitive to ignore Mexico's long history of struggle for rights by assuming the idea of human rights is a US or European imposition. Moreover, I continued, how would changing her research to US drug policy, certainly a worthy topic, help to illuminate women's rights in Ciudad Juárez?

This conversation only brushed the surface of my student's concerns, which warranted a longer and more complicated discussion. This chapter, therefore, is the continuation of my response that I want to share with that student, as well as with the many otherwise well-informed students, activists, and scholars who believe that the powerful states of the Global North proposed the idea of the international protection of human rights, wrote human rights laws, and imposed them on the weak states of the Global South against their will.[2]

Human Rights: A More Complex and Diverse Origin Story

We are all familiar with early national efforts to protect rights, such as the US Bill of Rights or the French Declaration of the Rights of Man and of the Citizen. Although these declarations gestured toward universalism by asserting the existence of natural or inalienable rights, the ultimate intention was for the US and French governments to protect the rights of their citizens. The emphasis of this book, however, is about the *international* protection of rights—the belief that, if your government fails to protect your rights, you have somewhere else to turn for recourse.

National protections have a longer history than international ones, and indeed originated in Western countries. Not until after World War II did governments begin to define rights deserving of international promotion and protections. Prior to World War II there were many campaigns involving the international protection of rights that later came to be grouped under the category of human rights, including the campaign to abolish the slave trade and slavery, the work within the League of Nations to protect the rights of minorities, efforts in the International Labor Organization to protect the rights of workers, and campaigns to promote women's rights. Powerful states such as the United Kingdom led some of these campaigns.[3] In particular, the United Kingdom led the way in the abolition of slavery and the slave trade, against its economic interests.[4] Indeed, as a leading historian of abolition argues, slavery was "at the peak of its economic success" in both the United States and the British West Indies when it was abolished.[5]

As important as these issues were, the campaigns fell far short of an international action to standardize and protect a broad set of human rights.[6] Most histories of the international protection of human rights emphasize the Universal Declaration of Human Rights (UDHR), passed by the UN General Assembly on December 10, 1948, as the founding moment of international human rights.[7] The UDHR, however, was not the first time that an intergovernmental organization had adopted a detailed enumeration of rights.[8] That distinction belongs to the American Declaration of the Rights and Duties of Man, approved unanimously by the twenty states of Latin America and the United States eight months before the UDHR, in April 1948, at a conference in Bogotá, Colombia.[9] The leaders in proposing the declaration were diplomats and jurists from Latin American countries such as Uruguay, Chile, Mexico, and Brazil, not the United States. The Latin American diplomats and jurists understood that they were creating something new, while drawing on a long Latin American tradition of concern for human rights and democracy. The American Declaration is just one example among many that I will discuss where the contributions of individuals and countries outside the Global North were pivotal in the development of human rights discourse, and yet continue to be ignored or downplayed.[10]

My arguments about the role of Latin America and other small states in the origins of human rights law and institutions are not new. I presented some of this material for the first time in a 1997 article, with other parts appearing in books published in 1998 and 2004.[11] Carefully researched books and articles by scholars such as Jan Herman Burgers, Paolo Carozza, Mary Ann Glendon, Greg Grandin, Rainer Huhle, Patrick William Kelly, Johannes Morsink, Liliana Obregón, Susan Waltz, and many others have also documented the historical trends presented here.[12] Yet somehow these voices have not been heard. Even well intentioned scholars working on the origins of human rights discourse sometimes disregard contributions from the Global South and from Latin America. For example, one of the most recent histories of human rights, *Revisiting the Origins of Human Rights*, completely ignores Latin American contributions. In its chapters, authors meticulously document many underappreciated sources of rights discourse, from Giuseppe Mazzini to André Mandelstam, from women's movements to peace movements to socialism, but there is not a single chapter about contributions from the developing world.[13]

Human rights scholars, pundits, and practitioners continue to assume and to argue that the idea of human rights comes from the Global North and is imposed upon the South. I used to threaten my students that the next person who made an unthinking comment that the UDHR was imposed by the powerful on the weak would have to read, word-for-word, the entire 375 pages of Johannes Morsink's book *The Universal Declaration of Human Rights: Origins, Drafting, and Intent*.[14] In it, Morsink traces the drafting history of each article of the UDHR, including the extensive debate over the exact content of each article. He writes of the diverse origins of the Declaration, detailing Latin American contributions. As the book was published in 1999, I'm not sure why we still are arguing about these issues in 2017; however, current debates in the field suggest that people have not yet paid attention to this historical scholarship, or perhaps prefer to read only the archives in the countries of the Global North.

Latin American Contributions to the International Protection of Rights and Democracy

Some Latin American politicians and jurists called very early on for international efforts to promote human rights and democracy.[15] Some scholars begin the story with the social reformer and Dominican friar, Bartolomé de las Casas (d.1566), who denounced the treatment of native peoples by the Spanish conquistadors in the colonial period, and then move on to describe Latin Americans' support of liberal ideals during their wars of independence.[16] These revolutions, like that of the United States, were motivated by Enlightenment ideas of rights, present at the moments of state creation, rather than as a result of later diffusion.[17] Rather than simply imitating the values inherited from their Spanish colonizers, Latin American revolutionaries used and transformed these ideas into a rallying cry to break their bonds with the Spanish empire. Some scholars would argue that these liberating ideas were tainted because Latin American revolutionaries were wresting themselves from empire while continuing to rely on slave labor, to subordinate indigenous peoples, and to deny women political representation, just as in the United States. Such problems, however, are not with ideas of rights, but with their incomplete application. Each of these groups—slaves, indigenous peoples, and women—would subsequently use rights discourses to begin securing their own emancipations.

Like the United States and France, Latin America was a laboratory for early experiments in democratic rule and was among the first regions where countries granted their citizens universal male suffrage.[18] As suffrage requirements fluctuated between countries, it is difficult to pinpoint which country was the first to grant and sustain male suffrage. Regardless, in the 1830s, more countries in Latin America than in Europe had male suffrage (with varying restrictions). By 1847, Mexico, El Salvador, and Greece were the only countries in the world with broad male suffrage.[19] Latin American activists also engaged in struggles relating to economic and social rights, precursors for post–World War II human rights demands.[20]

It was not enough to promote democracy or rights nationally; some Latin American countries also wanted to promote democracy and rights at the international level. Even as countries in the region suffered frequent interruptions to their democratic experiments, a vociferous minority of Latin American leaders and diplomats explored ways to use international pressures to promote democracies locally. Simón Bolívar, often called the "Liberator" of Latin America due to his role in freeing Latin American countries from Spanish colonialism, began this drive for international involvement. In 1826, Bolívar encouraged delegates to the Congress of Panama to draw up a treaty of confederation that would exclude non-democratic states from membership. While the treaty never entered into force, it was followed over the years by dozens of other proposals and resolutions by Latin American leaders for foreign policies that would promote democracy.[21] In particular, some leaders proposed that states should refuse diplomatic recognition to governments that came to power through coups or expel such governments from membership in regional organizations. Individual Latin American states and even the entire Central American region experimented with this policy, but did not sustain it.[22] Although the proposals for broader democracy promotion were unsuccessful, they illustrate early concern in the region with international policies supporting democratic values.

Latin American jurists and states also pioneered the defense of sovereignty and nonintervention as integral parts of international law.[23] It may seem counterintuitive that Latin American jurists supported sovereignty and nonintervention while arguing for the international protection of rights and the promotion of democracy, as the latter appears to invite some forms of intervention; yet many of these jurists did not think that their advocacy for the international promotion of democracy and human rights came into conflict with their belief in sovereignty. Instead, the jurists saw sovereignty as a means by which weaker countries might find refuge from the interventions of more powerful countries, especially the United States.[24] Latin American countries envisioned international law as one of the "weapons of the weak" which they could use to balance US power.[25]

The Calvo Doctrine and the Drago Doctrine, produced by two Argentine jurists, illustrate how Latin American jurists and activists saw the law as a form of protection for the weak. Argentine diplomat, historian, and international legal scholar Carlos Calvo was born in 1824 in Buenos Aires and educated in Argentina and Paris.[26] Early in his professional career, Calvo represented the Paraguayan government in a case against the British government, and he won. To Calvo, this case proved that a small country could win over a powerful one through arguments based on recognized principles of international law. This experience led Calvo to articulate an important international legal principle, the Calvo Doctrine, which stressed that countries should not use diplomatic or armed intervention to enforce the private claims of their citizens abroad. At the time, it was common for foreign states to interfere in the internal affairs of another country in order to protect their own citizens, and especially to defend those citizens' financial interests. Foreign powers would, at times, take over tax collection in a Latin America country until the country's debts were paid. The Calvo Doctrine, in turn, inspired the Argentine Minister of Foreign Affairs Luis María Drago to articulate the Drago Doctrine of 1902, forbidding the forcible collection of public debt. Both Calvo and Drago justified their doctrines as necessary to prevent powerful countries from abusing weaker ones. Both doctrines were widely incorporated into international and domestic law.

Latin American jurists such as Calvo saw the sovereign equality of states as a precondition for other goals, including the protection of human rights. Nevertheless, the doctrines of sovereignty and nonintervention complicated debates surrounding human rights throughout the twentieth century. The definition of sovereignty, and related issues, drove most debates. Traditionally, sovereignty has meant that the state has complete and exclusive power within its boundaries. This implies that how a government behaves towards its own citizens is not a matter for international attention, even if it violates citizens' rights. The doctrine of popular sovereignty, however, gave a tool to many early Latin American advocates of rights because it declared that sovereignty ultimately rested with the people.[27] Article 39 of the Mexican constitution of 1917 expresses it thus: "The national sovereignty is vested, originally and essentially, in the people. Public power comes from the people and it is institutionalized for the people's benefit. People, at all times have the inalienable right to change or modify its form of government."[28] This vision of popular sovereignty implies that a government cannot use claims of sovereignty to justify human rights violations against citizens since those citizens would then have grounds to revolt and alter their form of government.

Such popular sovereignty arguments form the basis for some of today's doctrines such as the Responsibility to Protect, which redefines sovereignty as creating the responsibility of the government to protect its citizens. Should governments fail in this responsibility, they may be subject to external pressures and assistance. Under such a doctrine, support for nonintervention and support for the international protection of human rights are not mutually exclusive. For Latin American lawyers, however, support for the international protection of human rights virtually never involved support for military intervention, since few envisioned military intervention as a tool for the international promotion of human rights.

The Interwar Period

Although work by lawyers such as Calvo provided important support for international law in the region, it was not until the period between World War I and World War II that lawyer-diplomats first introduced and promoted the idea of internationally recognized human rights. In 1917, Chilean jurist Alejandro Álvarez proposed the idea of the international rights of the individual to the American Institute of International Law.[29] Though historians continue to debate who first introduced the idea of the international protection of human rights, after exploring the topic at length, I am persuaded that Álvarez was indeed the first to propose the international protection of rights; his ideas were later expanded upon by others.[30] Another Latin America expert on international human rights, Ricardo Alfaro of Panama, who researched the topic deeply and was a contemporary of Álvarez, wrote:

> It was an American [i.e. Latin American] jurist, the illustrious Chilean Alejandro Alvarez, who for the first time, suggested in 1917, that the rights of the individual be internationally recognized. Dr. Alvarez made this proposal in his Draft Declaration of the Fundamental Bases of International Law in sessions of the American Institute of International

Law that took place in Havana in 1917. Alvarez's initiative attracted the attention of European scholars, resulting in a session in 1921 of the European Institute of International Law, where Professor de Lapradelle proposed and the Institute approved a draft declaration of the rights of individuals that was without doubt broader and more precise than the articles proposed by Alvarez.[31]

Note the order here—a Latin America jurist proposed an international legal idea, which attracted the attention of European scholars, who elaborated upon it further. By 1917 Álvarez was already participating in transnational judicial networks of experts bridging, at least, the Americas and Europe. This circulation of ideas is very different from the crude understanding of some scholars today, who claim that human rights ideas all started in the Global North and were imposed upon the Global South.[32]

Other jurist-diplomats active in the early proposals for the international protection of human rights include the Russian André Mandelstam and the Greek Antoine Frangulis, the latter of whom subsequently served as a delegate for Haiti at a number of international conferences.[33] Álvarez, Mandelstam, and Frangulis drafted and publicized the first declarations on the international rights of man as part of their work with three different nongovernmental legal organizations—the American Institute of International Law, the International Law Institute, and the International Diplomatic Academy, respectively. Frangulis, working at the time as the delegate from Haiti, tried to get governmental support for these declarations when he introduced an international human rights resolution at the League of Nations in 1933. Unfortunately, it received scant support from countries already in the midst of the crisis leading to German withdrawal from the League.[34]

At the same time that these lawyers first brought attention to the need for the international protection of individual rights, other rights were growing in prominence, especially the rights of minority groups. Eric Weitz has clarified that the international agreements during the interwar period approached the subject of rights from the perspective of group rights for the protection of minorities.[35] At times, protecting minorities was indistinguishable from protecting individuals—protecting a minority group as a whole could often result in the protection of the group's individual members. Yet this emphasis on collective rights created new problems as well. Although they can be seen as a stepping-stone to individual rights, such approaches were also used as a justification for the forced deportations and the genocides of minority populations, done in order to form a pure nation-state, that is, a state that contained only a single national group. This also reinforced the language of colonialism as some nationalities were seen as not yet prepared to have their own autonomous state.[36]

The concept of the international protection of groups continued with the work of a Jewish lawyer from Poland, Raphael Lemkin. Lemkin began a personal campaign to develop international law that forbade the purposeful destruction of groups, coining the term genocide.[37] Influenced as a boy by the massacre of Armenians in Turkey, Lemkin became convinced that the Nazis would carry out parallel outrages against Jews.[38] In 1933, Lemkin first proposed that an international treaty be negotiated making the "destruction of national, religious, and ethnic groups" an international crime akin to piracy, slavery, and drug smuggling.[39] Lemkin's emphasis on protecting groups was contested by those who focused on protecting individuals, a disagreement that would continue in the post-World War II period.[40]

Post–World War II Developments for Human Rights and Democracy

Aside from the work of this handful of individual lawyers and the work of the League on minority treaties, the concept of international protection for human rights received little attention prior to World War II. Although many policymakers and intellectuals were deeply concerned with democracy and freedom, they did not frame these issues in the language of human rights, nor did they call for the international protection of these rights.[41] During World War II, a flurry of new activity around human rights began first among academics and in civil society, and was later joined by diplomats. In the United Kingdom, for example, author H. G. Wells launched a major media campaign in 1939 to draft a new declaration on the rights of man that would clarify the war aims of the Allies. Wells sent the declaration to many people, including President Roosevelt, Gandhi, and Jawaharlal Nehru, all of whom answered.[42] At the same time, legal scholar Hersch Lauterpacht was working on his first book on human rights, *An International Bill of the Rights of Man*, published some time later, in June 1945, just as the San Francisco Conference, which composed the UN Charter, was ending.[43]

Near the end of World War II a global consensus began to emerge that human rights and democracy would need to be an essential part of the postwar order. No individual scholar or government led this global consensus; instead, ideas that had been circulating in the interwar period and during World War II converged. Most scholars are familiar with the initiatives taken by the Allies during the war to stress the importance of human rights. In particular, scholars point to Roosevelt's "Four Freedoms" speech and the inclusion of human rights language in the Atlantic Charter, both in 1941 and both influential in much of the world, not so much because of their originality, but because they promised renewed support of these ideals from the Allies in the postwar world. As mentioned previously, ideas about the international protection of human rights were already present in the interwar period. The endorsement of these ideals as part of Allied war aims generated high expectations for human rights and their protection in the postwar era.

Increasing support for human rights was not limited to Europe, the United States, and Latin America. In his book on Indian foreign policy in the post-World War II period, historian Manu Bhagavan calls this time "a true global Utopian moment, when anything seemed possible," and stresses that "there was virtually unanimous global consensus that an architecture of such human rights had to be created."[44] Such consensus extended to the new leaders in India, including Jawaharlal Nehru and his sister Vijaya Lakshmi Pandit, as well as the diplomat Hansa Mehta, who played key roles in the creation of the United Nations and in its embrace of human rights norms.

The atrocities of the Second World War called into question the doctrines of sovereignty and nonintervention, as the moral and political flaws of absolute sovereignty were revealed. For example, in the wake of World War II, the Uruguayan foreign minister, Eduardo Rodriguez Larreta, recognized the ways in which sovereignty and non-intervention could be misused when he wrote, "'Non-intervention' cannot be converted into a right to invoke one principle in order to be able to violate all other principles with immunity."[45] He argued instead that nonintervention had to be "harmonized" with the other principles important to the Inter-American system:

> [N]on-intervention is not a shield behind which crime may be perpetrated, law may be violated, agents and forces of the Axis may be sheltered, and binding obligations may be circumvented. Otherwise, at the very time when, since Mexico [Chapultepec Conference] and after San Francisco, we should be creating a new international and humanitarian conception, we would find ourselves tolerating a doctrine capable of frustrating and destroying that very conception.[46]

Dumbarton Oaks and the Great Powers

While the great powers stressed human rights in their war aims, they were much more hesitant to endorse the international protection of human rights through international law and institutions. The British, for example, following their common-law tradition developed without a written constitution, tended to oppose formal statements about rights.[47] The United Kingdom was also resistant because of its colonial holdings. When diplomats and jurists first proposed the international protection of human rights, powerful countries like the United Kingdom, France, and the Soviet Union were empires and did not want other countries or the new United Nations to scrutinize the rights of their subjects, particularly in the colonies. The United States, on the other hand, was more concerned with the implications of having international protections for human rights on segregation and Jim Crow laws in the southern states. Powerful groups within the United States wanted to prevent the United Nations from addressing racial discrimination within the country.[48] There were many champions of the idea of the international protection of human rights within these powerful countries, including jurists, diplomats, and activists, but they were having a hard time persuading their governments to support the cause.

The US and UK governments were both deeply divided about including human rights in the postwar order. US Secretary of State Cordell Hull had been willing to use human rights language during the war, but he opposed any efforts to promote human rights that would undermine national sovereignty in the postwar period.[49] Other members of the US government, especially the Undersecretary of State Sumner Welles, were committed to incorporating human rights into US foreign policy and into a new international organization, but these efforts were often impeded. Welles chaired one of the most important subcommittees of the Advisory Committee on Postwar Foreign Policy, which produced an international bill of human rights under his leadership in 1942, but the State Department never used or published the document.[50] Hull's opposition to the codification of international human rights eventually carried the day; the US delegation to the Dumbarton Oaks meeting was instructed to avoid any detailed discussion of human rights.[51] The initial US drafts of the UN Charter contained no references to human rights, and the proposals that emerged from the Big Four meeting at Dumbarton Oaks in preparation for the conference contained only one reference to human rights.[52] Due to conflicts within the US government and among the great powers, the Dumbarton Oaks meeting also did not discuss another crucial human rights issue that would dominate the post-World War II period—decolonization, and the related question of how to administer the colonies of the Axis countries as well as the territories inherited from the League of Nations mandate system.[53]

The reluctance of the great powers to include references to human rights in the UN Charter calls into question both a realist and a critical theory explanation for the origins of human rights norms. If human rights discourse emerged primarily from the goals and needs of powerful states, as realists claim, then why did these powerful states not include human rights language in the Dumbarton Oaks draft? Only China, the weakest of the four, pressed for the inclusion of an explicit statement against racial discrimination. This was rejected by the other great powers since the two other key governmental actors, the USSR and the United Kingdom, shared the United States' desire to limit possible infringement on domestic jurisdiction.[54] Although the human rights provisions did not have any teeth at this early stage, these powerful states were wary of the sovereignty implications of the human rights issue.

The Latin American Response

The exclusion of human rights language from the Dumbarton Oaks draft mobilized both the NGO community and a group of less powerful states, primarily in Latin America, but also the Philippines, Lebanon, New Zealand, and Australia. These countries were disappointed because they were not consulted about the Dumbarton Oaks plans for a postwar organization, and also because the draft for the UN Charter did not incorporate a number of ideals they supported, including human rights.[55] To voice their concerns and formulate a collective policy, Latin American countries called an extraordinary meeting at the Chapultepec Castle in Mexico City in February 1945—the Inter-American Conference on Problems of War and Peace—which ended just weeks before the opening of the San Francisco Conference to finalize the UN Charter.

Before the meeting, the Inter-American Juridical Committee prepared a detailed report of comments and recommendations on the Dumbarton Oaks proposal for the UN Charter. The committee argued for the Charter's inclusion of an international bill of rights. In perhaps its most radical statement, the committee suggested that "the community of nations has rights in its own name, that it is not the mere agent of sovereign and independent states." Furthermore, there needed to be some "machinery of international organization which could represent the will of the entire community and its collective interests."[56]

Delegates at Chapultepec raised a series of important issues: great-power dominance, the importance of international law, regional agreements for security, and economic and social problems. Human rights issues figured prominently in the speeches and resolutions.[57] Many Latin American states argued that World War II had created a worldwide demand that rights be recognized and protected at the international level.[58] Resolutions also emphasized the "necessity" of a declaration of the rights of man and the importance of having international machinery and procedures to put the principles of the declaration into action. Cuba and Uruguay even submitted draft declarations of human rights. Acting on these concerns, the delegates instructed the Inter-American Juridical Committee to prepare a draft declaration on the rights and duties of man.[59] States also debated proposals from Ecuador and Guatemala about whether member states should take a firmer stand against military coups by collectively agreeing to deny diplomatic recognition to governments that came to power through non-democratic means.

A careful examination of the coalition of Latin America states supporting human rights at this time reveals diverse political actors. Some scholars have argued that, in this period, human rights were primarily a project of the Christian right rather than the secular left, a claim refuted by the evidence from Latin America, where substantial support came from the secular left, as well as from some countries with more conservative, Catholic traditions.[60] The issue, as we shall see in chapter 4, was less about religion than it was about regime type. Authoritarian regimes, including those stressing their Christian orientation, opposed human rights, while democracies supported them.

The San Francisco Conference

As the delegates prepared for the San Francisco Conference in 1945—organized for the creation of the new postwar international organization—they were shocked and saddened to learn of the passing of President Franklin D. Roosevelt, who died of a heart attack just thirteen days before he was to travel to San Francisco to open the conference. Throughout the conference, whenever Latin American delegations—especially Uruguay, Chile, Panama, and Mexico—made arguments in favor of the international protection of rights, they often referenced Roosevelt's "Four Freedoms," both to honor his memory and also to prod the US delegation into taking a stronger position on human rights.

The largest diplomatic conference in history to that date, the San Francisco Conference lasted for over two months and included two thousand delegates, experts, advisers, and secretaries from fifty countries and 2,400 news and radio correspondents.[61] Of the fifty states at San Francisco, eighteen were from what we now call the

Global North, while thirty-one (or sixty-two percent) were from what we now call the Global South.[62] Twenty countries from Latin America made up the largest regional group at the meeting, while eleven countries from the developing world also joined, including the Republic of China (under Chiang Kai-shek, prior to the communist revolution), Egypt, Iran, Lebanon, the Philippine Commonwealth, Saudi Arabia, Syria, Turkey, Ethiopia, Iraq, and Liberia.[63] Many other countries were colonies at the time and thus were excluded, but, even so, the debate was more diverse than is often recognized.

Because the US government knew it would be difficult to get the Senate to ratify the UN Charter, it included senators in the delegation and invited a number of US-based NGOs to participate as consultants in the hope that they would later mobilize civil society to support the treaty. These NGOs backed demands for the inclusion of human rights and democracy in the Charter and lobbied the US government to endorse these proposals from Latin American and other small states.[64] The Latin Americans became the most important voting bloc at San Francisco; with each part of the Charter requiring a two-third majority to pass, the votes of the twenty Latin American countries were essential. In this brief historical moment, the region was composed mainly of democratic countries with a shared worldview.[65] The British government gave the Latin American bloc credit for changing the US government's position on human rights at San Francisco.[66] Without Latin American protagonism, it is unlikely that the Charter would have contained references to human rights.

The future of colonialism was another crucial human rights issue at San Francisco. Framed in the language of "trusteeship," or the temporary supervision of territories as they made their way from being colonies to independence, it was the "hottest subject" at the conference, in the words of Ralph Bunche, a member of the US delegation.[67] The United Kingdom and France opposed any efforts to promote the independence of their colonial possessions, while many of the countries present from the Global South believed that one of the most important roles of the new UN would be to promote the process of decolonization. Bunche, the only African-American on the US delegation, worked together with other anti-colonial advocates to craft a better system for trusteeship, despite opposition from the British, French, and some of the US delegation at San Francisco. Bunche would later serve as the first director of the Trusteeship Council at the new United Nations, before going on to be UN Undersecretary for Special Political Affairs, where he also promoted an anti-colonial agenda.[68]

The final version of the UN Charter testifies to the success of the NGO lobbying effort, the efforts of Latin American delegations in favor of human rights, and the work of the advocates of decolonization. The Charter contains seven references to human rights, including listing the promotion of human rights as one of the basic purposes of the organization. The Economic and Social Council (ECOSOC) is called on to set up a human rights commission, the only specifically mandated commission in the Charter. In particular, the initiatives of the Latin American countries helped extend the economic, social, and human rights objectives, especially in Articles 55 and 56, on which later human rights work of the organization rested. In addition, Chapter XI calls for UN members to promote "the progressive development of their free political institutions" in colonial territories.[69]

If the Charter, adopted at a high point of postwar collaboration, had not contained references to human rights and to a human rights commission, it is likely that the Universal Declaration of Human Rights (UDHR) would not have been drafted in 1948. The chapters of the Charter on trusteeship and non-self-governing territories "gave momentum and legitimacy to decolonization," which would in turn completely transform the membership of the organization over the next thirty years.[70] The inclusion of human rights language in the founding text of the United Nations was thus a critical juncture that channeled the history of postwar global governance in the direction of setting international norms and law about the promotion of human rights.[71] The language adopted was not the language of the great powers, but rather that of the Global South; it was only adopted by the great powers in response to pressure from small states and civil society.

Some Latin American states and NGOs demanded that the United Nations have more far-reaching power to enforce international human rights norms. The Uruguayan delegation, for example, proposed that the UN Charter contain a "Declaration of Rights" and "a system of effective juridical guardianship of those rights."[72] Uruguay proposed that it be possible to suspend from the organization countries which persistently violated human rights.[73] The final language of the Charter on human rights is less firm than many states and NGOs desired, since it calls on the UN to promote and encourage respect for human rights rather than to actually protect such rights.[74] Other broad, alternative visions for the new organization were presented and articulated at the San Francisco Conference, and the NGO consultants and a handful of democratic Latin American states were among the most eloquent spokespeople for them.

Colonial populations were also disappointed that the new United Nations did not contain more forceful language on the enforcement of human rights and the promotion of self-determination. Colonized peoples nevertheless used the new UN Charter to make their own demands for equality as well as economic and social improvements. For example, at the Fifth Pan-African Congress held in October 1945 in Manchester, England, just four months after the UN Charter was passed, delegates demanded racial equality, self-determination, and human rights; they also affirmed their support of the principles spelled out in the Charter.[75]

In the debate on the UN Charter, Latin American countries made it clear that they supported sovereignty and nonintervention, but also that these had to be subordinated to international law. For example, when discussing sovereignty, the Chileans clarified that, "The State is lord of its territory, can grant itself whatever *democratic* form of government it may desire *within standards which respect the inalienable rights of man*."[76]

Latin American countries were not alone in grappling with how to balance human rights and sovereignty. Almost as soon as the UN was set up, debates began to emerge about the conflicts between sovereignty and human rights that were embedded in the language of the Charter. In some of the early meetings of the UN, even before the UDHR was drafted, the Indian delegate, Madame Pandit, raised the issue of human rights violations in South Africa, where a large population of men and women from India faced legal discrimination. South Africa had been a training ground for Gandhi's activism,

FIG. 3.1. Madame Vijaya Lakshmi Pandit of India, in the Security Council chamber the day after being elected President of the United Nations General Assembly, 16 September 1953. With Dag Hammerskold. UN Photo / AF. Reproduced with permission.

so it held a special place in the minds of the new Indian leadership. In a General Assembly debate on the issue of sovereignty and human rights, India carried the day with the argument that the human rights of Indians in South Africa were not a matter only under the domestic jurisdiction of South Africa.[77] South Africa had argued that this was an issue covered by Article 2(7) of the Charter, which said, "Nothing contained in the present Charter shall authorize the United Nations to intervene in matters which are essentially within the domestic jurisdiction of any state."[78] Pandit persuaded the General Assembly that the human rights violations of Indians in South Africa were not solely within the jurisdiction of the South African state; rather, these human rights abuses were an issue that the UN could and should investigate. This move by India made the UN clarify, for the very first time, that violations of human rights were not protected by the doctrine of sovereignty. Nehru, writing to Einstein about this struggle, said that when India fought against policies in South Africa, it "stood on the broader plane of human rights for all in accordance with the Charter of the United Nations."[79]

The American Declaration of the Rights and Duties of Man and the UDHR

The UN Charter called on the new international organization to play a role in promoting respect for human rights, but no inter-governmental enumeration of such rights yet existed. The next step was to draft an agreed-upon, international definition of human rights. Two different processes got underway for drafting a declaration of rights at around the same time—an international process to draft the UDHR and a regional process to draft the American Declaration of the Rights and Duties of Man. These two processes were overlapping and complementary, but the process of drafting the American Declaration was always a step ahead of the drafting of the UDHR.[80] The Inter-American Judicial Committee produced a complete draft of the American Declaration, including twenty-one articles and another fifty pages of full commentary, by December 31, 1945, only six months after the San Francisco Conference had concluded. This document was published and circulated among member countries for comments in March of 1946, before the UN Preparatory Committee tasked with drafting the UDHR had even held its first meeting.[81] The American states later expanded the American Declaration beyond this draft declaration, but all core civil, political, economic, social, and cultural rights of the American Declaration were present in the 1945 draft.

The Bogotá Meeting

In April 1948, the American states met in Bogotá, Colombia, to address a number of regional concerns, foremost among them being the creation of a new regional organization, the Organization of American States (OAS). Just as the creation of the UN led to a long discussion about human rights and democracy, a similar debate continued in Bogotá. Once again, a minority of states wanted to include a human rights declaration as part of the OAS Charter, while other states argued for less legally binding options. The argument in favor of a separate declaration of rights and duties eventually won out over the idea of making human rights part of the binding OAS treaty. The draft American Declaration of the Rights and Duties of Man served as a starting place for the debate.[82]

Latin America's greatest contribution to human rights was an attempt "to combine and balance the individual and the communal aspect of human rights."[83] Latin Americans did this by incorporating attention to human duties as well as language on human rights; they also combined attention to civil and political *and* economic and social rights.[84] In doing so, Latin American jurists and diplomats drew on socialist, liberal, and catholic traditions to navigate between models of liberal capitalism and socialist collectivism.[85] The delegates in Bogotá considered the draft declaration prepared by the Inter-American Juridical Committee and added eight new articles on rights and ten articles on duties. Most discussions of duties in human rights law refer to the corresponding state duties that each right imposes. For example, if an individual has a right to education, the state has a duty to provide such education. But the duties in the American Declaration are of a different type. They are the complementary or supplementary duties that individuals have in addition to those of the state. In addition to the duty the state has to provide education, the American Declaration also says that "every person has the duty to acquire at least a primary education," and that parents have the duty to educate their children.[86] This attention to duties sets the American Declaration apart from the UDHR, which does not list specific duties, although it does mention them generally in Article 29. The earlier drafts by the Inter-American Juridical Committee did not include this list of duties; the decision to add them was made at Bogotá.

The American Declaration of the Rights and Duties of Man was built upon the existing traditions and constitutions of Latin American countries. In this sense, the rights and duties in the documents emerged from within Latin America, not as an imitation of the ideas of the United States or Western Europe. This is what one scholar has called "Inter-American Constitutionalism," or the interaction between human rights developments and progressive constitutional developments in the region.[87] Thus, the idea of human rights and of human duties was not a recent "legal transplant" in the region, but rather a nourished and cultivated local aspiration.[88]

Still, the inclusion of duties along with rights did not earn the declaration whole-hearted support from every Latin American state. More than any other country, Mexico was motivated by fear of intervention to oppose the strong, legally binding language proposed by other states. Located so close to the United States and the object of multiple US interventions over the years, Mexico had become the most rigorous defender of sovereignty and nonintervention in the region. The country's initial support for human rights declarations grew out of Mexicans' concern about US intervention to protect the rights of US nationals abroad, a problem anticipated by the Calvo Doctrine. If a declaration of the rights of man could lead to a single standard of rights protections for all people, such foreign interventions to protect rights would cease. This was Mexico's position at Chapultepec and in San Francisco. But after San Francisco, and after the election of a more conservative administration, Mexicans began to worry that the international protection of human rights could lead to more, not less, intervention. The Mexican government instructed its delegates to Bogotá to change directions. They were to support only a declaration of human rights, not a legally binding treaty, and to support national protection of human rights rather than international protection. For this reason, it would be important to change the title of the new declaration, tentatively titled "The Declaration of the *International* Rights and Duties of Man," by removing "international," thus leaving its purpose more ambiguous.

As a result of these kinds of disagreements, some of the delegations to Bogotá were disappointed with the human rights results of the conference. Some delegates had hoped that a declaration of rights would be included in the OAS Charter and that enforcement would be provided for the international protection of rights. Compared to this ideal of a legal document with provisions for enforcement, the head of the Uruguayan delegation, Dardo Regules, said the position states took on human rights was "the most timid and least obligatory." When he tried to explain why Uruguay and its allies had not succeeded in a more vigorous assertion of the rights of man, he suggested that authoritarian countries in the region were "alarmed at the creation of any institution that would oblige them to comply with international responsibilities." He also thought some Latin American jurists were so attached to the idea of nonintervention that they shied away from any new doctrine that might threaten it.[89]

The Influence of the American Declaration on the UDHR

The American Declaration was completed before the second round of drafting of the UDHR, and it was influential in the creation of the UDHR, particularly with regard to social and economic rights. In his book on the drafting of the UDHR, Morsink writes that the American Declaration "heavily influenced the drafting process and product of the universal one."[90] All of the rights in the UDHR appear first in the American Declaration, with the UDHR sometimes elaborating on them. The heavy influence of the American Declaration on the UDHR is not surprising as they share similar sources. When John Humphrey, the Canadian who served as the head of the UN Secretariat's Human Rights Division, wrote the Secretariat Outline (a draft bill of rights) for the UN Commission on Human Rights meant for use in producing the eventual UDHR, his models included drafts from countries, law professors, and NGOs, as well as from other intergovernmental organizations, including the Pan-American Union.[91] Cuba, Panama, and Chile were the first three countries to submit full drafts of bills of rights to the commission; each contained references to rights to education, food, health care, and other social security provisions.[92] Humphrey, a social democrat, was very sympathetic to the idea that the UDHR should include economic and social rights and used these drafts extensively in preparing the Secretariat's draft for the commission to consider. These submissions influenced his thinking so profoundly that "Humphrey took much of the wording and almost all of the ideas for the social, economic, and cultural rights of his first draft from the tradition of Latin American socialism," present in these Latin American draft bills of rights.[93] The involvement of Latin American countries in the inclusion of economic and social rights in the UDHR corrects a long-held belief that the economic and social rights in the UDHR were primarily the result of Soviet pressure.[94]

In the process of drafting the UDHR, Latin American delegates tried to insert articles on individual duties from the American Declaration, but with less success. The Cuban delegate Guy Pérez Cisneros, an ardent Catholic, pushed this most firmly. He said, "the individual must be reminded that he is a member of society and that he must affirm his right to be a human being by clearly recognizing the duties which are corollaries of his rights." The Brazilian delegate argued that it was "impossible to draw up a declaration of rights without proclaiming the duties implicit in the concept of freedom." Without the concept of duties, he continued, "freedom might lead to anarchy and tyranny." Delegate Peng-chun Chang from China also supported duties, especially since they aligned with Chinese collectivist ideals, as opposed to Western individualism. Other concepts introduced by Chang—such as two-man mindedness (translated as "conscience") and the "spirit of brotherhood"—reflected the responsibilities of an individual to his community and were incorporated into the UDHR, even though specific duties were not.[95]

The Latin American delegates failed to incorporate a detailed list of duties into the UDHR; they had to settle for a single line in Article 29 mentioning duties in general. Still, in the wording of that line, they believed that they had secured a victory for their more communitarian vision. The line read, "Everyone has duties to the community in which alone the free and full development of his personality is possible." The victory came with the word "alone," which, to them, recognized that community was necessary to the enjoyment of rights, and that duties were essential to the protection of that community.[96]

In addition to the economic and social rights and some mention of duties in the UDHR, Latin American delegates made other important contributions. Latin American delegations, especially Mexico, Cuba, and Chile, were the first to insist that the American Declaration include the right to justice. They then almost single-handedly inserted language about the right to justice into the UDHR, in what would become Article 8 of that Declaration. For them, the right to justice was the existence of judicial procedures that could protect the individuals against the abuse of authority by governments that violated their rights.

The *amparo* laws that existed in most, but not all, Latin American countries are probably the origin of Latin American proposals on the right to justice in the American Declaration and the UDHR.

Since there is no equivalent of full *amparo* law in common-law countries, it is difficult to translate. Habeas corpus is related, but habeas corpus only protects against unjust detention, while *amparo* laws offer protection for the full range of rights violations that may occur as a result of "acts of authority." Habeas corpus is like a species in a broader genus of protections, many of which are covered by *amparo* laws.[97] This is a clear example of normative innovation and protagonism in which Latin American delegations took legal procedures from their own constitutional traditions, which were not present in the constitutions of the large common law countries, and used them to craft an essential article of the new human rights declarations. The idea of a right to justice would later serve as the backbone for Latin American efforts to secure accountability through the Inter-American system. In this sense, there is continuity from the normative and legal contributions that Latin American states made to the UDHR and the American Declaration and the Inter-American system's later contributions to human rights law in the 1970s and 1990s. Without being pushed by Latin American delegates, the right to justice would not have been articulated in the UDHR.

Latin American countries were not alone in wanting stronger enforcement of human rights. The delegate from Yugoslavia attempted to include colonial populations explicitly in an article of the Universal Declaration that was "vehemently quashed by Great Britain in agreement with France."[98] The Indian delegate to the UN Commission on Human Rights, Hansa Mehta, also sought something more binding than a simple declaration of human rights. She proposed a framework for a special human rights committee, which would work with an international court to hear cases by and against individuals and states.[99] We see here that Mehta, with the support of Nehru, was a human rights visionary, suggesting ideas for enforcement that would not be adopted for another half century.

Women's Rights in the UN Charter and the UDHR

The story of how equal rights for men and women came to be included in the UN Charter illustrates how contributions from the Global South are often disregarded or even distorted. Some scholars

FIG. 3.2. Bertha Lutz of Brazil at the San Francisco Conference,
15 June 1945. UN Photo / Mili. Reproduced with permission.

simply assume that the small handful of women representing countries such as the United States and Canada made the difference.
Even the official UN story does not correctly recount the history; it
recognizes that, of the six official women delegates at the San Francisco Conference in 1945 (where the UN Charter was drafted), half
came from Latin America (the Dominican Republic, Brazil, and
Uruguay), one from China, one from the United States, and one
from Canada, but suggests that all the women delegates "worked
successfully together to include key wording for women's rights in
the UN Charter."[100] In reality, two Latin American women—Bertha
Lutz, the delegate from Brazil, and Minerva Bernardino, from the
Dominican Republic—took the lead in these efforts and received
more support from many of their colleagues in Latin America than
they did from the other women delegates.

The positions of the Latin American delegates at San Francisco were the result of their involvement, often decades long, with the Pan-American feminist movement, "a movement Lutz had helped start."[101] This movement's broad goals included not only the right to vote, but also social rights for women, labor legislation for domestic and rural workers, and greater multilateralism and global equality in international relations among states.[102] Lutz and Bernadino sponsored resolutions and amendments not only to promote women's rights, but also to support human rights and prohibit discrimination more generally. It is partly due to their efforts that the UN Charter mentions human rights in so many of its sections.[103] Lutz and Bernardino advocated for language supporting the equal rights of men and women, including what later became Article 8 of the Charter, which said, "The United Nations shall place no restrictions on the eligibility of men and women to participate in any capacity and under conditions of equality in its principal and subsidiary organs."[104] In promoting this language, Lutz and Bernardino were opposed by women delegates from the United States and Canada and by the women advisors to the UK delegation.[105]

Lutz, the daughter of a British mother and Brazilian father with Swiss-German roots, was a longtime Anglophile and anxious to meet the English-speaking women delegates. Shortly after Lutz arrived, she received an invitation to tea with US delegate Virginia Gildersleeve, Dean of Barnard College, and the two women advisors to the UK delegation. Lutz found them condescending.[106] Gildersleeve "peppered Lutz with questions about her qualifications, trying to "place her," to which Lutz responded, "Try Percy B. Martin's *Who's Who in Latin America*."[107] When Lutz told them her goal was to have a United Nations that would promote women's rights and include women in all its work, Gildersleeve warned Lutz that "urg[ing] any special measures for women in the charter" would be "very vulgar" and "unlady-like."[108]

In her notes from the conference, Lutz explained how the Latin American delegates, with the support of women advisors from the Australian delegation, fought for a general statement on women's rights, recognizing full equality of men and women before the law. She was bitterly disappointed in the failure of the US and British women to support a women's rights resolution. As Lutz reported:

The women delegates from the United States and Britain took the view that it was unnecessary—even undignified—for women to claim rights for themselves and that their presence at the Conference was proof positive that women were already in full status in the organisation. . . . The American delegate took the view that she was not there as a woman but as an expert. The British women maintained that as there were [women] Ministers [in the United Kingdom] women had no further vindications in Britain. . . . It was impossible to make the women from the great English speaking and war leading democracies see that there were women in other countries, not necessarily in South America which had contributed two women legislators to the Conference, where women had no rights.[109]

Lutz's memo also records humorous encounters with other delegations. The Soviet delegation, for example, had no women delegates; they explained to Lutz this was because "the trip over the polar regions was too strenuous for them." Nevertheless, Lutz later said that, of the big five sponsoring powers, "only Russia showed decided good will towards the women's amendments."[110]

US-based NGOs were much more supportive of the inclusion of women's amendments than were the US delegates themselves. Lutz met with US representatives of women's organizations who were present at San Francisco as consultants to the US delegation to ask them for their support of the Latin American amendments. These consultants in turn lobbied the US delegation and, despite continued opposition from Gildersleeve, they were eventually able to secure "a rather unwilling acquiescence" of the US delegation to the women's amendments. Finally, and surprisingly, the head of the South African delegation, Field Marshal Smuts, added a phrase to the Preamble of the UN Charter that reaffirmed "the equal rights of men and women and of nations large and small."[111]

Efforts to include references to women's rights in the UN Charter were followed by efforts to include women's rights in the UDHR. Hansa Mehta, the delegate from India both to the San Francisco Conference and to the drafting of the UDHR in 1948, made important contributions to the recognition of women's rights in both instances. A feminist who had been a strong advocate of India's independence and women's rights, Mehta served on the UN Sub-Commission on

FIG. 3.3. Commission members Hansa Mehta (right) and J. Marguerite
Bowie at the Fifth Session of the Human Rights Commission, 9 May
1949. UN Photo / Marvin Bolotsky. Reproduced with permission.

the Status of Women, where her contributions were informed by her
work with the All India Women's Conference in mid-1946.[112]

When Mehta saw that the original draft of Article 1 of the Universal Declaration said, "All men are born free and equal in dignity
and rights," she cautioned that terms like "'all men' . . . might be
interpreted to exclude women, and were out of date." Eleanor Roosevelt, chair of the UN Commission on Human Rights, did not see
the need for the change; the word men, she said, was generally accepted to include all human beings. But Mehta and other delegates
insisted and, through their persistent lobbying, the article was
changed to read "All human beings."[113]

Mehta also worked with Minerva Bernardino, the representative of the Dominican Republic, on the process of drafting the UDHR to make sure that the preamble of the UDHR reiterated the language of the preamble of the UN Charter by referring to the "equal rights of men and women." The Committee eventually voted 32-2 to include a reference to the "equal rights of men and women" with both China and the United States voting against.[114]

In summary, Bertha Lutz and Minerva Bernardino played important roles in getting women's rights into the UN Charter, the treaty on which all later UN human rights work was based; Mehta and Bernardino continued this work in strengthening the language of women's rights in the UDHR. Yet almost no one knows their names or remembers their achievements.[115] In Latin America, Lutz is not a well-known figure and, even in Brazil, it is only recently that her contributions are starting to be recognized, for example, in a wonderful "virtual museum" about her life put together by scholars at the University of Brasília.[116] Lutz was a feminist, a biologist, and a champion of women's rights and labor rights in many international conferences before and after World War II. In this sense, she had more international experience than Eleanor Roosevelt did when President Truman asked her to serve as a US delegate to the United Nations in 1945. I do not want to minimize Roosevelt's contributions—she was a courageous civil rights and women's rights advocate before she began her career in international human rights. But we need to make sure that all the attention to Roosevelt does not obscure the work of others.[117]

Agency and Authenticity of Human Rights Advocates

To direct our attention to the potential agency of individuals and states outside the Global North, we first need to see the complexities that are ignored by dividing the world into north and south and east and west. Many scholars use the terms "Global North" and "the West" as if they were interchangeable, referring to wealthy countries in Europe and North America. Latin America complicates this distinction because Latin American scholars and politicians have inherited the Western intellectual traditions of the Enlightenment and yet are geographically and politically part of the Global South.[118]

Many of the Latin Americans involved in the human rights movement and international law had a "creole" legal consciousness that blended elements of Latin American experiences and concerns with the international legal traditions of the time. Liliana Obregón, the scholar who coined the term "creole legal consciousness," explained it to me in these terms, using herself as an example: "You could say I am a modern creole in the sense that I have to write in English to get read, I have been at the center of academic power, but still feel tied to a certain particularity and sensibility of where I come from."[119] For Obregón, "creole" does not refer to an ethnic category, but rather to a legal and social category—a way of thinking about government and international law. Latin American legal elites participated in the international debates that took place at the center of power, while also challenging those at the center with ideas from their own regional perspective.[120] Arnulf Becker Lorca draws attention to a similar phenomenon that he calls "mestizo international law," which stresses the role non-Western international lawyers played in the construction of the international legal order. Lorca realizes that international law is often a discourse of power, but he shows that international law has been and can be one of resistance to power.[121] In the case of the San Francisco Conference, the majority of countries present were not from the Global North, yet they were able to make their concerns about development and rights present in the UN Charter in ways that had enduring influence on the work of that international organization.

Some critical theorists do not deny that individuals and political leaders from the Global South promoted human rights, but because these individuals were educated abroad or embraced western philosophies, they are seen as less authentic and not fully representative of their regions or traditions. In chapter 1, I presented the concept of "authenticity" as one part of legitimacy; by questioning the authenticity of some of these activists from the Global South, the legitimacy of human rights law is called into question. Thus, the contributions of a diplomat like Charles Malik—the representative of Lebanon who played an important role in the drafting of the UDHR—are discounted because he was a Christian educated abroad in American schools, eventually securing a Ph.D. in Philosophy from Harvard. For some scholars and activists, this makes him appear inauthentic, mimicking the ideas of the West rather than representing the Middle East—even though Christianity originated in the Middle East and Lebanon was founded as a majority Christian state in the early twentieth century. But one of Malik's key contributions to the UDHR arose directly from his preoccupation with issues relevant to Lebanon: the proposal that the freedom of religion article include the right to change one's beliefs. Malik based this idea not on a Western precedent, but on his country's experience accepting religious refugees, some of whom fled persecution resulting from religious conversions.[122]

Similarly, just before and during World War I, British-trained African intellectuals such as Osho Davis and Bandele Omoniyi argued forcefully against Britain's Native Authority system of exclusion of its colonial subjects from direct rule by allowing traditional rulers extensive powers over local African administrative units. These writers advocated for "the capacity of Africans to enjoy full political and civil rights," but because they were trained in Britain, some scholars may portray them as less authentic.[123]

Denying the authenticity of these scholars and diplomats means overlooking the already transnational character of the world in the mid-twentieth century—ideas were exchanged and people moved. All of the human rights champions discussed in this book took part in the global circulation of ideas and were part of transnational networks of activists, intellectuals, and diplomats.[124] Lutz, for instance, participated in what today we would call a transnational advocacy network.[125] She represented the Brazilian government at international conferences, but she was not just giving technical expertise. She was also an advocate for women's rights and was linked to other advocates in Brazil, Latin America, and around the world.

Like Malik and Lutz, General Carlos Romulo from the Philippines might be wrongly accused of having inherited and promoted the viewpoints of the United States, his country's past colonizer, during the drafting of the UDHR.[126] Yet closer examination reveals that General Romulo did the opposite. Instead of borrowing US foreign policy, he pointed to the "the spirit behind America's work in the Philippines" and molded it into what he called the "Philippine Pattern."[127] He encouraged the involvement of greater powers in the developing world, not through imperialism, but rather through the extension of rights and freedoms.[128] General Romulo, it is true, framed aspects of US imperialism as laudable, but he did so to strengthen his argument for the international promotion of individual rights.[129]

Not only are some of these delegates viewed an "inauthentic," but also as politically incorrect. Lutz, for example, abhorred Gandhi, did not support anti-colonial efforts in San Francisco, and privately held racist views. Both Bernardino and Lutz helped found middle class or upper middle class feminist organizations and were seen as too cozy with the dictators in power in their countries, Rafael Trujillo and Getúlio Vargas.[130] Bernardino and Lutz were people of their time in many ways and yet, at the same time, they were extraordinarily progressive in their demands for and work on behalf of women's rights.

To discredit the contributions of people like Malik or Lutz because they were educated abroad or held some conservative views misses the point. As we saw from Lutz's memoirs, delegates from parts of the Global South were proud of their positions and capable of standing up to powerful states.[131] This pride and autonomy has been lost in some of the postcolonial or subaltern scholarship. The idea of the subaltern highlights how people were excluded from established structures for political representation and denied a voice in refashioning their world.[132] Such exclusion was the norm in the 1940s, when many countries were still colonies and their people were excluded from representation and denied a voice at the new United Nations. But in their efforts to highlight the exclusion of the subaltern, some postcolonial theorists have ignored or downplayed important episodes of Southern protagonism, paradoxically marginalizing the contributions of delegates from the Global South who were active at the time.[133]

Many of the individuals discussed in this book were embodiments of a creole legal consciousness and hoped to refashion their world in part through mestizo international law. Here I don't limit the words creole or mestizo to Latin Americans; instead I use them to refer to individuals from any country or region who were fully engaged in the global legal debates, while questioning the terms of those debates from the perspective of the periphery of the system. Advocates of human rights and democracy from the Global South had the potential for full agency, as did their colleagues from the Global North. In other words, human rights activists from the Global South need to be seen as "autonomous beings who are responsible for many of their own actions."[134] They were not fully representative of their society, but neither were most human rights advocates. These individuals, moreover, were visionaries, so they were out ahead of majorities in their countries. Was Eleanor Roosevelt fully representative of the United States? Roosevelt lived at a time when the majority of Americans supported or tolerated legal discrimination against African-Americans. Roosevelt, on the other hand, committed herself to civil rights. Each of our protagonists reflected some strands of belief within his or her own country and rejected or challenged others. In their own ways, both Eleanor Roosevelt and Bertha Lutz were outliers in their own societies.[135]

To dismiss the authenticity of delegates from the Global South because they were in the minority—advocates of feminism, students abroad, etc.—is not only paternalistic, but also reflects a misunderstanding of the transnational nature of debates about rights in the twentieth century. Societies both in the Global South and the Global North were politically heterogeneous, and human rights activists often represented minority points of view. In the post-World War II period, these minority points of view were amplified by the great crisis the world had just passed through and the desire for a new beginning. Still, the ideas that surfaced at San Francisco had been percolating for a long time.

Conclusion

The post-World War II history of the human rights movement illustrates how the less powerful embraced the idea of the international protection of human rights in attempts to restrain the more powerful, not vice versa. These less powerful groups, however, were more likely to succeed when they had allies within powerful states. In the case of the UN Charter and the UDHR, the protagonists were Latin American states, other small states, and NGOs that took leadership roles in incorporating human rights into postwar institutions and eventually were able to persuade the United States to support them, not the other way around.[136]

Why have Latin America's role and the role of other small states in the emergence of global human rights norms and law not been more broadly perceived or understood by international relations scholars, including, at times, scholars from the Global South? There are a number of possible explanations. Many scholars of international relations have neither the training, the knowledge, nor the inclination to conduct field research in the developing world. They, therefore, turn to sources in the Global North. There is yet another paradox here: even scholars who critique how the Global North imposes norms on the Global South often do so on the basis of research conducted almost solely in the Global North, using sources available there. The research design of these scholars reproduces the very situation they critique. In their efforts to stress how the countries of the Global North have silenced voices in the developing world and imposed northern values on them, such scholars also have perpetuated the silence by not carefully investigating sources from the developing world. For example, one of the editors of *Revisiting the Origins of Human Rights*, a volume inspired by critical legal theory, tells us in her chapter on the UDHR that "it remains virtually impossible to find any decisive moments both prior to and after the adoption of the UDHR where one could argue that the underdogs . . . have genuinely been the primary actors themselves in the diverse global arenas instead of mere targets of action."[137] Yet, with the exception of a single mention of Simón Bolívar, none of the chapters pays any attention to Latin America, uses Latin American sources, or even uses sources from other parts of the developing world. The book never mentions the American Declaration of Rights and Duties of Man, nor its influence on the UDHR. This chapter has illustrated that the claim that one cannot find decisive moments where underdogs were primary actors is patently wrong. It is only impossible to find underdogs as primary actors if authors and editors do not look carefully and do not use sources from the developing world.

A survey of some of the great men and women who promoted human rights in the interwar period, during World War II, and in the postwar period shows that, while most were not underdogs in the sense of direct victims, many came from the semi-periphery of the world system, not from the center, and were personally aware of and affected by problems of exile, authoritarianism, and repression. Some, like Raphael Lemkin and Hersch Lauterpacht, were exiles from that part of middle Europe that historians have called "the Bloodlands" and lost their families in the Holocaust.[138] In other cases, key people such as Alejandro Álvarez of Chile, Ricardo Alfaro of Panama, Minerva Bernardino of the Dominican Republic, Peng-chun Chang of China, Antoine Frangulis of Greece, Bertha Lutz of Brazil, Charles Malik of Lebanon, André Mandelstam of Russia, Hansa Mehta and Madame Pandit of India, Dardo Regules of Uruguay, and Carlos Romulo of the Philippines were jurists and/ or diplomats from countries at the edges of power, some of whom had personally suffered exile, colonialism, discrimination, and/or marginalization.

There may be other reasons why the protagonism of Latin America has not been recognized, including a paradox at the heart of the Latin American defense of human rights that may have undermined its effectiveness. At the same time as many Latin American countries were advocating international human rights norms, practices on the ground fell far short of the human rights ideal. This paradox was conspicuously present at the 1948 conference at Bogotá where the American Declaration was first approved by the American states. In the midst of the conference, an important populist political leader in Colombia, Jorge Eliécer Gaitán, was assassinated on the streets of Bogotá, sparking protests and violence that temporarily suspended the conference proceedings. Gaitán, a leader of the left wing of the Liberal Party, was an eloquent speaker greatly admired by the poor of the city, who responded to his murder with riots, looting, and killings, which in turn provoked a violent response from the state security forces. This riot is known as the Bogotazo (Bogotá explosion); thousands were killed and a large part of the city burned to the ground. The Bogotazo is now seen as the start of the long period in Colombia known as La Violencia (the time of violence) during which hundreds of thousands of ordinary Colombians died.

Juxtaposed against the conference to set up a new regional organization and to proclaim the rights and duties of man is this scene of massive violence as the conference's host government trampled the rights of its citizens. The response of the world community, and

FIG. 3.4. Ninth International Conference of American States, Bogotá, 1948.
Property of the General Secretariat of the Organization of American States;

indeed of many in the region, may have been to dismiss the noble words inside the conference as they were apparently contradicted by the practices immediately surrounding it; or perhaps the events simply foreshadowed the pressing problems of security and violence that would dominate the Cold War period and lead to the disregard of general declarations. Either way, the gap between rhetoric and practice generated cynicism, recognized at the time. The Uruguayan delegate to Bogotá, Dardo Regules, wrote in his memoir of the conference, "We lift up the American man to make him a protagonist of peace. . . . And later we place in his hands a handful of unalienable rights; and, after all of this? After all of this, we leave him abandoned in the bottom of prisons, without trial, or exiled without resources?"[139]

Some scholars argue that Latin America has long been characterized by a "culture of non-compliance with law" which dates back to the colonial period. One author argues that "We Latin Americans live in a sort of schizophrenic society in which people talk a lot about

FIG. 3.5. The Bogotazo riots, April 9, 1948, at the same time as the Ninth International Conference of American States. Archivo fotográfico Sady González (Bogotá). 1938–1949 Biblioteca Luis Ángel Arango. Reproduced with permission.

what should be and enact many regulations about duty, but what is enacted is rarely practiced."[140] But as we shall see in chapter 4, although in the short term there was a disconnect between the new human rights declarations and state practices in the region, in the long term, the new human rights norms were institutionalized and became effective levers for change.

This historical work tracing the origins of international norms sheds light on current developments in human rights and can help students like the one mentioned at the start of this chapter to navigate the complexities of human rights work. Human rights protagonists from the Global South were not motivated by a single liberal philosophy. They came from different religious and political traditions. Some were secular, but many were not. Human rights were not a "secular replacement for the Christian god,"[141] but an ideal through which religious people and secular people motivated by various philosophical currents could find common ground. For a time in the mid-1940s, human rights discourse provided a meeting place, what philosophers later would call "an overlapping political consensus," among some liberals, socialists, Catholics, Hindus, and many other groups, rather than a victory by one or the imposition of secular morality upon all. This fragile consensus, however, was beset with fundamental disagreement, particularly about the degree to which the international protection of human rights should be embodied in treaties and enforced by courts, as we shall see in chapter 4.

In a book composed just after returning from serving as the head of the Uruguayan delegation in Bogotá, Dardo Regules wrote, "Does all this only represent an imperfect new phase full of brooding uncertainties? No one denies it. But even so, this was the best experience in the world, and the best opportunity Uruguay and all these countries have had to protect their independence and coexistence with the rule of law."[142]

The brooding uncertainties would turn out to be even more daunting than Regules imagined.

CHAPTER FOUR

The Struggles for Human Rights during the Cold War

IN 2013, A GUATEMALAN COURT convicted former President Efraín Ríos Montt and sentenced him to eighty years for genocide and crimes against humanity committed during his dictatorship in 1982 and 1983. This was the first time in the world that a national court convicted its own former president of genocide. Ríos Montt was found responsible for the massacres of thousands of indigenous Mayans in the bloodiest chapter of a long civil war. But, ten days later, the Guatemalan Constitutional Court vacated the verdict and ordered a partial retrial, a move that constitutional scholars and human rights activists view as illegal.[1] A lower court later determined that, because 89-year-old Ríos Montt suffered from dementia, he could be retried but could not be sentenced. In 2016, his trial reopened behind closed doors. In 2015 and 2016, Guatemalan courts also moved ahead on other prosecutions of crimes against humanity and other war crimes, also opening new corruption prosecutions against the former president and vice president of Guatemala. The twists and turns of the Guatemalan cases exemplify the history of human rights in the region—struggle, despair, setbacks, and, sometimes, astonishing results.

Human rights progress in Guatemala, as with anywhere in the world, has not happened quickly or easily. Progress takes time and hard work. In Guatemala, lawyers and victims initiated the first genocide complaint against Ríos Montt in 2000. Since Ríos Montt was a member of Congress at the time, he had immunity from prosecution; the trial could not begin until his congressional career ended in 2012. In the meantime, lawyers in the Ríos Montt case built upon work by other human rights lawyers beginning in the mid-1980s. These courageous individuals were embedded in national and international networks that supported their work of seeking accountability for human rights violations in Guatemala.

The fight for accountability continued during the transition to democracy in Guatemala in the 1990s, when the human rights movement lobbied to make sure that the 1996 amnesty law excluded acts of genocide and crimes against humanity. During the transition to democracy, activists cooperated with two crucial truth telling institutions in Guatemala: a truth commission sponsored by the United Nations as part of the peace agreement and a second commission set up by the office of the Archbishop of Guatemala. These truth commissions took testimony from victims and villages all over the country. The UN truth commission estimated that over 200,000 people had died or had been disappeared during the thirty-six-year civil war, over eighty percent from Mayan populations. The commission identified over 600 massacres and found that state security forces and paramilitaries were responsible for ninety-three percent of the violations. The UN report stated that, in the four regions most affected by the violence, "agents of the state . . . committed acts of genocide against groups of Mayan people." Despite the length and severity of the civil war, eighty percent of the human rights violations reported to the truth commission took place between 1981 and 1983, nearly half occurring during Ríos Montt's term in office in 1982.[2]

The Inter-American Commission of Human Rights and the Inter-American Court of Human Rights pressured the Guatemalan government to investigate massacres and provide remedies for victims. Various parts of the United Nations also urged the government to seek accountability.[3] Despite these national and international pressures, human rights and victims' groups continued to receive death threats from the still powerful members of the Guatemalan security forces. For each step forward, there was a full or half step backward. Even in the moment of apparent victory, as Ríos Montt stood convicted of genocide, the Constitutional Court undid the work of human rights lawyers by vacating the verdict and ordering a partial retrial. Despite all this, the Guatemalan human rights groups kept pushing. They received international help from the UN a second time when, at the urging of domestic groups, the UN set up the International Commission against Impunity in Guatemala (CICIG) to promote accountability and strengthen the rule of law.[4]

After thirty years, the task of holding perpetrators in Guatemala accountable is not yet finished. Still, the arc of this history in Guatemala is beginning to bend towards justice, as Martin Luther King Jr. said, echoing the words of nineteenth-century abolitionist Theodore Parker.[5]

When you try to tell such a story of human rights progress in the company of some international relations experts, you are likely to be labeled an optimist, an idealist, or simply naïve—someone who is not in touch with the political realities of the world.[6] To a critical theorist, you acquire the additional faults of telling a "teleological" or triumphalist history—in other words, of making it sound as if human rights progress is an inevitable endpoint that we should only celebrate.[7] More recently, yet another claim has been leveled—that human rights movements go hand in hand with the rise of neoliberalism and thus are either complicit with or helpless in preventing the rise of inequality in the world.[8]

Though it is challenging to telescope forty years of Guatemalan history into a few paragraphs, the Ríos Montt case illustrates my point about the complexity and the halting nature of human rights progress. This chapter situates the forty-year Guatemala story in the longer history of the Cold War, a story of developments that are both improbable and real. This is not a naïve or triumphalist history, but rather a possibilist one that tells not what was probable but what, with extraordinary effort, was eventually possible.[9] Ríos Montt was the most powerful man in Guatemala in 1980. No one even dreamed he might be held accountable for his crimes and yet, eventually, he was.

To situate current events in Guatemala in the relevant history, we have to look to the 1950s, shortly after where we left off in chapter 3. Some scholars, including Moyn as mentioned previously, argue that nothing much happened in regard to human rights during the 1950s and 1960s.[10] However, developments in Latin America, Europe, the former Soviet Union, Asia, and recently decolonized states in the Global South fill in the gaps of the human rights story and reveal the historical links between developments in the 1940s and in the 1970s. Though most often associated with the struggle of social movements in the streets, human rights work also happens as diplomats negotiate human rights treaties and create new institutions. In the first part of the Cold War, diplomats from different countries, including from Latin America and newly decolonized countries in Africa and Asia, led the way as they worked to construct human rights law and treaties.[11]

The delegates who gathered in Bogotá and Paris in 1948 to approve the American Declaration of the Rights and Duties of Man and the UDHR did not believe that creating a declaration of rights would be sufficient to provide international protection for rights; it was, however, a crucial first step. After all, how could you protect human rights if you didn't even have agreed-upon definitions of what human rights meant? The delegates knew that they would then need to embed such definitions in binding treaties and set up institutions, including international courts, to enforce the treaties. For decades, jurists and diplomats fought to ensure the creation of institutions with the power necessary to enforce human rights. At the same time, the governments of other countries, including authoritarian regimes backed by the United States, feared legal institutions with the strength to enforce human rights and worked hard to *block* the creation of these institutions. As a leading historian of human rights and decolonization argued, "The human rights project of the 1940s was not stillborn but it arrived on the international scene without any privileged birthright. It would have to make its own way through the world."[12] That process of making its own way through the world was fraught with barriers and backtracking.

Although Latin American countries had passed the first intergovernmental declaration of human rights in 1948, Europe moved more rapidly to produce the first overarching human rights treaty, the European Convention on Human Rights. The Convention went into effect in 1953, establishing two connected institutions to enforce its provisions—the European Commission and the European Court of Human Rights. Europe had good reason to move quickly; it had just suffered the worst human rights violations of the twentieth century. More than European virtue or enlightenment, the crises of World War II and the Holocaust drove the creation of a regional human rights regime. Many Europeans believed that the international protection of human rights was essential to reestablishing peace and well-being in the region. Moreover, the post–World War II Soviet control of Eastern Europe made it all the more important for Western Europeans to define human rights as key to a unique, and threatened, European identity. Countries in the region hoped to use a human rights treaty to "lock in" their democratic regimes and corresponding rights.[13] Despite this push for international protections for human rights, the European Convention on Human Rights almost did not happen. In 1949, the French and British Foreign Ministers tried to take the European Convention off the agenda; only the work of the Danes and the Irish was able to keep the issue alive.[14] Although Great Britain was later the first to ratify the Convention, in March of 1951, it was only because the British viewed their approval of the convention as a symbolic gesture. The British leaders believed that there were no human rights abuses in their country to be investigated and that actions outside of their domestic jurisdiction were off-limits.[15]

In Latin America, progress on a human rights treaty ground to a halt as more countries suffered military coups. In the twenty years after the American Declaration of the Rights and Duties of Man, every single Latin American state of the twenty at the meetings of the 1940s suffered at least one authoritarian regime that resisted the idea of international protection of human rights. In the case of Guatemala, its brief democracy of the 1940s and early 1950s was overthrown by a US-backed coup in 1954. The left's inability to secure change through electoral means convinced leftist supporters that armed struggle was the only tool they had to pursue their goals. Increasingly repressive regimes in the region became locked in conflict against leftist insurgents. At the same time, governments engaged in increasingly brutal campaigns against any civilians believed to be sympathetic to the insurgents. The wave of authoritarian regimes eventually hit not only the poorer and fragile states in Central America and the Caribbean, but also robust democracies, including Uruguay and Chile, which had advocated for human rights at San Francisco and Bogotá.

But I get ahead of myself. Let's slow down, go back to the beginning, and point out how, at every step along the way, the human rights story involved agency, contestation, struggle, and contingency.

The Slow and Contested Path from Human Rights Declarations to Treaties and Institutions

A lack of political will stymied the human rights proposals that came out of Bogotá in 1948. Brazil, in the first proposal of its kind, had argued for the creation of an Inter-American Court of Human Rights as a means of enforcing human rights norms.[16] Many states in the Americas thought the Brazilian proposal was premature, yet they forwarded it to the Inter-American Juridical Committee for study and elaboration. Though it did not produce any results at the time, the Brazilian proposal shows that one of the big democratic powers in the region thought that international human rights had to be backed up with an *international* court.[17] This example is just one of many in this chapter that illustrates one of the main points of chapters 2 and 3—human rights proposals and innovations came from countries in the Global South, not only from the United States and other more powerful countries.

The Inter-American Juridical Committee, when it considered the Brazilian resolution, informed the member states that they were putting the cart before the horse. A court must have law to enforce. The American Declaration of the Rights and Duties of Man was not legally binding soft law—for the court to function, the American States needed hard law in the form of a human rights convention or treaty.[18] As more countries began to move from democracies to dictatorships, the political will to forge a human rights treaty disappeared, and Brazil's proposal for a court lay dormant for years, forgotten even by Brazilians.

Struggles to secure a regional human rights treaty and regional human rights institutions took place at the Inter-American conferences of the 1950s and 1960s. Both theater and practical politics, the meetings followed a long tradition in Latin America where high-level officials from across the Americas spent weeks debating with their colleagues. The cast of characters in these conferences included many colorful figures of the period. The Cuban revolutionary Ernesto "Che" Guevara, in his characteristic fatigues and smoking a cigar, was the star of the Punta del Este conference of 1962. Also present was Che's ideological opponent from the nearby Caribbean island of the Dominican Republic, Joaquín Balaguer, a protégé of dictator Rafael Trujillo. In contrast to the flamboyant excesses of Trujillo, Balaguer was a "meek-looking intellectual" who had been a poet, scholar, and civil servant before he became Trujillo's right-hand man, but he was as staunchly anti-communist and pro-US as his boss.[19] Justino Jiménez de Aréchaga of Uruguay attended a number of the meetings as well, representing the more liberal thinking prevalent in his country.

The life and work of Jiménez de Aréchaga, a Uruguayan jurist and diplomat, illustrates the direct links between the human rights work of the 1940s and the 1970s. From a family of respected jurists, Jiménez de Aréchaga was educated in the Law School at the University of the Republic in Montevideo, later serving there as a professor. He was the Uruguayan delegate at the meeting of the UN Commission on Human Rights that elaborated the final version of the UDHR in Paris in 1948. A former student and colleague of Jiménez de Aréchaga's said human rights "was his life's purpose" and that his "only bit of vanity" was to have participated in drafting the UDHR in 1948, although he would later play an even more important role strengthening the Inter-American Commission on Human Rights in the 1970s.[20] Jiménez de Aréchaga embodied the type of liberal common to Uruguay in the 1940s and 1950s. Uruguayans prided themselves on the stability of their liberal democracy and their welfare state—stability that was maintained through much of the twentieth century, in contrast to the more tumultuous and often authoritarian politics of neighboring Argentina.

By the time delegates gathered in Caracas at the Tenth International Conference of American States in 1954, the possibilities for a regional human rights treaty were more remote than they had been in 1948. Alongside the long-term dictators in the region, such as Anastasio Somoza of Nicaragua, military coups had toppled several governments that had supported demands for human rights in 1948. Venezuela's democracy ended in November of that year with a military coup that brought to power the dictator Marcos Pérez Jiménez. In Cuba, a military coup in 1952 ushered in the dictatorship of Fulgencio Batista. Moreover, one of the few remaining democracies in the region, Costa Rica, refused to even attend the 1954 conference since the Venezuelan host government was so repressive.[21]

The great flaw of US foreign policy in this period was that the main US allies in the region were these dictators, Pérez Jiménez, Batista, and Trujillo, as well as Somoza in Nicaragua, instead of democratic countries like Brazil, Uruguay, Chile, and Costa Rica.[22] These dictators argued that their struggle against communism and the preservation of "our Christian civilization" trumped all other issues facing the region. According to Balaguer, every other topic on the agenda, including the creation of an Inter-American Court of Human Rights, was secondary when faced with "the gravity of the sinister threat that communism represent[ed] to the countries of the Americas."[23] At the Caracas meeting, Balaguer praised the United States lavishly, arguing that, if the region "survives the catastrophe that threatens humanity, there is no doubt that this miracle will be due almost entirely to the United States, which is not omitting any sacrifice to stop the communist conspiracy to save civilization, our civilization, from this destructive plot of history."[24]

At the same time, the US position on human rights had shifted and hardened. In 1952, President Eisenhower took office after a campaign influenced by the rise of McCarthyism and accusations that the Democrats had been weak against the communists and had "lost" China. An alliance within the United States between segregationists and Cold Warriors, each with their own reason to dislike the idea of the international protection of human rights, had forced Eisenhower and his Secretary of State, John Foster Dulles, to concede to Congress that the United States would not ratify any of the international human rights treaties that the UN was in the process of drafting.[25] As a result, the United States offered little support to regional efforts to create human rights institutions. The best the

United States could do under the circumstances was to vote in favor of the human rights resolutions and "raise no objection" to other states entering into human rights conventions:

> While the United States, because of the structure of its Federal Government, does not find it possible to enter into multilateral conventions with respect to human rights or with respect to an Inter-American Court of Human Rights, it, of course, raises no objection to other states' entering into conventions on these subjects should they find it possible to do so.[26]

By mentioning the "structure of its Federal Government," the United States referenced the states' rights arguments Southern states were making then, which included the claim that the federal government did not have the power to regulate southern policies of racial discrimination.[27] Lawmakers' fears, especially those of southern lawmakers, that international human rights treaties could be used to undermine states' rights put the United States on the sidelines of international and regional efforts to build human rights law from 1953 to 1973.

By the 1954 meeting, the voices for institutionalization of human rights law had shrunk to a handful of states that were still under democratic regimes—Uruguay, Chile, Brazil, and Costa Rica. Though also concerned about communism, these democracies had a different approach to combat it. The Chilean delegation in Caracas, for example, argued, "One has to take the communist microbe out of the broth in which it reproduces best, which is the misery and the ignorance of the people. Communism is the ally of sadness, necessity, and pain; it can't emerge among prosperous and happy people."[28] Countries like Chile and Uruguay thought that their economic and political reforms would help make them immune to this "communist microbe."

The United States had other ideas. The main US goal at the Caracas Conference was to seek multilateral support for an anticommunist agenda, including covert support for an invasion against the elected government of Jacobo Árbenz in Guatemala, which it characterized as communist. Árbenz was a leftist whose greatest passion was the need for agrarian reform in his country, which he saw as a tool to overcome poverty and inequality. Árbenz, although sympathetic to the Guatemalan communist party, did not think that a communist state could or should be established in Guatemala at that time.[29] Yet Árbenz earned the enmity of the US government and accusations of communism because of his agrarian reform and, in particular, because he nationalized the property of the United Fruit Company, a US business, compensating them only for the value of the land they declared on their tax returns.[30]

Eisenhower's Secretary of State, John Foster Dulles, and his brother, Alan Foster Dulles, the Director of the CIA, were not making fine distinctions between democratically elected leftists and USSR communists. The Dulles brothers saw Árbenz as an outpost of Soviet power in Latin America and were intent on removing him. Their heavy personal economic involvement with the United Fruit Company fueled their ideological certainty. Latin Americans knew John Foster Dulles was using the Caracas conference to lend legitimacy to sanctions against Guatemala and to a future covert invasion. Despite the fact that many Latin American states were not sympathetic to the Guatemalans, they dreaded setting a dangerous precedent which could lead to more US intervention in the region.[31] After long debates, the United States succeeded in persuading seventeen member states to vote in favor of a declaration against "International Communist Intervention" in the region, a statement aimed at Guatemala without mentioning the country by name.[32] Hypocritically in the eyes of many, the conference also reaffirmed regional commitment to democracy, even as the countries present understood that the elected government of Árbenz was about to be overthrown. Argentina and Mexico abstained; only Guatemala voted against.

Even though Uruguay did not vote against this resolution, its delegates were aware of US intentions, explicitly opposing them. Jiménez de Aréchaga, representing the Uruguayan government in Caracas in 1954, asked during one the sessions:

> [W]hat kind of thing is our democracy that we have to kill it to defend it? ... We don't want to underestimate the dangers, but should we let hysterical fear win out (in which the people of my country and all countries participate with sincerity and good intentions) that allows us to legitimize any policy that, under the guise of anti-communism, can become an additional threat to the freedom of the people of the Americas?[33]

Jiménez de Aréchaga warned against "hysterical fear" that could be used to justify a military coup against a democratically elected government. His fears were prescient; such tactics would increasingly be employed in justifying authoritarian regimes throughout the region, eventually even in the apparently stable Uruguay.

The aggressive anti-communist policy of the United States polarized the region. When the Árbenz government was overthrown with the support of the CIA in 1954, leftists became radicalized. Che Guevara in particular, who was in Guatemala City when Árbenz fell, became further radicalized. It was around this time that both Che Guevara and Fidel Castro became convinced that only armed revolution could succeed in bringing about change. In this sense, the US failure to tolerate a democratically elected government of the left created almost a self-fulfilling prophecy; as leftists became convinced that they would not be allowed to come to power through elections, they focused on coming to power through armed struggle. As the new authoritarian regimes that took the place of Árbenz in Guatemala became increasingly repressive, leftists there formed guerrilla groups to struggle for power.

Related Developments around the World: Decolonization

Latin America was not the only region of the developing world that made important contributions to the idea and practice of the international protection of human rights. In fact, just as the momentum for human rights institutions in Latin America slowed to a snail's pace, the newly decolonized states in the Global South took up the human rights cause. This story has been told brilliantly by the latest historians of decolonization; here I offer a slender summary of their well-documented and carefully argued histories.[34]

Recent scholars have demonstrated that decolonization was *both* about sovereignty and about human rights, as opposed to earlier claims that decolonization was about sovereignty and *not* about rights.[35] According to Roland Burke, "Decolonization was the most powerful shaping influence on the human rights program between 1950 and 1979. In virtually every significant debate, Arab, Asian, and African delegations played a leading role, with their contributions central to the creation of major pillars of the modern human rights system."[36] Similarly, Steven Jensen argues, "Decolonization made a crack in the world running from South to North and East to West. From this tectonic shift, the issue of human rights emerged and over time achieved global prominence." This transformation was the result of "a story of agency where the lead protagonists were, in fact, a group of states from the Global South."[37]

In the face of this agency exercised in particular by former colonies and other countries in the Global South, European colonial powers worked hard to maintain a "divided world," where the international protection of human rights would not spread to their colonies and thereby undermine the legitimacy of colonial rule.[38] European colonial powers blocked rather than promoted the international protection of human rights. Indeed, it was decolonization that made it possible for countries of Europe to be able to reclaim their role in global human rights, lost after World War II: "Decolonization was a precondition that 'Europe' might again be associated with and worthy of an egalitarian universalism."[39] As Frederick Cooper said on a related issue, actors from the Global South "were not simply entrapped in a framework of European beliefs; they profoundly changed what Europeans thought they believed."[40]

The link between anti-colonialism and human rights was evident at the 1955 Bandung Conference hosted by Indonesia. Representatives from twenty-nine Afro-Asian states attended, as did other representatives from territories that were not yet independent. The conference was important because of the attention devoted to self-determination as a human right.[41] Self-determination as a collective right of peoples had become the powerful mobilizing slogan for anti-colonial nationalists, and the nationalists present at Bandung saw human rights and self-determination as mutually reinforcing.[42] At the same time, the representatives acknowledged a wide range of issues concerning human rights, exemplified by the conference's endorsement of the UDHR.[43] Though the Chinese delegation to Bandung tried to block some of this attention to human rights, particularly regarding the UDHR, which communist China had not helped to write, they were unable to change the language.

Some African leaders, especially those associated with Pan-African transnationalism—like Julius Nyerere, the first president of

Tanzania, and Kwame Nkrumah, leader of the newly independent Ghana—expressed support for human rights as an integral part of their work for independence and regional unity. Under Nkrumah's leadership, the first All-African Peoples' Conference was convened—a regional gathering of independent African states and delegates of independence movements held in Accra, Ghana, in 1958. The conference aimed, among other things, to "mobilize world opinion against the denial of political rights and fundamental human rights to Africans."[44] The countries of the Global South reaffirmed their belief in the link between decolonization and human rights in the 1960 Declaration on the Granting of Independence to Colonial Countries and People.

The Anti-Apartheid Campaign and an International Treaty against Racial Discrimination (CERD)

During the Cold War, perhaps the most important early and sustained human rights struggle was the anti-apartheid campaign. In chapter 3, we saw how Indian diplomats in the early days of the UN made use of the new doctrine of human rights to protest legal discrimination against Indians in South Africa and to persuade the General Assembly that the UN could and should investigate. This was the first of many times that the UN would be an arena to demand human rights for people in South Africa.

The anti-apartheid campaign, initiated by activists and governments from Africa and other countries from the Global South, was one of the first great transnational human rights campaigns. By the 1940s, the African National Congress (ANC), the main movement against apartheid, "explicitly embraced human rights as a fundamental goal of its struggle for racial justice" in its charter, called Africans' Claims, in the ANC Basic Policy statement, and in the ANC's Youth League Manifesto, authored by new young leaders who later led the ANC, including Nelson Mandela and Oliver Tambo.[45] The ANC's demands for rights were taken up by transnational actors who tried to put pressure on the South African government. The meeting of the All-African Peoples' Conference in 1958 was the first international convention to propose sanctions against South Africa.[46]

In 1965, anti-apartheid sentiment played an important role in leading Asian and African leaders to spearhead passage of the second major international human rights treaty (after the Genocide Convention)—the International Convention on the Elimination of All Forms of Racial Discrimination (CERD). Two years later the issue of apartheid pushed the UN Commission on Human Rights to create its first ever special procedure, the Ad Hoc Working Group of Experts on Southern Africa.[47] This special procedure set the precedent for later ones, and became one of the main tools the UN uses to investigate and address a wide range of human rights issues. The UN also devoted attention to the situation in Southern Rhodesia, another white supremacist regime that, in 1966, became the first country to face economic sanctions under Chapter VII of the UN Charter. Just as it had spoken out against apartheid in 1947, India continued to work against white supremacists in South Africa and Southern Rhodesia. In 1966, India urged all states to break off political and economic ties to the white minority regime in Southern Rhodesia and, in 1968, the Indian government promoted a draft Security Council resolution condemning the execution of prisoners in Southern Rhodesia as a threat to international peace and security.[48] A country from the Global South thus provides one of the earliest examples of efforts to get the Security Council to take action on human rights issues.

The developments were about much more than apartheid. Jamaica, one of the main postcolonial leaders promoting human rights in the United Nations in the 1960s, had only been a member of the UN for three weeks when it called on the organization to intensify its efforts on behalf of human rights by creating an international human rights year, among other things.[49] Jamaica also helped to push forward the drafting of the Convention on the Elimination of All Forms of Racial Discrimination (CERD). Because many states from the Global South felt so strongly about racial discrimination, CERD was drafted and ratified in record time. Countries from the Global South also wanted to be certain that CERD had enforcement mechanisms. The countries promoted the creation of a special committee of independent experts on racial discrimination to receive state reports on compliance with the treaty, what later became known as a "treaty body." In the case of CERD, the treaty body was called the Committee on the Elimination of Racial Discrimination. Additionally, in the context of negotiating CERD, Lebanon championed another institutional innovation—the right of individuals to petition the treaty body. Thus, the Committee on the Elimination of Racial Discrimination could receive not only state reports, but also petitions from individuals.

Southern leadership on CERD helped create precedents for institutional implementation and enforcement for the entire human rights treaty system. Jamaica and other allies used the rapid success of CERD to revitalize the two general human rights covenants, which had been languishing in the UN General Assembly. Once the precedent had been set in the CERD for treaty bodies, the two covenants and all subsequent human rights treaties were set up with their own treaty bodies for enforcement. CERD's new provision for individual petitions would likewise reappear in various other human rights treaties, usually as a separate protocol.

Support for Human Rights in the Global South Wanes

In Latin America, the Middle East, and Africa, support for human rights waned as the number of authoritarian regimes increased. US foreign policy during the Cold War contributed to this trend as the country helped overthrow democratically elected leftists around the world, not just in Latin America. On August 19, 1953, to cite an early example, a coup overthrew the government of Iranian Prime Minister Mohammad Mosaddeq—a year prior to the coup in Guatemala. Mosaddeq was a nationalist elected to the parliament in April 1951.[50] These elections were unusually democratic for Iran at the time; they were held after rigged elections organized by the Shah had been publicly rejected. Public protests against the initial election results continued until the Shah promised to hold a new round of fair elections.[51] During the protests and the elections, Mosaddeq emerged as the leader of the National Front coalition, organized in support of democracy and against foreign intervention. Mosaddeq was later elected prime minister from within the parliament with a vote of 79 to 12.[52] His willingness to nationalize the oil industry, and thus free Iran from continued British domination, earned him most of his support.[53] For decades the public knew little about the US role in Mosaddeq's removal, but recently uncovered evidence places the United States at the center of operations in Iran, making it clear that the CIA would have carried out the coup even if the Shah himself had not been on board.[54]

The US justification for actions against Iran was a fear of communism, imagining the possibility of Iran falling to internal communist influences or of the USSR invading Iran and starting a global war.[55] Yet, according to historian Ervand Abrahamian, "'communist danger' was more of a rhetorical device than a real issue."[56] Instead, the topmost US concern was oil and the country was drawn into the conflict by the Anglo-Iranian oil crisis.[57] Oil was needed for the West's economic recovery after World War II, and in case of war with the USSR.[58]

The coup ended democracy in Iran and led to political repression, especially of the Tudeh Party.[59] The apparent success of the coup in Iran led to it becoming the "blueprint" for future covert operations to topple democracies, including Guatemala in 1954.[60] According to historian Shiva Balaghi, "covert operations to overthrow liberal democratic governments became a cornerstone of US Cold War strategy." The CIA and the US government discovered that coups were short, cheap, and deniable.[61]

The CIA later became involved in operations in the Congo in 1960 and 1961, assisting in overthrowing the government and assassinating its leader, Patrice Lumumba.[62] Lumumba, a nationalist with a wide base of popular support, was the first leader, and to date the only one, democratically elected in the Congo.[63] As in Iran, the most cited reason for US interference was its policy of containment in the face of communism.[64] Congo had come into conflict with the United Nations, and this disagreement led the country to side with the Soviets, at least in terms of aid.[65] Yet the US fear of communism in the Congo appears to have been based more in economics than in a desire to defend democracy—Congo's geographic centrality and importance to US business interests drove US involvement, according to the most recent research.[66] As an added incentive, the CIA chose to overthrow Lumumba because it was relatively easy. African countries had recently gained independence and the democracies were fragile; their regimes were not difficult to topple.[67]

The CIA's top priority, to use the words of the CIA itself, was "The election of a government oriented to the West, friendly to the United States, devoted to ideals which may best guarantee stability and order," not democracy per se.[68] After Lumumba's assassination, Congo was left in the hands of Mobutu, a dictator who favored the West, instead of a new, democratically elected leader. Mobutu eliminated the country's democratic traditions (even staging a second coup in 1965 to gain power as the sole ruler of the country) and destroyed its political culture.[69] In Africa, the memory of Western involvement in the Congo serves to make Lumumba a proud symbol of pan-Africanism. Yet, in the Congo itself, Mobutu warped history by simultaneously claiming and erasing Lumumba's memory, so much so that the public has only a vague idea of who Lumumba was and retains none of his nationalistic or democratic legacies.[70]

Coups were not the only method of US intervention during the Cold War. As Gary Bass has meticulously documented, in the name of anti-communist policy the White House illegally supplied arms to Pakistan in 1971, thereby supporting a regime that carried out a largely forgotten genocide on the scale of Rwanda.[71] At the time, Pakistan was split geographically into two main regions: West Pakistan and East Pakistan, present-day Bangladesh. A Bengali leader, Sheikh Mujibur Rahman of the Awami League, won the elections held in December of 1970.[72] This was a free and fair election in which all adults could vote, including women.[73] However, politicians from West Pakistan were unwilling to transfer power to politicians from Bangladesh and, in 1971, the Pakistani army began a systemic genocide against the Bengali people that lasted about nine months. India invaded to stop the genocide, in what one Indian scholar said is "widely and fairly regarded as one of the world's most successful cases of humanitarian intervention against genocide."[74] Bass points out that "India's brief for saving Bangladeshis provides a crucial opportunity to hear the legal and moral voices of non-Westerners" on human rights issues.[75] While India intervened to stop the genocide, the United States actively supported Pakistan as it crushed democracy in this region; Bangladesh, weak from violence and corruption, has not achieved truly democratic politics since.

At the same time as a number of African and Latin American countries turned towards authoritarian regimes, efforts continued in the UN and the OAS to build more support for human rights.

Jamaica, for example, pushed for the 1968 First International Human Rights Conference to mark the twentieth anniversary of the UDHR. One great irony of the 1968 Conference was that it was held in Tehran, Iran, where the Shah was then suppressing dissent and violating human rights.[76] Perhaps not surprisingly, the Tehran Conference did not live up to the high expectations of its planners. Developments during the tumultuous year of 1968, including the reform movement in Czechoslovakia ("the Prague Spring") as well as student unrest around the world, overshadowed the conference.[77] Struggles against apartheid and the Israel-Palestine conflict took up most of the meeting, forestalling discussions on a wider range of human rights issues.[78] Moreover, representatives from the increasingly authoritarian countries of the Global South prioritized independence and development over individual rights.[79] Although the Tehran Conference was considered a failure by many, the process leading up to it signals the beginning of a human rights legal agenda in the UN. Looking closely at this history reveals that Africa was a "driving force" in the process through which "human rights acquired real meaning" as legally binding universal standards.[80]

African states were more outspoken about human rights violations in apartheid South Africa than in other independent African states. After Idi Amin came to power in Uganda though a military coup in 1971, the president of neighboring Tanzania, Julius Nyerere, repeatedly called for the Organization of African Unity (OAU) to condemn Amin's massive violations of human rights. Nyerere sometimes explicitly contrasted the OAU's criticism of South Africa's abuses with its failure to condemn violations by newly decolonized African states, such as Uganda. Nyerere said, "Amin . . . has killed more Africans than the Boers under apartheid rule."[81] When criticism of Amin went unheeded by other African leaders, Tanzania went to war with Amin in 1978–79 to oust him, a war often counted as another early case of unilateral humanitarian intervention.[82]

Impact of the Cuban Revolution in Latin America

A decade earlier, in the 1960s, the success of the Cuban Revolution provoked a reevaluation of human rights issues in Latin America. After the rebels under Fidel Castro defeated the Cuban military in January of 1959, dictator Fulgencio Batista and his inner circle fled to the Dominican Republic, where Trujillo received them. The new Cuban government accused Batista and his government of being "war criminals" and attacked Trujillo for sheltering them.[83] These events came to be labeled "disturbances in the Caribbean" and led to the calling of a special meeting of the Foreign Ministers of the Americas in Santiago, Chile, in August 1959.

Interpreting the minutes of the Santiago meeting requires reading between the lines as, in the diplomatic tradition of the time, nothing public was said explicitly. The new revolutionary Cuban Minister of Foreign Affairs, Raúl Roa García, delivered the most candid of the speeches. His words show how the new Cuban government was still defining its approach to international affairs and had not ruled out the international protection of human rights. In his speech, Roa García explained that Cuba had voted in favor of the resolutions concerning human rights and the exercise of representative government. Still, he signaled that his government's principle concerns were the "existing relations between economic underdevelopment and political instability . . . Historical experience shows that without a solid economic structure and an equitable distribution of wealth, the exercise of democracy and respect for human rights are exposed to serious risk and mystification." Roa García was expressing an opinion increasingly common among the Latin American left about the economic causes of human rights violations and authoritarianism. He spoke in favor of human rights and the "triumphs of free peoples of the Americas against the dictatorships."[84] Some countries were quite sympathetic to this argument. Mexico, for example, although authoritarian at the time, recalled its own revolution when it expressed support for Cuba, "whose aspirations for economic improvement and social justice have the fullest support of the government and people of Mexico."[85] Likewise, Bolivia, under a left-leaning, semi-democratic government, agreed that the stability of democracy and the protection of human rights "will be possible when the great inequalities of development existing among American nations have been overcome."[86]

One conclusion that other states in the Americas derived from the Cuban Revolution was that reform would be necessary if revolution were to be avoided. Believing that dictatorships led to the deprivation of human rights in the Americas, the Latin American countries passed two key resolutions in Santiago supporting the regional mechanisms for human rights protection that had languished for over a decade. The first resolution reignited progress on a binding regional human rights treaty by calling on the Council of Jurists to complete a draft of the American Convention on Human Rights. At the same time, since it would take some time for the Convention to be drafted and ratified, the states of the Americas supported a second resolution to create a stopgap institutional measure—the Inter-American Commission on Human Rights (IACHR)—to act under the American Declaration of the Rights and Duties of Man and to provide some international supervision of human rights practices in the Americas. While some countries hoped the new IACHR would be used to stigmatize and single out Cuba and other leftist regimes, even in its early years the IACHR devoted attention to widespread human rights violations by right-wing authoritarian regimes, including the Dominican Republic, Haiti, Guatemala, Paraguay, and Nicaragua.

Unstable politics in the region, and especially the Bay of Pigs fiasco, further delayed progress on a binding regional human rights treaty and led to the postponement of the Eleventh Inter-American Conference. When the states finally gathered for this conference in 1962 at the Uruguayan beach resort of Punta del Este, the battle lines were drawn between the Cuban regime and the new US government of John Kennedy. This eventually led to the expulsion of Cuba from the Inter-American system.

Despite the US-Cuban conflict, the star at the Punta del Este conference was Che Guevara, the only delegate to be greeted by applauding crowds upon his arrival in Uruguay. But Guevara was worried about the survival of the Cuban Revolution. The Bay of Pigs invasion had failed, but he anticipated another invasion, or a full quarantine, this time with the support of other Latin American states. In his first speech to the conference, Guevara denounced US intervention in Cuba and in other countries of the region. Although Guevara made no explicit references to rights in his speech, he spoke at length about democracy, saying that the Cuban conviction was

that democracy cannot consist solely of elections that are nearly always fictitious and managed by rich landowners and professional politicians,

but rather it lies in the right of the citizens to determine their own des-
tiny . . . democracy will come to exist in Latin America only when people are really free to make choices, when the poor are not reduced—by
hunger, social discrimination, illiteracy, and the legal system—to the
most wretched impotence.[87]

Guevara's words fell on fertile soil among the young people in
Latin America, not only in places with so-called fictitious democracies, but also in places like Uruguay and Brazil, where reformers
began to see their own relatively robust democracies as inadequate.
Meanwhile the United States contributed in its own way to discred-
iting democracy in the region. By throwing its weight behind the
dictators in the region as a bulwark against communism and by
promoting coups against democracies that brought leftists to power,
as in Guatemala, the United States fueled the idea that only armed
revolution could bring about change. Once again, human rights and
democracy were relegated to the margins as the battles of the Cold
War were fought out within the conferences of the OAS. But while
human rights ideas were neglected at the OAS conference, they
gained new life in the creation of the fledgling Inter-American Commission on Human Rights.

The Inter-American Commission on Human Rights

Although created in 1959, the Inter-American Commission on
Human Rights (IACHR) took years to set up and begin functioning,
as is common with human rights institutions. It was not until 1965,
when states amended the IACHR's statute so that it could receive
petitions, that the IACHR began to have the tools necessary to do
its work. The IACHR may seem a small thing today because we live
in a world inundated with human rights commissions, but in Latin
America this was the first time countries had ever agreed to create
an independent commission to look into the human rights practices
of sovereign states. As such, it had few models on which to draw. As
one expert explained, the IACHR "was set up as a hasty improvisa-
tion and with no well-thought-out role or procedure."[88] Its initial
rules did not even allow the commission to send communications
to governments inquiring about human rights violations or to re-

ceive individual complaints. But from the moment it was set up, people from around the region saw the commission as an institution to protect their rights and began to write to it to denounce human rights violations.[89]

In 1968, the democratic Uruguayan government nominated Jiménez de Aréchaga as one of seven experts to serve on the IACHR. By that time, the IACHR had established and expanded its procedures and methods of work, but had not accomplished much along the lines of protecting human rights in the region. To the surprise of many observers, this changed under the leadership of Jiménez de Aréchaga as he, together with some of his colleagues, converted the IACHR into a tool for the international protection of human rights, particularly through the documentation of abuses and recommendations for improvements. The IACHR took a stand against human rights violations not only in small states of Central America or the Caribbean like the Dominican Republic, Honduras, or Cuba, but also in larger countries like Brazil, which became increasingly repressive after experiencing a military coup in 1964.

The activation of the IACHR was the result of a combination of actions by civil society organizations, which turned to the IACHR to address gross human rights violations, and the responsiveness of commissioners to these complaints. Civil society needed the Commission, and the Commission needed civil society. In the late 1960s, academics and church organizations in Brazil began sending information to their contacts abroad about the torture of political prisoners. These academics and church groups had launched a publicity campaign about torture in Brazil by publishing articles and op-eds in the newspaper, but they sought additional means to protect political prisoners in Brazil. I still recall hearing how two religious human rights activists in Washington, D.C., trying to find ways to help their imprisoned colleagues in Brazil, came across the name of the Inter-American Commission on Human Rights and called them up on the telephone to see if they could offer any help.[90] The IACHR said that NGOs could make submissions to the Commission, and, beginning in the 1970s, several NGOs submitted important communications to the IACHR on behalf of human rights victims with allegations of torture, political imprisonment, and political executions in Brazil.[91] The US Catholic Conference and the National

Council of Churches, for example, wrote to the IACHR that there were 12,000 political prisoners in Brazil and documented their conditions.[92] The IACHR, under the leadership of Jiménez de Aréchaga, rose to the challenge. When the Brazilian government questioned its jurisdiction, the IACHR replied that it had the authority to examine general situations of human rights violations, such as large-scale torture and imprisonment, in addition to individual complaints.[93]

Commission member Genaro Carrió later credited Jiménez de Aréchaga for being the "noble and valiant architect" of the IACHR's "major positive modification in the efficient protection of human rights."[94] After helping to draft the UDHR in 1948, Jiménez de Aréchaga played a key role in turning the new human rights institutions into effective tools to respond to the social movements of the 1970s, providing almost a human bridge between the 1940s and the 1970s and illustrating how the social movements of the 1970s relied on laws and institutions begun in the 1940s.

Jiménez de Aréchaga was dismayed to see his own Uruguay fall to a military dictatorship in 1973. The coup in Uruguay shared many similarities with that of the same year in Chile, where the elected government of socialist Salvador Allende was also overthrown. Both Chile and Uruguay had maintained democratic traditions through much of the twentieth century. The two countries also had high levels of education, a large middle class, and relatively stable politics compared to most other countries in the region. Yet the youth of Uruguay nevertheless were caught up in the tide of revolutionary thought sweeping through Latin America. The youth came to view democratic institutions as formal and bourgeois and their welfare state as unable to address the poverty of the sugar cane cutters in the north or of the people in Uruguay's shantytowns, and turned to violence. The violent acts of the Tupamaro guerrillas in Uruguay were in turn used by the government to justify military intervention.

After the rightist military coup in Uruguay in 1973, the regime began imprisoning and sometimes killing its opponents—not only insurgents, but also the members of the parliamentary left and center. Family members of victims no longer had recourse through domestic institutions and searched desperately for someone who could help. This, along with the brutal events in Chile after its 1973 coup, led to an unprecedented number of complaints to the IACHR.

In 1974, the IACHR issued the first in a series of reports on human rights in Chile, criticizing the Pinochet government for torture, summary executions, and disappearances. In the 1974 report and for the first time, the IACHR proposed that a member state prosecute and punish individual perpetrators. The IACHR made similar recommendations in another report on Chile in 1977, as well as in reports on El Salvador and Haiti in 1979.[95] In 1980, the IACHR issued a country report on Argentina based on its on-site visit in 1979 and became the first to call in print for human rights prosecutions in Argentina.[96]

The initial call for prosecutions in Chile may seem a simple, straightforward recommendation, but it was not. In fact, it was groundbreaking. When the IACHR first recommended trials to Chile in 1974, it did so before any country in the world had held its own leaders criminally accountable for human rights violations. At this time, the IACHR was still acting under the American Declaration because a human rights treaty was not yet in effect in the region. Thus, the recommendation to investigate, prosecute, and punish drew on the idea of the right to justice and other rights written into the 1948 American Declaration, not on a human rights treaty. The commissioners were ahead of their time, but they were not inventing law out of whole cloth. They were reaching back and infusing new meaning into an older demand in the region for a right to justice that individuals had vis-à-vis their governments, and that the American Declaration affirmed could and should be internationally protected.

At a special meeting in San José, Costa Rica, in 1969, the OAS finally approved and opened for ratification the American Convention on Human Rights, also called the Pact of San José. This was ten years after the Convention was first introduced and drafted in 1959 and another almost ten years would pass before the required number of states ratified the Convention. Eleven states had to ratify it; given the number of authoritarian regimes in the region at the time, this took a while. The American Convention on Human Rights finally entered into force in 1978.

At this point, US policy made a positive impact on the protection of human rights in the region. The newly elected government of Jimmy Carter took office in 1977 and announced a new human rights policy. Although Carter knew he would be unable to secure the votes of two-thirds of the US Senate needed to ratify the American Convention, his administration encouraged Latin American countries to ratify human rights treaties, with many doing so in 1977–78, after Carter had taken office. The Carter administration also provided funds to the IACHR so that it could expand its staff. As a result of this and other policies the Carter administration put into place, many activists throughout the region have long been grateful to the administration for its support of human rights in the Americas.

The American Convention finally put into effect Brazil's 1948 proposal for an Inter-American Court of Human Rights. The Convention also provided a new role for the IACHR as an antechamber to the Court, much like the model in Europe. The Inter-American Court, like the European Court before it, took years to get up and running. Almost a decade after the Convention had gone into effect, the Inter-American Court of Human Rights issued its first pathbreaking decision in 1988 on a Honduran disappearance, the Velásquez Rodríguez case. The Court found that the Honduran government was responsible for the disappearances and ordered it to pay compensation to the families of the victims. Moreover, the Court concluded that governments have an obligation to respect the human rights of individuals and to guarantee the enjoyment of these rights. As a consequence of this obligation, the Court found that "states must prevent, investigate and punish any violation of the rights recognized by the Convention."[97] This landmark decision was the first time a human rights court anywhere in the world had found that states had a duty to prosecute.

Despite its apparent originality, the Velásquez Rodríguez decision was the culmination of a series of incremental developments starting with the articulation of a right to justice in the American Declaration of the Rights and Duties of Man in 1948. The lawyers in Guatemala then working on the Ríos Montt genocide case were buoyed by the findings in the Velásquez Rodríguez case. The Guatemalan government had ratified the American Convention in 1978, before Ríos Montt took power. Although Guatemala did not accept the compulsory jurisdiction of the Court until 1987, the Convention provided firm international law on which to base their case.

The Development of the International Protection of Human Rights

While the regional human rights system in the Americas lagged far behind the European system by the late 1970s, the pace of human rights law development in the Americas coincided almost exactly with that of human rights law internationally. In the Americas, as in the broader world, the post-World War II momentum in favor of the international protection of human rights was interrupted by the Cold War. With the exception of the Genocide Convention, passed in 1948, the institutionalization of international human rights law was also hostage to the Cold War.

The main overarching treaty that was to put the UDHR into hard law was first divided into two treaties—the International Covenant on Civil and Political Rights (ICCPR) and the International Covenant on Economic, Social and Cultural Rights (ICESCR). Contrary to popular perception, India proposed splitting the single human rights treaty into two different covenants. In this, they supported the US position and opposed the USSR, which lobbied strenuously in favor of a single treaty including both sets of rights. At the time India was working hard to maintain its non-aligned status and negotiate between the two superpowers. Why divide the two covenants? India had already incorporated human rights into its new constitution and, in that constitution, there existed a distinction between some justiciable civil and political rights and other economic and social rights that were perceived as not justiciable, though equally important. India was drawing on its own experience in its support of two different but equal covenants.[98]

It took almost fifteen years to draft the two treaties and they were opened for ratification in 1966. In 1970, democratic Uruguay was the fourth country in the world to ratify the ICCPR and the third country (after Colombia and Costa Rica) to ratify its First Optional Protocol, which allowed individuals to bring claims against their governments to the UN Human Rights Committee, the treaty body that oversaw the ICCPR. But the Human Rights Committee could not start its work until enough countries had ratified the treaty for it to enter into force, which took until 1976. Thus, the timelines of the first general-purpose international human rights treaties and the first overarching regional treaty in the Americas coincide in the mid-1970s.

The previous discussion of the IACHR and the role of NGOs in reporting human rights abuses in Brazil demonstrated how a mutually beneficial situation developed between human rights institutions and human rights NGOs in the Inter-American system. In the case of Uruguay and the UN Human Rights Committee there existed a similar dynamic. Civil society and victim demands from Uruguay helped "activate" the Human Rights Committee by giving it some of its first cases and, at the same time, the Human Rights Committee offered support for those individuals who brought complaints. The victims and their families, targeted by their own states and bereft of protection, turned to emerging human rights institutions. The family members of the imprisoned and the disappeared had few places to turn for help, but word spread that organizations called the UN Human Rights Committee and the Inter-American Commission on Human Rights would take their cases. Some of the families with more resources were even able to travel to Geneva or to Washington, D.C. to talk directly to members of these organizations about their cases.

To the surprise of the Uruguayan dictatorship, after the ICCPR and the ICESCR went into effect in 1976 Uruguay quickly became the country with the most cases against it in the UN Human Rights Committee. The large number of cases did not mean that Uruguay had a greater number of violations than other violent regimes; it only meant that Uruguay had gone further in guaranteeing human rights than most countries before the 1973 coup. The country had already ratified the First Optional Protocol to the ICCPR and thus allowed individual Uruguayan citizens to send complaints to the UN Human Rights Committee. The democratic Uruguayan government of 1970 had nothing to fear from oversight by the Human Rights Committee, but its commitment also bound the later authoritarian government, which found out, to its displeasure, the impact of international scrutiny.

The case of María del Carmen Quinteros illustrates how the process worked. María del Carmen Quinteros was the mother of Elena Quinteros, who was disappeared in Uruguay in 1976. Elena was a teacher, an anarchist, and the founder of a small guerrilla group in Argentina and Uruguay. In her petition to the UN Human Rights Committee, María del Carmen Quinteros described the facts as follows:

> My daughter (born on 9 September 1945) was arrested at her home in the city of Montevideo on 24 June 1976. Four days later, while she was being held completely incommunicado, military personnel took her to a particular spot in the city near the Embassy of Venezuela. My daughter would appear to have told her captors that she had a rendezvous at that place with another person whom they wished to arrest. Once she was in front of a house adjoining the Embassy of Venezuela, my daughter succeeded in getting away from the persons accompanying her, jumped over a wall and landed inside the Embassy grounds. At the same time, she shouted out her name so as to alert passers-by to what was happening in case she was recaptured. The military personnel accompanying her then entered the diplomatic mission and, after striking the Secretary of the Embassy and other members of its staff, dragged my daughter off the premises.[99]

The government of Venezuela subsequently broke off diplomatic relations with the government of Uruguay as a result of this incident. Embassy property is inviolable, so when Uruguayan military personnel forcibly entered the property they violated international law. The violent way that Elena Quinteros was dragged off the premises of the embassy and the fact that her captors assaulted Venezuelan officials in the process exacerbated the conflict.

Elena's mother was never able to obtain from the authorities any official information about her daughter's whereabouts, nor was Elena's detention officially acknowledged. Elena Quinteros was never heard from again, and her body never located. Presumed dead, she became one of the countless disappeared people in the region. Later, two witnesses who knew Elena recalled hearing her voice in their detention center, where they were kept blindfolded and systematically subjected to torture. One reported that she recognized the voice of Elena Quinteros in "the despairing cries of a woman who kept saying, 'why didn't they kill me, why didn't they kill me.'" It was clear to the witness that Elena was being brutally tortured."[100]

When Elena's mother began to search for her daughter, she turned first to her labor union, where the union lawyers helped her file a case with the Inter-American Commission on Human Rights and later with the UN Human Rights Committee. The Human Rights Committee considered the case and concluded that "responsibility for the disappearance of Elena Quinteros falls on the authorities of Uruguay" and that, consequently, the government of Uruguay should take immediate and effective steps to secure her release, bring to justice any persons found to be responsible for her disappearance and ill treatment, pay compensation, and ensure that similar violations do not occur in the future.[101] The case became some of the earliest case law on disappearances, letting governments know that disappeared people would not be forgotten by the international community or its human rights institutions.

The European human rights system also addressed abuses by repressive regimes. At the time, Spain, Portugal, and Greece were under dictatorships. The regimes in Spain and Portugal had existed for so long that they had never been invited to join the Council of Europe, where democracy was a precondition for membership. Greece, on the other hand, was one of the early members of the European human rights system, so when it fell to a military junta in 1967, it provoked general consternation in the region. How would the European states and institutions react to a situation similar to what the IACHR had been facing for a number of years?

Greece and the European Commission

The case of authoritarianism and torture in Greece illustrates how human rights change happened slowly not only in Latin America, but also elsewhere in the world, including in Europe. The 1949 Statute of the Council of Europe made respect for human rights and the rule of law conditions of membership. Greece, then under a democratic government, joined the Council of Europe the year it was founded, helping the Council draft the European Convention on

Human Rights. Greece also participated in the creation of two regional human rights institutions, the first of their kind—the European Commission of Human Rights and the European Court of Human Rights. Greece was one of the first to ratify the Convention in March 1953, and the Convention came into effect by September of that year. Greece was also one of the first countries to use the Convention, bringing suit against Great Britain over abuses in Cyprus in 1956.[102] After the 1967 coup, Greece's relationship with the European human rights system began to change. As with the dictatorships in Latin America, the new authoritarian regime justified its coup with "national security ideology," which saw internal leftist and communist groups as a major security threat and justified authoritarianism and repression as legitimate, indeed necessary, means to confront subversion.[103]

In 1968, Norway, the Netherlands, Denmark, and Sweden filed a joint suit with the European Commission of Human Rights against the military government of Greece for violations of a number of human rights provisions found in the European Convention. An Amnesty International January 1968 report on torture in Greece later prompted the Scandinavian governments to add charges of torture to their original suit.[104] Since the previous democratic Greek government had been an early and active supporter of the Commission and the Convention, it was difficult for Greece to refuse the Commission permission to conduct a thorough investigation of the human rights situation in Greece. In its final report, the Commission concluded that the Greek military government had indeed violated a number of the articles of the Convention. The large second volume of the Commission's report deals entirely with torture and inhumane and degrading treatment.[105] As a result of the report, Greece eventually withdrew from the Council of Europe to avoid being ousted from membership.

Just as in the case of Latin America, when Greek prisoners and their families and Greek exiles in other European countries began to fight against the Greek dictatorship, one of the main tools they had at their disposal was the European Commission of Human Rights. If the diplomats of Europe had not worked in the 1950s to write the Convention and set up the Commission, the activists of the

1970s would not have had this valuable tool and ally in the struggle against repression and torture.

As human rights institutions responded to cases in Greece, Chile, and Uruguay, there was a stunning failure of states and institutions to take action on human rights in Cambodia, in 1975–1978, when the brutal Khmer Rouge took power and carried out a genocide against the Cambodian people. The emerging UN human rights system was unable to provide any adequate response. The apparent paradox that the human rights system began to respond in earnest with cases like Greece and in Uruguay, where violations were much lower, but could not respond to worse violations in Cambodia was the result of the nature of a system that relied on state consent. It was exactly those countries that had been democratic, that had ratified the relevant treaties and accepted principles of international supervision of human rights, with lively civil societies accustomed to rights, that first put into place international supervision of their human rights records when they suffered military coups. Cambodia had ratified the Genocide Convention in 1950, but that treaty had no treaty body or enforcement mechanism. At the time, Cambodia was almost off the international radar, as it closed its borders to all travel and scrutiny.

Around the same time, the signing of the Helsinki Final Act in 1975 provided a major impetus for change in the USSR and Eastern Europe. The agreement aimed at improving relations between the Communist bloc and the West. The Soviets wanted the Helsinki agreement because it recognized the sovereignty and the inviolability of countries' borders. In exchange, the Soviets agreed to human rights commitments, including freedom of movement. The United States and other Western governments were initially skeptical about, even hostile to, the Helsinki agreement, because they felt they had given away too much with regard to borders with only vague human rights commitments in return. But, contrary to what many of the drafters anticipated, the Final Act initiated the "Helsinki Process," which came to have human rights at its core and contributed to the demise of communism in the Soviet Union and Eastern Europe.[106] The Helsinki agreement gave tools to human rights activists in the region that enabled them to demand that their governments live up to their written commitments.

The Role of the United States

The United States played important, if varying, roles in the human rights movements in Greece, Latin America, Cambodia, and the USSR. Instead of being global leaders in the area of human rights, President Richard Nixon and his Secretary of State, Henry Kissinger, supported the Greek Junta and ignored the practices of torture, just as they had supported the anti-communist dictators in the Americas. Greece was a NATO member and received substantial military and economic aid from the United States, which treated it as a bulwark against the expansion of the Soviet bloc. Greece in turn provided valuable military bases to the United States.[107]

Crucial leaders in the United States opposed this policy. In the House of Representatives, Donald Fraser (D-MN) was so opposed to US support for repressive regimes that he launched the new US human rights policy in Congress in 1973. Jimmy Carter picked up on these ideas and brought his own to inaugurate the first US human rights policy from the executive branch when he took office in 1977. Such support from within the US government eventually made a huge difference for Latin American activists. Nevertheless, as regards the *institutionalization* of the international protection of human rights, the United States did not take a strong role, except, as discussed previously, when the Carter administration encouraged other countries to ratify human rights treaties and supported the IACHR both politically and financially.

In the case of Latin America, governments were hesitant to attack the IACHR after Carter took office in 1977 and announced his new human rights policy. Under the Carter administration and, for the first time since Latin American states created the IACHR in 1959, the Commission received the full support of the US government. The Carter administration also coincided with increased activism on the part of Latin American human rights social movements.[108]

Latin American governments found it difficult to fight back against human rights institutions because international law stipulates that, once ratified, a treaty binds that state in the future regardless of regime change, unless the new government formally withdraws from the institution. Thus, the ratification of the American

Convention on Human Rights by states (often during moments of democracy) bound later authoritarian rulers. Likewise, when states nominated individuals like Jiménez de Aréchaga to serve on human rights institutions, either as members of the IACHR or as judges on the Inter-American Court, these individuals could not be removed from their positions until their term expired, even when a new government came into power. Commissioners nominated to the IACHR by Uruguay and Argentina before the 1973 and 1976 coups in their countries continued to serve their terms after the change of governments, joining the commissioners from Venezuela and the United States in the mid-1970s to form a four-member majority in favor of vigorous human rights reports. The authoritarian regimes did not wish to be bound by legal obligations to respect human rights, but to repudiate the obligations publicly by withdrawing could have yielded exactly the unfavorable publicity they were trying to avoid.

Human Rights and Neoliberalism

As neo-liberal economic policies were very much part of the story of the Cold War period in Latin America, it is useful to evaluate the claim that human rights were complicit with neoliberalism.[109] The authoritarian regimes in Chile, Brazil, Argentina, and Uruguay in the 1960s, 1970s, and 1980s were motivated by an interconnected political and economic agenda. The governments wanted to impose what began at that time to be called "neo-liberal" economic policies—policies that lowered tariff barriers to promote trade, provided for free exchange of currencies at international market rates, and made conditions more welcoming to foreign investment. These neo-liberal policies also worked to eliminate government deficits by cutting state spending, often through curtailing social welfare policies. In many cases in Latin America, aspects of these economic policies were later continued after transitions to democracy.

The new military regimes in Argentina, Brazil, Chile, El Salvador, Guatemala, Uruguay, and others began to imprison, torture, and sometimes disappear their political opponents. The governments targeted members of guerrilla movements, political parties of the left, labor unions, and also centrist political leaders who opposed authoritarian rule. In Latin America, the human rights movement emerged *in response* to authoritarian regimes that had adopted neo-liberal economic policies and in response to the complaints made by the families of these regimes' many victims. The neo-liberal dictatorships were repressing all political opposition, in particular labor leaders and leftist activists, including the armed left.

Because of this history, when I hear scholars and activists today say that human rights and neoliberalism somehow go hand in hand, one complicit with the other, I am convinced they have misunderstood or misread history.[110] This chapter has demonstrated how the debate over economic models in Latin America has a long and complex history. The revolutionary left in the 1960s increasingly believed that it was necessary to overthrow bourgeois democracy and the capitalist system to promote development and rights. Meanwhile, many conservative economic and political actors began to believe that neo-liberal economic policies could not be enacted under democratic governments operating with strong labor movements. Political repression, they argued, was necessary for economic stability. So, paradoxically, in the 1970s, in Latin America both the left and the right increasingly believed there was an affinity between free market economic policies and the harsh authoritarian regimes that violated human rights. This is exactly the inverse of the argument that human rights are complicit with neoliberalism. This position was also supported by some of the most brilliant scholars of Latin American politics in the 1980s and 1990s, such as the Argentine political scientist Guillermo O'Donnell, who argued that a particular stage of capitalism required new forms of "bureaucratic-authoritarian" regimes with repressive policies.[111] Essentially, O'Donnell argued that neoliberalism was complicit with human rights *violations*, not human rights ideas.

When I was a graduate student studying Latin American politics at Columbia University in the 1980s, bureaucratic authoritarianism was one of the main theories I absorbed. I was grateful once again to Albert O. Hirschman, this time for questioning the rigidity of O'Donnell's argument in its emphasis on the economic determinants for political regimes. Hirschman saw bureaucratic authoritarianism as yet another example of social scientists being too anxious to find negative, unintended consequences and disenchantment. He said O'Donnell made it seem as if the "effort to achieve growth, whether or not successful, brings with it calamitous side effects in the political realm, from the loss of democratic liberties at the hand of authoritarian, repressive regimes to the wholesale violation of elementary human rights."[112] Hirschman suggested instead that the link between economics and politics was much more complicated, interesting, and open-ended. Hirschman's 1991 critique has been supported more recently by research on the emergence, survival, and fall of democracy in the Americas, which finds that beliefs about democracy itself, including international beliefs, are a crucial part of the explanation for why democracies break down or survive.[113] In other words, rather than continuing to look for the economic determinants of democracy, we should look for more proximate causes, such as people's normative preferences for democracy. My dissertation field research on economic policymaking in Latin America in the 1950s and 1960s, where I saw that the debates over economic models and political regimes were as complex and open-ended as Hirschman suggested, reinforced the ideas I had gleaned from him.

Even so, having grown up hearing arguments that neoliberal capitalism had an elective affinity for repressive authoritarian regimes made me incredulous when I heard it all reversed—that some scholars now think human rights is "complicit" with neoliberalism. On the contrary, I have found a new appreciation for both human rights and democracy was one effect of the period of neoliberalism and authoritarianism in Latin America, where thousands of activists, mainly the young, were disappeared and killed. The initial move by the left to adopt human rights language may have grown out of a desperate need to find any acceptable language in which to couch demands to stop disappearances and release political prisoners. But, for some men and women, human rights protections and the value of democracy became a genuine conviction, not just a useful slogan. During this period, the Latin American left moved away from revolution and towards more reformist solutions. Cuba, once a model for every young leftist in the region, lost some of its luster. Yes, Che was eloquent about the defects of democracy in poor countries, but the single-party alternative that he had embraced back in Cuba was not able to produce any alteration in power for Fidel Castro, nor a means to express vigorous dissent with the government. By the 1980s, in Chile, Uruguay, Argentina, El Salvador, Guatemala, and other countries in the region, there was a profound rethinking of democracy that moved the left to embrace human rights as a moral vocabulary for oppositional struggles. The stability of democracy in the region is thus largely the result of a stronger normative preference for democracy, partly born of the experience of harsh authoritarian regimes that massively violated rights.[114]

The increasing support for democracy in Latin America also meant that some ground had been cleared for tolerating pro-market economic and social policies, as long as these were advocated by elected governments. Many human rights groups were part of this rethinking. Some came to see themselves as alternatives to revolution, as Sergio Aguayo pointed out in chapter 1. They had seen firsthand the many deaths that followed the call to revolution in the region and were less willing to romanticize the revolutionaries than they had been in the 1960s. Human rights groups adopted a nonviolent, gradualist approach to social change based on demanding all types of rights. Some call this approach "minimalist" because it did not call for violent revolutionary upheaval, but as I will discuss in chapter 7, while their methods are gradual, there is nothing minimalist about the goals of human rights movements.

Given the complex relationship between the support for human rights and democracy and the experience of neoliberalism in Latin America, I find it unacceptably simplistic to claim that human rights have been "complicit" with neoliberalism.

Conclusion

After the emergence of the norm of international protection of human rights in the 1940s, 1950s, and 1960s, every part of the world except Europe yielded to turmoil and discord, with the struggles of the Cold War sometimes drowning out the voices supporting human rights. Yet developments in the 1970s are politically and institutionally linked to and made possible by what happened in the 1940s, 1950s, and 1960s.

A number of countries in the Global South worked hard to keep the concept of human rights alive during the Cold War. In the words of Jensen, they "delivered the human rights project onto the doorstep of the 1970s."[115] When the First International Conference on Human Rights in Tehran, Iran, failed, one of its architects, the Jamaican Ambassador Egerton Richardson, recognized one of the great shortcomings of what had been done up to that point on human rights: "Tehran was our moment of truth, when we came face to face with the nature of our beast—when we saw what it means to be promoting the cause of Human Rights by working mainly through governments."[116] The great paradox of human rights is that governments are both the main protectors of human rights and the main violators. This Janus-faced nature of the state vis-à-vis human rights means that one needs states, but can never depend on them to be the sole champions of rights. Richardson recognized that the way forward had to involve a greater role for civil society and NGOs.[117]

During the Cold War, human rights debates in a variety of regions and countries, including Africa, Latin America, the Soviet Union and Eastern Europe, converged. There was a multi-centric shift going on in Cold War politics that gave human rights more traction. The social movements that emerged in the 1970s were very much connected to earlier efforts to draft laws and create human rights institutions.

But worldwide, the normative and institutional developments that occurred in the period of 1950–1979 could not be fully activated until civil society organizations began to make use of them. Human rights did not, therefore, begin in the 1970s as some claim. Rather, the 1970s were the moment when new human rights NGOs around the world began to use the institutional arrangements that diplomatic struggles of the 1940s, 1950s, and 1960s had put at their disposal: the agreements, treaties, treaty bodies, provisions for individual petitions, commissions, and courts. This convergence made it possible for transnational anti-apartheid activists to use the United Nations to denounce and secure sanctions against South Africa, for Latin American human rights activists to bring their cases forward at the IACHR and at the UN Human Rights Committee, and for civil society groups and states to bring their concerns to the European Commission of Human Rights. In the Soviet Union and Eastern Europe, the Helsinki agreement likewise provided institutional means for activists (from the Helsinki committees in the Soviet Union to Helsinki Watch in the United States) to pursue their agendas. When human rights social movements in Latin America, South Africa, Eastern Europe, and the United States began during the 1970s and 1980s, they had laws and institutions at their disposal that traced their origins to the 1940s and 1950s.

The stories of the Cold War also offer cautionary tales for policy-makers and publics in the United States today. Important lessons from the Cold War include that you cannot save democracy by destroying it; nor can anyone build democracy from the outside. Democracy must be homegrown to take root. But international actors can do much to destroy democracy, as the United States did in Guatemala, Iran, and the Congo. International actors can also help create a climate where democracy can survive and slowly strengthen.

After 9/11, US citizens sometimes act as though we need a whole new set of rules to deal with the apparently new threat of terrorism. Terrorism, however, is not a new threat. Virtually all of the military regimes of the Americas referred to their opponents as terrorists. The regimes argued, similar to what the Bush administration argued in response to 9/11 and the Trump administration has argued more recently, that the battle against terrorism requires us to go beyond the realm of rights and turn to new tools and tactics to confront it. After 9/11, Vice President Cheney famously said that the US had to "take off the gloves," by which he meant that the United States would need to engage in illegal practices like torture and extraordinary rendition.[118] But long before Cheney, authoritarian regimes had already taken off their gloves and used illegal counterterrorism tactics, often with US support. Latin Americans know well how going outside of the rule of law to fight terrorism carries the risk of causing more suffering and civilian deaths than do terrorists themselves. Such actions also risk delegitimizing the very cause of freedom as well as providing recruiting tools to those who advocate violent change. The Cold War experience reminds us of the devastating, if unintended, consequences of the decision to use illegal means to fight terrorism.

Human rights and democracy are intimately related and, so far in human history, it is hard to have one without the other. That does not mean that democracy inevitably leads to human rights; it just means that democracy is a necessary, but not at all sufficient, condition for human rights progress. We do not yet have any examples in the world where full sets of economic, social, civil, and political rights are protected under a non-democratic regime. Thus, undermining democracy, as the United States helped to do in Iran, Guatemala, the Congo, Brazil, and Chile, is a shortsighted policy. However imperfect and fragile, if a democracy is destroyed by a military coup, it may take decades, perhaps even half a century, to reconstruct it.

What would have happened in Iran, the Congo, or Guatemala if the United States had seen the elected leftist administrations as governments they did not like and did not trust, but that they could tolerate and work with? For years, the United States has been stymied by the revolutionary regime in Iran. Would allowing Mosaddeq to stay in power have led to a different outcome? Congo is one of the most violent countries in the world today. If Lumumba had stayed in power, would the Congo have been more stable and less violent? If Árbenz had not been overthrown, would Guatemalan democracy have been able to avoid the polarization and violence that led to the genocide under Ríos Montt in the early 1980s? These are all counterfactual questions. We can never know. But it is worth noting that, in all three cases, we can hardly imagine a more violent and dangerous history than those that followed US-backed coups. In 1982 in Guatemala, a US diplomat was heard to muse, "What we wouldn't give to have Arbenz back now."[119] In Iran or the Congo today, some might say the same about Mosaddeq or Lumumba.

What we do know is that human rights progress and democratic change take time. Such progress is to be measured in decades, not in years, and the breakdown of a genuinely elected democratic regime sets the process back immeasurably. One reason human rights movements work slowly is because they progress through the incremental creation of law and institutions. Social movements and citizen action are necessary to mobilize these institutions and put them to work. By the late 1980s, the countries of the Americas had finally put such institutions in place, both nationally in many countries and regionally, finally securing a difficult-to-alter path to greater protection of human rights.

By the 1990s, activists and states had added a new feature to the human rights institutional landscape: individual criminal accountability for past human rights violations, such as the trial of General Ríos Montt that opened this chapter. Most of the UN human rights system and the regional human rights courts in Europe, Latin America, and Africa, used "state accountability" for past human rights violations. But state accountability often felt inadequate because the actual perpetrators of violence were never held individually accountable and sent to prison. This all began to change in the 1980s when a handful of the post-Cold War states discussed previously—such as Greece, Argentina, and Guatemala—began to hold their own former officials criminally accountable in domestic courts. By the 1990s, with the fall of the Soviet Union and the outbreak of war in the former Yugoslavia, demands arose for international tribunals to hold accountable those responsible for mass atrocities; in response, the UN set up ad hoc tribunals for the former Yugoslavia (ICTY) and Rwanda (ICTR). In 1998, states set up the first permanent international criminal tribunal, the International Criminal Court (ICC). A third type of human rights criminal trial gained attention when General Augusto Pinochet of Chile was arrested in London by British police executing a Spanish extradition request: foreign prosecutions in domestic courts outside of the country where the human rights violations occurred. The Spanish court wanted Pinochet to stand trial in Spain for crimes committed in Chile during his military dictatorship. The Law Lords (the British Supreme Court) decided that Pinochet could be extradited to Spain, but let him return to Chile for humanitarian reasons, where he was facing prosecutions for corruption and human rights violations when he died in 2006.[120]

Together, these three kinds of prosecutions comprise an interrelated, dramatic new trend in world politics—holding individual state officials, including heads of state, criminally accountable for human rights violations.[121] I call this trend the "justice cascade."[122] By justice cascade, I do not mean that perfect justice has been or will be done, or even that most perpetrators of human rights violations will be held criminally accountable. Rather, justice cascade means that there has been a shift in the *legitimacy of the norm* of individual criminal accountability for human rights violations and an increase in criminal prosecutions on behalf of that norm.[123]

Just as with all the other political and legal developments discussed in this chapter, the justice cascade was not an inevitable reaction to unprecedented violence or to the emergence of human rights norms. The human rights movement, working together with like-minded states, fueled these changes. The cascade started with the concerted efforts of small groups of public interest lawyers, jurists, and activists who pioneered strategies, developed legal arguments, recruited plaintiffs and witnesses, marshaled evidence, and persevered through years of legal challenges. The work of these norm entrepreneurs was facilitated by two broader structural changes in the world: the third wave of democracy and the end of the Cold War. The first multiplied the number of transitional countries open to the trends described here, and the second opened space for countries to consider a wider range of policy options. These new practices of accountability would not have emerged without the combination of new human rights movements, new human rights law, and regional institutions to implement the law that we have discussed in this chapter.

Understanding this is crucial for modern debates about the future of human rights because so many scholars are arguing about the "endtimes" or "twilight" of human rights based on erroneous ideas about their origins and institutional development. Human rights institutions give continuity to human rights norms and policies that last beyond the power of those that set them up. This is what historical institutionalists mean when they say institutions are "sticky." In other words, institutional choices from the past can persist, or become locked in, thereby shaping and constraining actors across time.[124] Even as the original coalitions that led to the formation of institutions disappear, these institutions have power in their own right and can sustain policy.

Human rights institutions can help protect human rights activists and sustain human rights work. Though not without problems of their own, such institutions are viable resources to which victims can turn when they suffer abuse and neglect in their own countries. There has often been an affinity between human rights institutions and human rights movements, but such affinities will not be realized if the institutions are staffed with unfeeling bureaucrats only interested in collecting a comfortable salary, or if movements disdain such institutions to focus on what they consider the more genuine, direct activism in the streets. Human rights institutions can also be "captured" by the governments of repressive countries. Fortunately, in the cases of Latin America in the 1970s, Greece, or the Helsinki Committees, the affinity between human rights movements and human rights institutions was realized.

This chapter illustrates the open-ended and conflictual nature of processes leading to human rights change. At every point, some states, including many powerful states, attempted (often successfully) to delay human rights progress. Yet, even in the throes of the Cold War, some states managed to craft treaties, create institutions, and secure the state ratifications that put these institutions into effect. Such legal developments sometimes had unintended consequences for later governments and presented political and legal opportunities for other governments and social movements. All this implies that the distinction between idealists and pessimists is too static and misses buildups, eruptions, backlashes, and backsliding. Rather, we need to take a perspective of what historians call the *longue durée*, or long-term, like the one offered in this book, to see how human rights works over time.[125] In this case, the history I seek to tell is particularly attentive to sources and institutional developments from the Global South.

Jiménez de Aréchaga never lived to see the transition to democracy in Uruguay, nor in most of Latin America. When he died in 1980, the majority of countries in the region were still under authoritarian regimes and the human rights practices in many had worsened. In a series of talks and newspaper interviews he gave in the mid- to late 1970s, as the region grew ever more repressive, Jiménez de Aréchaga's voice was that of an increasingly outraged man able to speak out when others could not.[126] But, even in those dark days of Latin American authoritarianism, Jiménez de Aréchaga still saw the possibility for hope. He was interviewed in 1978, on the day after the tiny island state of Grenada ratified the American Convention on Human Rights, which was the last ratification needed for the Convention to finally enter into force. Jiménez de Aréchaga was proud to see the achievement of something he, along with many other jurists, had worked to secure for almost all of his professional lifetime. When asked to sum up his reaction, he said he saw it as "a splendid victory in the best legal Uruguayan tradition . . . and a new hope for those who believe in the sacredness of human liberty."[127]

PART III

The Effectiveness of Human Rights Law, Institutions, and Movements

CHAPTER FIVE

Why Is It So Hard to Measure the Effectiveness of Human Rights?

THE FIRST HALF OF THIS BOOK has addressed the legitimacy of human rights ideas, institutions, and movements, largely through an exploration of human rights history.[1] But as important as questions of legitimacy are, so too are questions concerning the effectiveness of human rights, the focus of the second part of this book. Do human rights law, institutions, and movements actually improve human rights? Discussion of effectiveness, like that of legitimacy, has been pervaded recently by significant pessimism, so much so that some refer to the current period as a human rights crisis. Moreover, just as with legitimacy, issues of effectiveness are raised not only by academics and governments, but also and more importantly from within human rights movements.

Lucia Nader, former head of Conectas, a human rights organization in Brazil, said that one of things that most discouraged her and her colleagues about human rights work was the feeling that "in some cases, we have important results but we don't have structural and lasting changes." Nader said:

> Some of the people I talk to in the human rights movement and me too, we sometimes feel this exhaustion. We use all of our tools—we approve

laws, we have campaigns, we use the UN and yet there is still such a long way to go. I am positive we would be in a worse place without it all and I truly believe that human rights are the only way to fight for a better world. But sometimes it is hard to keep the daily optimism, especially if we compare the results with the world we dream about. At the international level, for instance, we are seeing Trump talking about law as an obstacle to what he wants to do to terrorist suspects. We hear in the latest polls that fifty-eight percent of the American public agrees with him. What can change this mentality? Six in every ten people in America support torture. Is this sustainable? Can we live in this world?[2]

A recent survey of 346 individuals currently or previously working in the field of human rights found that this work is associated with elevated levels of depression and Post-Traumatic Stress Disorder (PTSD) and that one source of this appears to be negative self-appraisals about human rights work.[3] This suggests that one of the most difficult parts about being a human rights activist is the doubt about whether you are contributing to positive change. Is it true that the human rights movement has seen some results but not structural and lasting changes? How would we know? This chapter takes up that challenge.

In previous chapters, we saw how individual diplomats, jurists, and activists struggled to develop human rights norms, draft human rights law, and establish courts and commissions to enforce these rights. By the early twenty-first century, most states around the world had accepted human rights law, at least on paper. Almost every state had signaled its support for human rights by ratifying at least one of the core international human right treaties.[4] However, countries' ratifications of treaties do not mean that the countries will comply, especially since many of these treaties do not have strong enforcement mechanisms. Nevertheless, to date, many countries have ratified treaties that enable enforcement through established courts and 122 countries have ratified the treaty with the potential for the most stringent enforcement: the Rome Statute of the International Criminal Court. State officials who violate the Rome Statute risk being criminally prosecuted and sent to prison.[5] Most states in regions with strong regional human rights systems—Europe, Africa, and the Americas—have also ratified their regional human rights conventions and accepted the compulsory jurisdiction of their regional human rights courts.[6]

The question remains, however—how, if at all, do these legal commitments influence the actual behavior of states? The US use of torture, kidnapping, and arbitrary detention after 9/11, despite prior commitment to international treaties that absolutely prohibited torture whether in wartime or peace, gave rise to some of the current pessimism about the relevance of human rights law.[7] The election of Donald Trump, with his disregard for human rights law, has provoked a new round of fear and anxiety among many human rights organizations in the United States and around the world.

Global Human Rights Trends

An examination of global human rights trends reveals that the record is far more positive than current pessimism suggests. I argue that the issue of improvements in human rights is an empirical question, requiring us to look closely at the best data we have on issues that most of us would agree constitute measures of human rights progress—for example, data about the number of individuals killed in wars, the use of the death penalty, the number of children who die before their first or fifth years, or the percentage of girls and women in school around the world.

When we analyze these trends, we discover that human rights is characterized by some areas of retrogression and worsening, such as the current refugee crisis in Europe, or the US use of torture and rendition during the Bush administration. Yet there are many other areas of increasing awareness and improvements, such as the decline of deaths in war and conflict, as well as improvements in gender equality, the rights of sexual minorities, and the rights of people with disabilities. Despite some worrisome trends in some areas, such as the rise of economic inequality, my survey of the current data suggests that overall there is *less* violence and *fewer* human rights violations in the world than there were in the past.

As stated throughout this book, and particularly in chapter 2, I measure human rights violations in comparison with the past because, as a social scientist, I am more interested in empirical comparisons than comparisons to the ideal. In this section, I will briefly present a series of graphs in support of my argument, before turning to the main subject of this chapter: why so many people are pessimistic in spite of positive human rights trends. Because the data may be problematic in any one case, I use many different data sets that point to similar trends in drawing my conclusions.

There is a lot of variation in the human rights data—between regions, between countries, and even within countries. We must understand the general trends, however, before talking about how certain groups, cases, or countries are doing better or worse in relation to those trends. For instance, life expectancy has been rising all over the world, including in Africa, but in some countries, such as Zimbabwe, life expectancy declined in the early and mid-2000s. Therefore, whenever we talk about broad trends we know that there is ample variation, but to understand and study the variation, we need to start with the general trends.

There are two big questions here—first, are there positive human rights trends in the world? And second, what are the explanations for these trends? These are separate issues; in some cases, we see positive human rights outcomes without any clear evidence that human rights law, institutions, or movements played a role. Positive human rights outcomes in these cases are still relevant for a discussion of pessimism, however, since critics such as Posner deny both that any positive human rights change has occurred *and* that human rights law has made any impact. I will try to indicate clearly where I have found evidence that human rights law, institutions, and movements have contributed to the trends I portray.

The Refugee Crisis

In chapter 6, I will provide data about the decline of international and civil war in the world, as well as about the related decline in the number of battle deaths. Here, however, we must acknowledge that, even though there are now fewer international wars and fewer battle deaths, the current wars in Syria, Iraq, and Afghanistan have produced more refugees than at any time since World War II. This situation is not principally about death—although many people have died en route—but about people relocating to avoid conflict and to seek a better life.

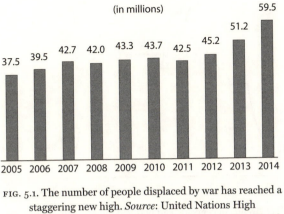

FIG. 5.1. The number of people displaced by war has reached a staggering new high. *Source*: United Nations High Commissioner for Refugees. Adapted from chart in "Worldwide Displacement Hits All-Time High as War and Persecution Increase," *UNHCR*, June 18, 2015, http://www.unhcr.org/news /latest/2015/6/558193896/worldwide-displacement-hits-all -time-high-war-persecution-increase.html.

In Figure 5.1 we see that the number of displaced people increased dramatically between 2004 and 2015. These numbers are estimates from the Office of the UN High Commissioner for Refugees (UNHCR), which has been tracking displaced people for decades, and, therefore, we consider its numbers reliable. There is strong reason to believe that this trend is a genuine expression of a human rights and humanitarian crisis of unprecedented proportions.

The causes of the crisis are complex. People move because of a combination of push factors, especially war, and pull factors, including a new information environment where people around the world know about better possibilities elsewhere and can more easily connect both with legal channels and with criminal networks that assist such movement. There is no reason to believe that human rights ideas or institutions somehow contributed to the flow of refugees, though better policies could have improved the reception of refugees and diminished their suffering.

Genocide and Politicide

On other issues, including genocide—one of the most serious of human rights crimes—evidence shows fewer episodes of violence

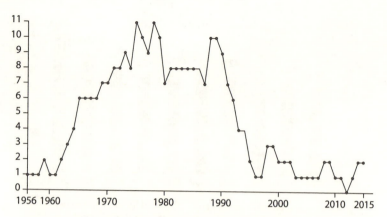

FIG. 5.2. Trends in genocide and politicide, 1955–2015. *Source*: Max Roser, *Trends in Genocide and Politicide 1955–2015*, n.d. Genocide Indicator of the Political Instability Task Force (PITF) State Failure Problem Set, 1955–2014. http://ourworldindata.org/data/war-peace/genocides/.

than in the past. Genocide, by definition, involves situations where there is "intent to destroy, in whole or in part, a national, ethnical, racial or religious group."[8] Since genocide does not include people targeted for destruction because of their political beliefs or ideology, scholars have created an additional category called "politicide," which refers to the murder of any person or people by a government because of their politics or for political purposes.

Figure 5.2 charts global trends in genocide and politicide, using the Political Instability Task Force State Failure Data.[9] This figure measures what we call "events-based data," which means the data counts episodes of genocide and politicide. Because the events included are big events, they are hard to hide and we can have some confidence in the data. But focusing on "episodes" of genocide could obscure the number of people affected; even if the number of genocides and politicides is declining, the number of affected people could be increasing. To address this concern, the data in Figure 5.3 contains the estimated number of people killed in "one-sided" violence in the world, defined as "lethal attacks on civilians by governments or formally organized groups."[10] This category goes beyond genocide and politicide to measure the number of people killed by a broader range of violence.

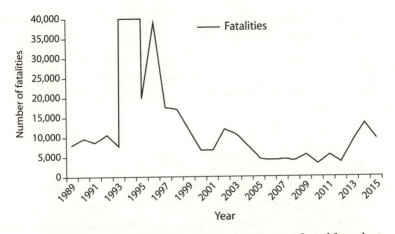

FIG. 5.3. Fatalities in one-sided violence, 1989–2015. *Source*: Adapted from chart in Erik Melander, Therése Pettersson, and Lotta Themnér, "Organized Violence, 1989–2015," *Journal of Peace Research* 53 no. 5 (2016): 727–742. Uppsala Conflict Data Program One-Sided Dataset.

Whether we use episodes or try to count actual deaths, evidence supports the conclusion of a decline in one-sided violence in the world. Genocide and politicide increased in the period 1960–1990, but significantly decreased after that time. Explanations for improvements in core human rights issues like genocide are complex, and identifying the risk factors that lead to worsening or improvement is not an easy task. Still, studies of possible risk factors show that war and authoritarianism are key trigger mechanisms for genocide.[11] Therefore, not surprisingly, the decline in trends in genocide corresponds with a decline in civil war and a decline in authoritarian regimes during the same period (see Figures 6.1 and 6.3 in chapter 6). Many leading scholars of genocide have also found that an upsurge in exclusionary and dehumanizing ideologies and language is associated with genocide.[12] Human rights ideas are the exact opposite of dehumanizing and exclusionary ideologies; they are humanizing and inclusive. As such, human rights ideas provide an alternative to the ideologies that contribute to genocide.

Human rights work also has a potentially measurable impact in the struggle to end genocide. My research shows that criminal accountability for human rights violations is associated with improvement in core human rights practices.[13] In the 1990s, state leaders and insurgents were held criminally accountable for the first time for the crime of genocide, in the ad hoc tribunals for Rwanda and the former Yugoslavia. This rise of accountability could be part of the explanation for the decline in genocide, although this conclusion is not yet certain.[14]

Capital Punishment

The death penalty is an issue where the link between human rights law and activism and improvements in human rights is more obvious. Amnesty International (AI) has had campaigns against the death penalty worldwide as one of its core mandates since 1977, when only sixteen countries had abolished it in law or practice.[15] Today, as we can see in Figure 5.4, that number has increased to 140, nearly two-thirds of the countries in the world. If we look at the ratification of various death penalty protocols in human rights treaties, we see that a large plurality of countries in the world have agreed that the death penalty is a violation of human rights.[16]

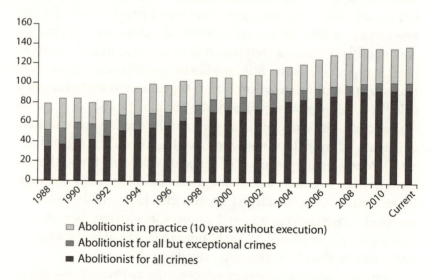

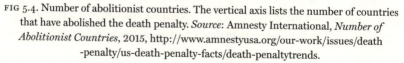

FIG 5.4. Number of abolitionist countries. The vertical axis lists the number of countries that have abolished the death penalty. *Source*: Amnesty International, *Number of Abolitionist Countries*, 2015, http://www.amnestyusa.org/our-work/issues/death-penalty/us-death-penalty-facts/death-penaltytrends.

Human rights law has made a difference in this case because research shows that countries that have ratified the death penalty protocols are more likely to abolish the death penalty in law or practice later.[17]

The death penalty, like genocide, can be measured using events-based data—that is, counts of specific countries that have abolished the death penalty either legally or in practice. Because these laws and practices are often public (with the exception of China, which practices an unknown number of executions each year), we can have confidence in the trend this data signals—a significant decrease in the use of the death penalty over time. Using this data, researchers have been able to ask and answer questions about the impact of human rights law and activism as it relates to capital punishment.[18]

Famine, Hunger, and Malnourishment

It is sometimes difficult to measure violations of economic and social rights, but famine is a measure of the most extreme deprivation of an economic right—the right to food—that is in turn a violation of the right to life. Increasingly, we understand that famine is usually not caused by an absence of food, but rather by a failure to get the food to those who most need it, or an inability of those who need the food to claim it. Amartya Sen described famine as primarily the result of the hungry lacking entitlements to food, in other words, as a human rights issue.[19] Sen demonstrated that famines do not occur under democratic leadership because, in democracies, the existence of a free press and regular elections ensure that governments know about any severe lack of food and they take action to prevent it so that they will not be voted out of power.[20]

Figure 5.5 shows the overall decline in great famines in the context of global population growth. Past theorists led us to believe that dramatic increases in population would inevitably lead to famine, but we see from the chart that this is not the case. Most of the figures included in this chapter also could have incorporated these population figures as a reminder that declining trends in violence and suffering occur in the context of increasing population pressures. In this sense, the declines in the absolute number of battle deaths,

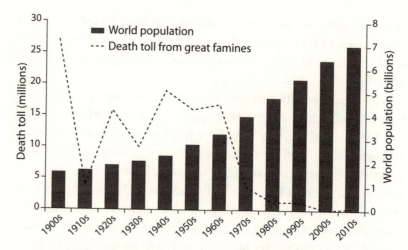

FIG. 5.5. World population growth and death toll from great famines, 1900–2015. *Note*: Each great famine killed more than 100,000 people. *Source*: World Peace Foundation. "Famine Trends Project." Boston: World Peace Foundation, 2016.

genocide, one-sided violence, and famine worldwide are all the more impressive in light of the dramatic increase in population.

We are, of course, not only concerned about famine, but also about less extreme forms of deprivation of the right to food. When Sen pointed out how democracy ended famine in India, he also noted that endemic malnutrition has endured there since independence. Famine grabs headlines and demands a political response, malnutrition does not. But, as discussed in chapter 2, hunger or malnourishment is also declining in the world, although not as dramatically as famine and with different trends in different regions. In this, as in all trends, it is important to distinguish between the absolute number of people affected and the number of people affected as a percentage of total population. As Figure 5.6 shows, both the absolute number of malnourished people in the world *and* the percentage of malnourished people in the total world population are declining. Yet while worldwide there is progress, in some regions the numbers are discouraging. In Africa, for example, while the number of malnourished people as a percentage of the population is declining, the absolute number of hungry people is increasing.

Figure 5.6 also reveals that the decline in hunger has not met some of the goals set by the international community. The decline

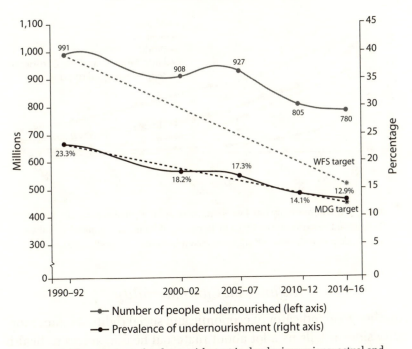

FIG. 5.6. The trajectory of undernourishment in developing regions: actual and projected progress of absolute number of malnourished people and malnourished people as a percentage of population. *Source*: Food and Agriculture Organization of the United Nations, "The State of Food Insecurity in the World 2015," http://www.fao.org/hunger/key-messages/en/.

in the prevalence of malnourishment has met the Millennium Development Goal (MDG), but the governments at the 1996 World Food Summit (WFS) in Rome set a target that was missed by a large margin: "to eradicate hunger in all countries, with an immediate view to reducing the number of undernourished people to half their present level no later than 2015."[21] This provides yet another illustration of how the different types of comparison can result in different evaluations of the same situation. Relying on empirical comparison, we see that malnourishment has declined in the world in both absolute and percentage terms since 1990. But, using the WFS target—which we can think of as an explicit comparison to an ideal (reducing the number of hungry people in the world by half in nine years)—we see a big gap in the chart between the ideal and the reality.

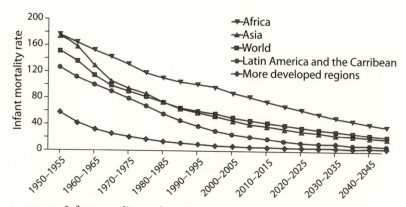

FIG. 5.7. Infant mortality rate by region, 1950–2050. Source of data: UN World Population Prospects, 2008. Chart by Rcragun / Wikimedia Commons (Creative Commons license, http://creativecommons.org/licenses/by/3.0).

Infant and Child Mortality

Another good indicator of economic and social rights is infant mortality since it tells us a lot about maternal health, access to health care, and access to clean water. As we see in Figure 5.7, infant mortality is declining in all regions of the world. This chart includes a prediction for the future, projecting this positive change through 2045, assuming current trends will continue. Once again, there is substantial regional variation. We see, for example, that Africa lags significantly behind other regions, yet it still shows a trend towards improvement.

Progress in measures of infant or child mortality may not be a result of the effectiveness of the human rights institutions or movement. The World Health Organization (WHO) and the United Nations Children's Fund (UNICEF) have demonstrated that more than half of early child deaths can be prevented with simple, affordable interventions, including exclusive breastfeeding, safe water, vaccinations, and oral rehydration therapy.[22] Many of these interventions are the result of public health measures, not of human rights campaigns. However, if we find that improvements in breastfeeding or use of oral rehydration were made, for example, in part as a result of a successful human rights campaign—such as the boycott against the Nestle Corporation and the resulting code of conduct for transnational corporations on the marketing of breast-milk substitutes—

we could say that human rights movements were one factor that contributed to improvements in infant mortality.[23]

Women's Rights

Human rights movements also have had an impact on women's rights. In Figure 5.8 we see an important trend: the decrease of inequality in education for women. This chart uses a standard measure of inequality, the Gini coefficient, to measure this decline at all levels of education—primary, secondary, and tertiary. Though improvements in education for women are affected by diverse issues, Beth Simmons has shown that the ratification of the Women's Convention (CEDAW) is an important factor.[24] Prior to ratification, countries often had legislation that set different requirements for obligatory education for girls and boys. For example, boys might have had to go to school until eighth grade, but girls only needed to go until sixth grade. When a country ratified CEDAW, the treaty body told them that such requirements were discriminatory and contrary to their obligations under the convention. Some countries

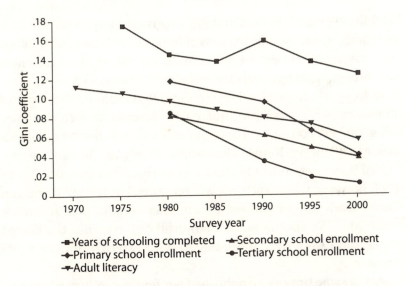

FIG. 5.8. Change in global gender inequality: five education indicators. Data drawn from Shawn F. Dorius and Glenn Firebaugh, "Trends in Global Gender Inequality," *Social Forces* 88, no. 5 (2010): 1953.

then changed their legislation, equalizing the mandatory age of education. When families followed the new law, countries saw increases in girls' education, increases that can be appropriately attributed to human rights law. When it comes to the impact of human rights law, Beth Simmons, Daniel Hill, and Yonatan Lupu have all shown that CEDAW has been one of the most effective human rights treaties to date.[25]

I could include many additional graphs, for example, on child mortality (the number of children who die in the first five years of life), which looks very much like the infant mortality graph, or on global trends in education, literacy levels, and life expectancy, all showing strong improvement, albeit with significant regional variation. My hope is that I have provided sufficient evidence to suggest that, on many issues, people around the world are better off than they were before. The remainder of this chapter focuses on to what degree human rights law, institutions, and movements have contributed to these trends.

Effectiveness of Human Rights Law, Institutions, and Movements

Establishing trends in human rights progress is only a starting place for talking about the effectiveness of human rights law, institutions, and movements. I began examining this question of effectiveness over fifteen years ago with my colleagues Thomas Risse and Stephen Ropp when we edited two volumes that explored the power of human rights by means of qualitative comparative case studies using various countries. Based on research on diverse countries such as Indonesia, Kenya, Guatemala, Morocco, Tunisia, and the United States, we concluded that human rights law did not work by itself; however, where such law was reinforced by transnational and domestic advocacy, improvements in human rights practices often occurred.[26] We also found that powerful countries like the United States and China were most able to flout external human rights pressures.[27]

At the same time as we published our findings, other researchers revealed a tension within the field of human rights scholarship. Studies more narrowly focused on quantitative data suggested that the ratification of some human rights treaties did not have a positive impact on human rights practices, sometimes even appearing to be counterproductive. For example, some studies showed that ratification of the Convention against Torture (CAT) was associated with increases in torture.[28] In a review essay called "Seeing Double: Human Rights Impact through Qualitative and Quantitative Eyes," two colleagues asserted that scholars who did field research were more optimistic about human rights progress, while scholars using quantitative research were more pessimistic.[29] The undercurrent of the article was that those of us doing field research were engaged in wishful thinking, while our colleagues who relied on numbers were more objective.

Beth Simmons's prize-winning book, *Mobilizing for Human Rights*, called into question the dichotomy between optimistic field researchers and pessimistic number crunchers. Using sophisticated quantitative techniques, Simmons showed that human rights treaties do lead to advances in human rights, provided the type of government in a country is taken into account. Though Simmons's book, published in 2010, was the best work to date on how international law influences state practice, it did not put to rest the debate about effectiveness. Three years later, Posner's *The Twilight of Human Rights* largely ignored Simmons's work as Posner claimed that human rights law and advocacy have failed to bring about results. Despite Simmons's contributions, no consensus has emerged. If anything, scholars and critics appear to differ more now than ever before.

Why can't we agree? In chapter 2, I explained one of the main causes for disagreement: the different conclusions reached by people using comparison to the ideal vs. empirical comparison. To further answer this question, I discuss three other issues that influence the debate about effectiveness, even among people doing empirical comparisons:

1. Invisible harms and the information paradox.
2. Heuristics or biases that lead us to pay more attention to prominent negative information.
3. A changing standard of accountability, where what we mean by human rights keeps expanding.

Invisible Harms and the Information Paradox

Some rights can be measured by fairly straightforward calculations, such as the information on women's education mentioned previously. As my colleague Malcolm Sparrow points out, however, many human rights issues are part of a larger set of problems, what he calls "invisible harms." These harms are difficult to discern and analyze because they tend to be underreported; thus, the bulk of the problem is hidden.[30] Examples of invisible harms include torture, disappearance, extrajudicial executions, rape, and political imprisonment. UN surveys, for example, show that one third of all women in the world will face either physical or sexual abuse by a partner or sexual violence by a non-partner during their lifetimes.[31] Because domestic abuse is a type of hidden harm that is harder to document than infant mortality or the number of girls in school, it is difficult to make conclusions about progress, regression, or something between.

One of the goals of the human rights movement is to make invisible harms visible, but in the process of doing this, they may make it seem as if human rights violations are more prevalent. In our 1998 book *Activists beyond Borders: Advocacy Networks in International Politics*, Margaret Keck and I grappled with how to define and measure the effectiveness of transnational advocacy networks, including those of human rights. We pointed out that to measure the influence of advocacy networks, you have to go beyond thinking about their influence on actual behavior and look at their ability to create new issues, to set agendas, and to influence legal and policy changes.

Keck and I argued that the most important tool of advocacy networks is "information politics"—credibly producing politically usable information and moving it to where it can have the most impact. We introduced the term "information paradox" to describe how activists, by creating new issues and producing new information, can sometimes give the impression that practices are getting worse, when in reality people just know more about them.[32] As we see in Figure 5.9, the number of human rights international nongovernmental organizations (INGOs) in these advocacy networks has continued to grow. The main tool of these INGOs also continues

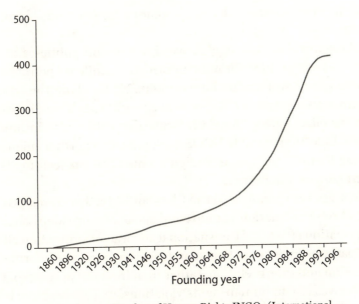

FIG. 5.9. Average Number of Human Rights INGOs (International Nongovernmental Organization) Working within States. The data comes from publically available coding of Yearbook of International Organization INGO data by Jackie Smith and Dawn Wiest. Thanks to Amanda Murdie for permission to adapt this chart.

to be information politics; more and more human rights NGOs continue to research, to publish more reports, and to post and tweet about them.

The information politics of human rights networks in turn provoke a response from repressive governments and other perpetrators, who try to keep their "invisible harms" hidden and to delegitimize the messengers—especially NGOs. Perpetrators use drastic means to keep human rights violations hidden. For example, several weeks after Serbian groups massacred thousands of men and boys in Srebrenica, Bosnia, in 1990 and buried their bodies, those responsible for the murders sent in bulldozers to exhume and disrupt the mass graves and rebury them in order to make the forensic identification of bodies impossible. Human rights organizations turn to increasingly sophisticated technology to respond. In this case, they harnessed a new DNA technique that permitted the identification of bodies from even tiny bone fragments in the disrupted graves, information that later was used in the ad hoc tribunal for war crimes in the former Yugoslavia to convict some of those responsible for the massacre.[33]

There are always struggles over information politics, not just with activists working for more information while perpetrators try to hide it, but also among human rights NGOs about the types of information they report. Repressive governments have discovered that one effective way to fight information politics is to intimidate and exclude human rights NGOS, including through draconian laws forcing them to register as foreign agents or by prosecuting them for treason or other crimes.

In a 2013 article, Ann Marie Clark and I further developed the idea of the information paradox and spoke of a broader issue: the "information effects" of transnational advocacy. Information effects are "patterns in the data that stem from the process of information collection and interpretation, rather than from the process that actually gives rise to human rights violations."[34] This problem is not limited to human rights research; it plagues other areas of research, such as current debates over autism. Researchers are still uncertain whether there has actually been an increase in autism or merely an increase in the diagnosis of autism, or some combination of both. Human rights researchers, however, for the most part seem unaware that such a phenomenon might also affect our field.

The situation in Brazil that is discouraging some women's rights defenders is an example of the information paradox. As NGOs in Brazil began to highlight violations of the Maria da Penha Law, which sought to protect women from domestic abuse, it sometimes appeared that violence against women was getting worse when it was not—we simply had more information about it.[35] Women in Brazil, increasingly aware of the new law on violence against women, are reporting violence at new levels. Eventually, the data should settle down so that we can observe trends. But I suspect that ten years later is too early to establish reliable data on violence against women and, therefore, that we cannot know yet whether it is violence or the reporting of violence that is truly increasing. The information paradox challenges human rights activists to make sure their skills in information politics and issue creation do not become tools for demonstrating a lack of effectiveness in leading to behavioral change.

There were very few sources of reliable human rights information in the 1970s, so we don't have a baseline against which to measure human rights progress. Since the 1980s, the number of NGOs, states, and international organizations reporting on human rights has proliferated. Violations are less likely to be hidden and unknown than they were before, and researchers have many more sources to draw on. For example, NGOs, other organizations, and the media have drawn increasing attention to violence against women, especially the widespread prevalence of rape and particularly of rape in wartime. But is there really a new global epidemic of violence against women or do victims, organizations and the media simply report it more than before?

When we try to get good information about whether violence against women is increasing, we sometimes get data like that in Figure 5.10 on rape, produced using figures from the UN Office on Drugs and Crime. The map makes it look as if the countries in the world with the most rapes are Sweden, New Zealand, South Africa, and Botswana. It also appears that rape occurs more often in the UK and France than in the former Yugoslavia. There are great swaths of countries for which there is no data (the light grey striped areas on the map). This data is a snapshot of a single period of time, telling us nothing about trends over time or about the actual prevalence of rape in the world. Rather, it shows which countries are collecting data, including which countries are doing a better job collecting data than others, or simply have different procedures. For example:

> In Sweden there has been this ambition explicitly to record every case of sexual violence separately, to make it visible in the statistics. . . . So, for instance, when a woman comes to the police and she says my husband or my fiancé raped me almost every day during the last year, the police have to record each of these events, which might be more than 300 events. In many other countries it would just be one record—one victim, one type of crime, one record.[36]

We might applaud the Swedish government for its commitment to making rape more visible, even while recognizing that such a unique commitment makes it impossible to compare Sweden's practices with other global data.

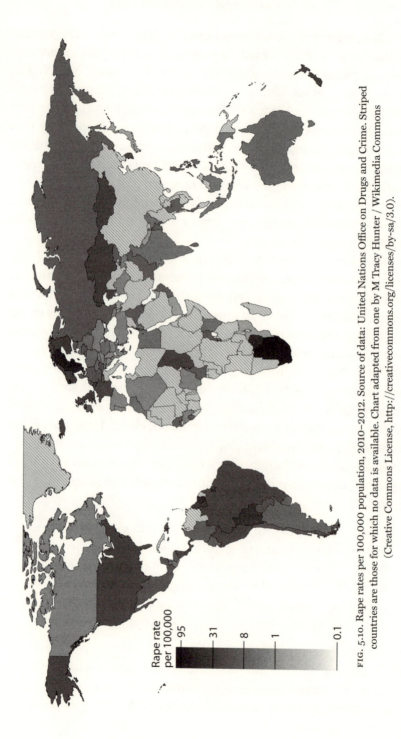

FIG. 5-10. Rape rates per 100,000 population, 2010–2012. Source of data: United Nations Office on Drugs and Crime. Striped countries are those for which no data is available. Chart adapted from one by M Tracy Hunter / Wikimedia Commons (Creative Commons License, http://creativecommons.org/licenses/by-sa/3.0).

Rape rate
per 100,000

95
31
8
1
0.1

Most invisible harms are "invisible by design"—that is, the perpetrators take steps to avoid detection.[37] Because of that, we can't measure these human rights violations, only reports of them. For example, when academics are coding Amnesty International reports, they produce a data set of Amnesty International alleged violations, "not a census of actual violations."[38] Violations by governments, such as US efforts to hide torture during the Bush administration, as well as violations by non-state actors, such as domestic abuse, can be seen as invisible harms by design.

Human rights violations in particular are complex because the government itself is often committing the harm. This is different from cases of government corruption, for example, where individual government officials might engage in corruption even though the government as a whole is interested in detecting and even prosecuting the crime. In the case of mass human rights violations, the government as a whole may be committing the crimes and doing everything possible to keep them hidden. When the Argentine government was disappearing thousands of its own citizens, the entire security apparatus was devoted to committing and then hiding these invisible harms.

Invisible harms present measurement problems for policymakers that are serious and yet also predictable.[39] In the short term, new reporting makes it appear that the situation is worsening. But if the campaign succeeds in the long term, the volume of reporting of incidents of violence should eventually decline. The issue that remains, however, is how long human rights change takes. How soon should human rights activists expect to see a decline in human rights violations if law, institutions, and activism are working?

Why We Pay More Attention to Prominent Negative Information

Another reason why activists, policymakers, and even scholars often can't agree on whether human rights are improving has to do with a series of psychological heuristics and biases that make humans prone to pay more attention to prominent information and to notice and believe negative information more than positive information.

In his book *The Better Angels of Our Nature: Why Violence Has Declined*, Steven Pinker first drew my attention to these cognitive illusions and biases.[40] Pinker cited the work of Nobel prize-winning economists Daniel Kahneman and Amos Tversky and their descriptions of psychological mechanisms that influence how people judge the probability or frequency of events in situations of uncertainty.[41] This is exactly what is at stake in the debate over human rights effectiveness—we judge, for example, how frequent practices like torture or violence against women are from a position of uncertainty because governments or individuals try to hide these practices. Tversky and Kahneman pointed to a number of heuristics, or shortcuts, that people use to reduce complex judgments like this to simpler ones.

The most relevant heuristic for us is the *availability heuristic*: if it is easier to imagine or to remember an example, people think it is more likely.[42] The availability heuristic can help us understand the puzzling discrepancies between the actual likelihood of an event and people's perceptions of its likelihood. For example, people in the United States today are extremely worried that they might be victims of jihadist terrorism, even though an average of only four people a year are killed in the United States by such terrorism. A person's chances of being murdered with a firearm are almost 3,000 times greater—even the chances of being killed by lightning or by a falling object are far greater than that of being the victim of a terrorist attack.[43] Yet, per Kahneman and Tversky's model, dramatic events are more available to our cognitive memory and thus more likely to be remembered than less dramatic events.[44] Because terrorism is so horrific, is covered relentlessly in the news, and is harped upon by political candidates, individuals are led to believe that it is far more likely to occur than it actually is.

Human rights activists are especially prone to the availability heuristic, and for good reason. Day in, day out, they hear dramatic stories of human rights abuses. Those stories are constantly, painfully available to them. Activists' very profession and their political commitments require them to ruminate about awful events and to bring them to the attention of the public. In one sense, the availability heuristic is almost an underpinning of human rights work; its purpose is to make human rights violations more available to the general public and to policymakers. Success in making human rights violations available, however, may have the unintended consequence of making it appear that these violations are becoming more frequent than ever before.

In *The Idea of Justice*, Amartya Sen discusses a related cognitive bias, which he calls "objective illusion." Sen argues that when there is manifest injustice, it is taken for granted to such an extent that people can't see it. But, as the situation gradually improves and becomes more just, people are more aware of the original problem. Those who complain the most may be those who have already seen change. He gives the example of the Indian state of Kerala, where people complain more about morbidity even though they have longer life spans than elsewhere in India.[45]

A second kind of cognitive bias that affects judgments about the frequency of human rights violations is the *negativity bias*: people pay more attention to negative information than positive information. Social psychologist Roy Baumeister and his co-authors captured this idea in the 2001 article "Bad Is Stronger Than Good." They wrote, "Bad emotions, bad parents and bad feedback have more impact than good ones. Bad impressions and bad stereotypes are quicker to form and more resistant to disconfirmation than good ones."[46] Baumeister noted that "many good events can overcome the psychological effects of a bad one," but it may take many good pieces of news to balance out one bad piece of news.[47] Behavioral economists have confirmed a negativity bias by showing that people are much more concerned about loss aversion than about pursuing gain; for example, people are much more likely to care about losing money than about gaining it.[48]

All this illustrates how humans are "cognitive misers"—because we cannot process all information equally, we prioritize what we are going to process.[49] People spend more time and care processing bad information, with this more extensive processing often leading to enhanced memory.[50] One study found that people were more than twice as likely to remember bad events as they were to remember good ones.[51] There may be good evolutionary reasons for both the availability heuristic and the negativity bias—humans who paid attention to and remembered information about bad things, such as predators, would have been more likely to survive.[52]

Humans also have more detailed and systematic analysis and vocabulary to explain negative experiences and their resulting emotions than positive ones, which may be related to the fact that we process positive and negative information in different hemispheres of the brain. Positive emotions trigger top-down, heuristic processing, while "negative emotions trigger bottom-up, systematic processing in which an individual engages in more fine-grained, detailed analysis of experience."[53] As a result, "we tend to ruminate more about unpleasant events—and use stronger words to describe them—than happy ones."[54]

Not only do people pay more attention to and retain more information about bad events, but we also tend to see people who say negative things as smarter than those who present positive views. Thus, we are likely to give greater weight to criticism. One researcher found that "If I tell you that you are going to give a lecture before smarter people, you will say more negative things."[55] This may explain why some of the negative books about human rights that I discussed in chapter 2 are getting so much attention—the authors seem smarter for focusing on the negative! I'm taking this piece of research particularly hard. I have long been characterized as an "optimist" by colleagues; now I suspect that this is also a code word for "not very smart." I've also sometimes noticed that my colleagues who are more negative seem to benefit from a certain mystique of elegance and sophistication. Psychological literature helps explain why this is the case. I'm taking a risk with this book in the hope that readers can be persuaded to acknowledge negativity bias and give me the benefit of the doubt.

Hirschman's Perversity, Futility, and Jeopardy Theses

Not surprisingly, negativity bias with regard to human rights progress is far from new. In *The Rhetoric of Reaction: Perversity, Futility, Jeopardy*, Hirschman wrote about the historical reactions to three waves of demands for rights in countries around the world: the basic civil rights of man in the eighteenth century, the expansion of male suffrage in the nineteenth century, and the rise of the welfare state and of social and economic rights in the twentieth century.[56] All of these waves involved the national protection of the rights of citizens. The international protection of human rights could be seen as a fourth wave of rights that started in the mid-twentieth century and continues today.[57]

Hirschman spoke of three different types of negative arguments that frequently appeared in response to each of these waves of rights: the perversity thesis, the futility thesis, and the jeopardy thesis. According to the perversity thesis, "any purposive action to improve some feature of the political, social, or economic order only serves to exacerbate the condition one wishes to remedy."[58] For example, Hirschman showed how the expansion of male suffrage in the eighteenth century was portrayed as likely to undermine the very freedom it sought to advance. Conservatives argued that increasing democracy through universal male suffrage would lead to the despotism of the masses and future tyranny.[59] In other words, they argued that democracy exacerbates the condition it seeks to remedy. The perversity thesis is perfectly captured in modern human rights debates by Jack Snyder and Leslie Vinjamuri's claim that proponents of legalistic justice "cause more abuses than they prevent."[60] Snyder and Vinjamuri say that prosecuting state officials exacerbates the precise condition that the proponents wish to remedy—widespread human rights violations. This is a clear causal statement and thus lends itself to empirical testing. My research on the effects of such prosecutions and that of other scholars using our new data on human rights prosecution has found no evidence of such a perversity effect, but this has not prevented critics from repeating the claim.[61]

The futility thesis holds that attempts at social transformation will "simply fail to make a dent" in the problems they are meant to address.[62] For example, critics of the welfare state in the twentieth century, such as Milton Friedman, claimed that many programs aimed at the poor were futile, tending instead to benefit the middle and upper classes.[63] The futility thesis is expressed today by Eric Posner, who concludes simply that human rights law doesn't work: "we should face that fact and move on."[64] Similar futility arguments are expressed by Samuel Moyn when he argues that human rights "have been the powerless companion to market fundamentalism" because they "simply have nothing to say about inequality."[65]

The jeopardy thesis "argues that the cost of the proposed change or reform is too high as it endangers some previous precious accomplishment."[66] In the nineteenth century, for example, the expansion of male suffrage was portrayed as fatal to Britain's "ancient liberties," especially the right to own and accumulate property.[67] Stephen Krasner and Jack Goldsmith similarly present a jeopardy argument today when they say, "an insistence on criminal prosecutions can prolong . . . conflict, resulting in more deaths, destruction, and human suffering."[68] In the case of human rights, peace is often the "previous precious accomplishment" that these critics argue will be endangered by trials. Krasner and Goldsmith's is, however, a modified jeopardy thesis because in most of these cases peace has not yet been secured. Since peace has been elusive for a long time in the countries they study, Krasner and Goldsmith do not argue that trials jeopardize a "precious previous accomplishment," but rather a much-desired future one.

Hirschman also understood that reformers sometimes brought criticism upon themselves by making exaggerated promises, which in turn led to exaggerated assertions of total failure. He saw that such reactions came not only from conservatives, but also from radical reformist writers whose critiques emerged from their hope for more fundamental change.[69] At this point, Hirschman's argument in *The Rhetoric of Reaction* hearkens back to his earlier work on Latin America, including *Journeys Toward Progress*, where he explored responses to development policy, including land reform. In this work, he became aware that policy analysis in Latin America at the time was imprinted with what he called "fracasomania," or a "failure complex."[70] Many of these reformmongers were engaged in what I have called comparison to the ideal. They insisted that the efforts for development in Latin America had completely failed because the results had not lived up to their high ideals and expectations of growth with equity. But for Hirschman, it was not enough to draw attention to crises; one also needed to think about the possibilities of escaping them.[71] For him, "social change was riddled with chance and choice."[72]

Hirschman was often suspicious of the motivations of writers who insisted only on these negative effects. He suspected that it gave them a feeling of superiority and they "revel[ed] in it." He said, "Once again, a group of social analysts found itself irresistibly attracted to deriding those who aspire to change the world for the better." Hirschman anticipated by a couple of decades—and stated more elegantly—the insight in psychological literature that people presenting negative information are seen as smarter than those talking about positive change. The perversity effect, he said, "has a certain elementary sophistication and paradoxical quality" that appeals to those in search of "instant insight." All three effects—perversity, futility, and jeopardy—add up to project "a certain worldly wise wit as opposed to the alleged earnestness and humorlessness of believers in progress."[73] Hirschman's intuition may also be relevant with regard to modern perversity and jeopardy theorists. When I asked Patrick Ball, one of the world's leading experts on the measurement of human rights violations, how he explained recent pessimistic literature, he almost echoed Hirschman—he said that everyone likes to cut do-gooders down to size.[74] Human rights activists are do-gooders and yes, at times both self-righteous and humorless.

Both the perversity and the jeopardy theses involve unintended consequences, to which Hirschman was quite attracted because the concepts introduce "uncertainty and open-endedness into social thought."[75] Hirschman clarified that "none of this is meant to deny that purposive social action does occasionally have perverse effects," but he did not understand why unintended consequences should always be perverse or negative.[76] I agree with Hirschman that we need to be attentive to unintended negative consequences. In fact, I think that the information paradox is exactly such an example of an unintended negative consequence in the human rights realm, one with important consequences for the field.

In a later chapter of *The Rhetoric of Reaction*, Hirschman warned against progressive arguments that are the mirror image of the three theses. For example, progressives can make arguments that appear naïve ("all good things go together") or have an inverse perversity thesis (the failure to act will have disastrous effects).[77] This warning is particularly relevant for human rights activists and researchers as we may be tempted at times to make these kinds of claims.

Other psychological phenomena that may affect evaluations of human rights progress among activists include both direct trauma and the "vicarious traumatization" of human rights workers. We know that many victims of human rights violations have been deeply traumatized by their experience and that this trauma can manifest itself in ways that make people feel "survivor's guilt," questioning why they survived and others died. Survivors may believe that they must not rest until they have done whatever they can to remember the dead and denounce ongoing violations. At the same time, survivors may feel depressed and hopeless. Those who work with victims of human rights violations may be indirectly traumatized and suffer from some of these same symptoms. These people are known as secondary trauma survivors. The authors of the aforementioned survey of 346 human rights workers found that such trauma exposure had a negative effect on their well-being.[78] This effect was exacerbated when respondents also had negative self-appraisals of the efficacy of their work. To measure respondents' self-appraisals, the researchers constructed a series of positive and negative statements about working in human rights, including items such as "I have been able to make a positive difference through my work," "I feel inspired by my work," and "I feel that my work is pointless."[79] Individuals who answered these questions in a manner that showed they had a negative self-appraisal of their efficacy were prone to experience more severe symptoms of PTSD. It is important that human rights workers have resilience, an "ineffable quality that allows some people to be knocked down by life and come back stronger than ever." Psychologists have identified some of the factors that make someone resilient, among them a positive attitude, optimism, and an ability to learn from failure.[80] Both hope and the ability to see failure as helpful feedback may contribute to more resilient and less traumatized human rights workers.

The cognitive biases and psychological effects discussed here can make it hard to perceive progress in human rights. It can be even more difficult when we add to this the news bias. What we see on the news is more available to us than what we do not see on the news. If the news viewed or heard is dramatic, we are more likely to remember it. In addition to that, the news has its own version of the negativity bias—in the classic words of a news editor, "if it bleeds, it leads."[81] Whether we get our news from newspapers, TV, or online, it likely consists of dramatic and negative events, i.e. violence, rather than the mundane and the everyday.[82] This combination of various cognitive and news biases contributes to the perception that the world has more human rights violations than ever before.[83]

It is not only the news that is negative, so too are the reports of human rights organizations. Stephen Northfield, the Digital Director for Human Rights Watch, previously a seasoned journalist, is concerned about the negative messages of human rights organizations: "There is an endless drumbeat of negativity. You start to numb your audience with the parade of bad news. It creates a negative feedback loop. It is one of the things we need to figure out as a process." Northfield went on to explain some alternative ways to communicate a greater sense of hope:

> We can't wait till we get to Nirvana, but there are ten steps to get there. We move the ball down the field. If you can train your audience to understand, you can break this sense of the monopoly of negativity. If you think of gay rights, for example, profound progress has been made in the last five years. But once we make progress, that gets banked and forgotten. It is deeply in the DNA of human rights groups to orient themselves around problems. But there are internal and external dangers of not being able to measure progress. It is disempowering for people working on human rights.[84]

Changing Standards of Accountability

Finally, measuring human rights progress is affected by a changing standard of accountability that occurs when human rights activists and lawyers begin to expand the notion of what constitutes a human rights violation.[85] International human rights law is both comprehensive and incomplete. Since the UDHR was passed in 1948, many campaigns have worked to establish new human rights norms and laws while also expanding our understanding of existing law. The power of the human rights movement is that it contains within it the seeds of its own expansion.[86]

The UDHR, for example, does not mention the rights of sexual minorities or of people with disabilities, yet today's activists have helped expand our understanding of rights and draft new conventions to include these issues. This is one of the great strengths of human rights as a moral vocabulary and a legal process. When I started working on human rights as a young student over thirty-five years ago, it did not occur to me that the absence of an accessibility ramp was a violation of human rights. Today I am fully persuaded that for people with disabilities or the elderly to enjoy their rights to health and education, or the right to vote, for example, they have to be able to enter clinics, schools, and voting stations. When I accompany my father, who is legally blind and also recently consigned to a wheelchair, I thank the movement for disability rights for their contributions to his ability to live a life with dignity. The Convention on the Rights of Persons with Disabilities shows how the human rights movement is constantly raising the bar of what constitutes a human right. That is good news for human rights, but unless activists and scholars understand the implications of this practice when we measure progress and effectiveness, we may live with more pessimism than is warranted.

The process of constantly raising the bar of what constitutes a human rights violation can cause problems for human rights measurement and is one of the reasons that many people believe human rights practices are worsening. As we raise the bar, it can appear that the implementation gap is ever wider.

Standards of accountability also change when the definition of what constitutes a violation of existing rights alters. Previously, we called a killing an extrajudicial execution when a government killed its political opponents, but today we use the term to refer to high levels of indiscriminate police killings. The European Court of Human Rights, for example, has changed its understanding over time of what constitutes an act of torture.[87] Increased information and higher standards are both good news for human rights victims, but they can be bad news for data sets and measurement, which try to compare numbers about human rights performance over time. The next section will illustrate how this works using examples from Brazil and Guatemala.

Quantitative Researchers and Information Effects

The information paradox takes two main forms. The first is straightforward: members of the public, scholars, or policymakers who read the reports and follow the news are left with the impression that violence and human rights violations of all kinds are increasing in the world. These general impressions are affected by the availability heuristic, negativity bias, and news bias.

The second form of the information paradox is more hidden and involves technical issues of how human rights information gets coded into quantitative measures and then used by scholars to measure the effectiveness of human rights law, policy, and activism. The danger of this type of information paradox is particularly acute for scholars who do quantitative analysis, relying only on one or two key measures of repression. Such data is not intentionally wrong or distorted, but may nevertheless be misleading because of our increased knowledge about human rights violations. Examples in Brazil and Guatemala explain how more information and higher standards affect quantitative evaluations.

BRAZIL

Brazil had an authoritarian military regime from 1964 until 1985, with its most repressive period from 1968 to 1974; almost 2,000 individuals later testified in military courts that they had been tortured during this period.[88] Roughly, we can think of the mid-1960s through the 1970s as authoritarian rule, the 1980s as a period of transition toward democracy, and the 1990s and 2000s as democratic. Between 1995 and 2016, Brazil was governed by democratic governments of the center and the left.

Brazil would appear to be an example of the kind of change that the human rights movement hopes to promote. Brazilians elected former opposition figures as presidents and their governments carried out policies of gradual political and economic inclusion. Most experts on Brazil know that serious human rights problems have continued after the transition to democracy, but virtually all would argue that the democratic period has had better human rights practices than the military regime. In spite of this, the main quantitative measures of repression—the Political Terror Scale (PTS) and the Cingranelli and Richards (CIRI) Physical Integrity Rights Index—indicate that there was less torture and fewer executions, imprisonments and disappearances during the last years of the military government than in the current democratic period. How do we explain this puzzle?

To read the data correctly, we have to understand the process through which these measurements are created. First, what the quantitative measures of repression seek to document are invisible harms, as governments try to hide information about their human rights violations. During the military dictatorship in Brazil, for example, the government concealed its practices of torture, disappearance, and summary execution of political opponents. Because of this, analysts turn to nongovernmental organizations, international organizations, and even other states for reports on human rights practices. Evidence suggests that reports of outside monitors, however imperfect, come closer to revealing the nature of repression than states' self-reporting.[89]

The two sources most commonly used by academics for measuring state repression are Amnesty International's annual reports and the US State Department's annual country reports on human rights practices, both of which have been issued regularly for several decades. Both AI and the US State Department produce combined annual reports that try to summarize the human rights practices of most countries worldwide. We are fortunate that two such series exist, one by a government and one by a respected nongovernmental organization, although there is, of course, still bias: The US State Department has political goals that may affect human rights reporting, although its reports have become more accurate over time, and Amnesty International is committed to a human rights ethos that may make it difficult for it to speak of "improvement" in the context of serious on-going violations of human rights.

Researchers use these sources to create a "time series" on human rights practices, allowing us to compare change over time, in this case from 1980 to the present. The PTS and CIRI human rights data projects use the reports to produce scales of human rights violations of core physical integrity rights. Both of these scales are composite measures of four human rights violations: torture, extrajudicial killings, disappearance, and political imprisonment. We call these the standard-based measures because they assign human rights scores to every country in the world every year, based on subjective criteria applied to primary source documents. In other words, research assistant coders read the narrative Brazil text in the Amnesty International or State Department report for every year and give it a number in a scale created by the project. The PTS has a numerical scale from one to five, with five as the worst human rights performance and one as the best. The CIRI Physical Integrity Index is a somewhat more complex eight-point scale, with its own set of cod-

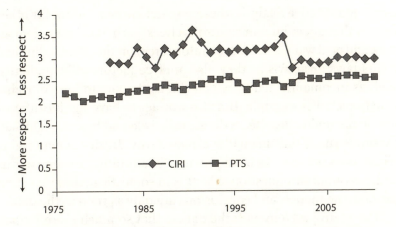

FIG. 5.11. Global average standard-based human rights scores. *Note*: The CIRI
Physical Integrity Scale is 0–8 and the PTS scale is 0–5. The PTS line here
represents the average combination of PTS scores derived from Amnesty and
State Department reports. For the source data in this chart see the CIRI
Human Rights Data Project (http://www.humanrightsdata.com) and the
Political Terror Scale (PTS) database (http://www.politicalterrorscale.org).

ing instructions that are precise, but sometimes problematic. The
CIRI measure of extrajudicial killings, for instance, is designed in
such a way that the index simply cannot measure any improvements
until the number of violations falls below fifty. Thus, a country that
has two hundred extrajudicial killings one year and the next has
only eighty, would not show any improvement. Together, these
scores produce a database of core human rights practices that are
available online for researchers to use.

When charted over time, these popular datasets tend to show
unchanging global levels of repression. Figure 5.11 shows that, despite minor fluctuations, global average scores on PTS and CIRI
have stayed mostly flat from the late 1970s to 2010. Based on this,
many scholars have argued that the human rights movement has
been a failure.[90]

After the databases have been published, quantitative researchers insert them into their models in order to address several important questions: What impact do human rights laws have? Do human
rights prosecutions improve human rights? Can transnational advocacy groups create positive change? Researchers then use quantitative methods to test their hypotheses. Perhaps most importantly,

using quantitative analysis, these researchers can control for other factors that affect human rights practices, such as poverty, democracy, and civil war. Scholars look into more than the effects of human rights laws or activism; they also analyze factors independently, such as income inequality, which can contribute to human rights violations.[91] For example, Brazil continues to have significant economic inequality despite its democratic rule and human rights activism. Perhaps this inequality explains why Brazil's human rights record does not seem to be improving. Quantitative research lets us address important questions like this in sophisticated ways; yet, in the end, the models and conclusions are only as good as the data.

The main problem with the data is that so much more human rights information is being produced today than in the past. Today, when the reports are written, there are hundreds of groups working on human rights in Brazil in situations of relative security; they are able to document and publish more far-reaching reports than ever before.[92] Human rights officers in US embassies are in routine contact with a large range of human rights groups inside and outside the country. Compare this to when Amnesty International and the State Department first began to report on human rights in Brazil in the late 1970s. As there were few sources of human rights information, they relied on a small number of sources in Brazil and communicated with only a handful of other human rights organizations. Thus, the early years of the CIRI and PTS measures are less reliable due to several factors—the reports were the shortest at this time, fewer human rights NGOs existed to produce good information, and the political bias in the State Department reports was the strongest.[93]

Perhaps because of these data problems, the human rights situation in Brazil according to CIRI and PTS was a full point better during the authoritarian and transition period than it has been during the recent democratic decades. Brazil has an average PTS score of three for the authoritarian and transition decades of the 1970s and 1980s, and a score of four for the fully democratic period of the 1990s through 2013.[94] The average CIRI physical integrity rights score for Brazil during the military government period (1981–1985) is also almost a point better than the average score for the democratic period of the 1990s and the 2000s. Because CIRI breaks the score down further by specific type of violation, we can see more precisely the kinds of violations that are driving the scores. Although democratic Brazilian governments rarely practiced disappearances or held political prisoners, from the data they appear to be engaged in more extrajudicial killing and torture than the dictatorship. This differs from other reports of deaths and disappearances for the same periods.[95] Why do CIRI and PTS record more killing and torture under democracy? The difference lies in the changing standard of accountability. Earlier US State Department and Amnesty International reports (and the Brazilian government report mentioned above) only documented *government* killing and torture of *political opponents*. By 1985, human rights organizations and the US government expanded their focus from a narrow emphasis on direct government responsibility for death, disappearance, torture, and imprisonment of political opponents, to consideration of a wider range of rights, including the right of people to be free from police brutality and the excessive use of lethal force, as well as the duty of the state to prevent, investigate, and prosecute violence by non-state actors.

In their first reports on Brazil, both Amnesty International and the State Department focused on gross human rights violations, especially political imprisonment, torture, and summary executions committed directly by state officials. The early State Department reports on Brazil were short and largely positive, commending the government on improvements in state-sponsored deaths and disappearances in the early 1980s. By 1987, however, during the transition to democracy, both AI and the State Department began to take a harsher tone. Amnesty became able to travel to Brazil for on-site visits and, as a result, produced a specific report on rural killings. AI clarified that such killings were carried out by "hired gunmen in the pay of local landowners," but also stressed that it was concerned that "full and impartial investigations into such killings are not being carried out and this failing may amount to acquiescence, and even complicity with the crimes."[96] A second AI investigation focused on the torture and ill treatment of detainees in police stations and prisons throughout the country, including the killing of suspects. This was a new approach for human rights organizations at the time because it focused on the treatment of criminal suspects rather than that of political prisoners, whose protection was previously the core mission of AI.

From a human rights perspective, the changing standard of accountability was a positive development. From a data and measurement perspective, it caused problems. AI's expansion of its mandate and improved capacity to conduct on-site investigations led to an increased documentation of human rights violations that could make it seem as though the situation in Brazil was getting worse after democratization. However, it is possible that the situation was the same or even better; it only seemed more severe because of an expanded notion of what constitutes a human rights violation and because of increased capacities for in-country reporting. This more thorough attention to a wider range of victims translated into worse PTS and CIRI scores because both measures now count extrajudicial killing and torture whether it is against political opponents or against criminal suspects. Similar changes were made to the State Department reports, which, taking their cue in part from NGOs, were expanding their focus on rights violations in Brazil to include the treatment of peasants and indigenous people involved in land disputes, as well as of criminal suspects.

We still do not know if the Brazilian police kill or mistreat more victims than they did in the 1970s and 1980s. In the earlier decades, human rights organizations were not collecting data on rural violence, nor were they investigating the excessive use of force against common criminal suspects. Organizations within Brazil recently have turned their attention to police violence. For example, the Observatório das Violências Policiais-SP (Observatory of Police Violence in São Paulo) uses news sources to compile a monthly report of all victims of police violence. The Observatório argues that all of these deaths are "extrajudicial executions," and represent the excessive use of lethal force of the Brazilian police.[97] Many of these killings are of poor and marginal populations living in the *favelas* of São Paulo. This human rights work calls our attention to violations against groups who were not the original focus of the human rights movement. Yet, from the point of view of measuring effectiveness, such expanding standards of accountability can paint a more pessimistic picture than is warranted. Police violence in Brazilian *favelas*, for example, is the first example that Eric Posner uses in the opening paragraph of his book *The Twilight of Human Rights Law* to illustrate his point that human rights are not respected more today than in the past, unaware that he has chosen an issue that clearly illustrates how the information paradox and the changing standard of accountability affect human rights data.[98]

GUATEMALA

It can be difficult to discern human rights improvements in Guatemala as well. After the transition to democracy in Guatemala in the 1990s, two different truth commissions, one sponsored by the United Nations and the other by the Guatemalan Catholic Church, took extensive testimony on repression under the dictatorship.[99] Using the information from those commissions, the UN, with the assistance of Patrick Ball, arrived at much more precise estimates for the number of deaths and disappearances that had occurred in Guatemala than those that had appeared in AI or State Department reports. These estimates allow a year-by-year comparison of event-based data (in this case, actual counts of killings and disappearances) with the standard-based data produced by the CIRI and the PTS scales. While repression was severe during this entire period, there was a marked surge in killings and disappearances from 1980–1982 (during the Ríos Montt government), with 1982 being the worst year by far. Guatemala logged 25,928 identified and unidentified deaths and disappearances in the years 1980–1983, roughly seventy-nine percent of all deaths and disappearances that occurred between 1970 and 1995. This figure, large as it is, is likely an undercount; undoubtedly, some violations went unreported to the commissions.

Amnesty International and the State Department were not able to capture an accurate picture of the repression as it was occurring, despite the fact that they wrote their reports at nearly the same time as the events. The score based on the AI reports reflects the actual trend of repression, giving its worse possible score for the period of the genocide in 1980–1982, but the State Department reports, for reasons of political bias during the Reagan administration, failed to document the genocide as it occurred. Even so, the scales based on both the AI and State Department reports are "sticky" and not able easily to record a subsequent decline in deaths and disappearances. The repression in Guatemala in the period 1980–1982 was also so severe that the government eradicated or silenced human rights organizations, thus eliminating an important source of information about repression.

In the mid-1980s, domestic human rights organizations began functioning again in Guatemala, although they still faced intense repression. The process of re-democratization in Guatemala after 1985 contributed to a more information-rich environment. Human rights organizations in turn did a better job documenting ongoing repression and that better documentation was reflected in the standard-based measures. According to the actual counts of deaths and disappearances, the number fell from 17,000 people affected in 1982 to 350 in 1993. Looking at the CIRI and PTS scores, however, it appears that there was virtually no improvement. A human rights activist might argue that, as long as there are 350 dead and disappeared, we should not speak of any improvements. But a social scientist would say that movement from 17,000 dead and disappeared to 350 constitutes improvement. The inability of the CIRI and PTS scales to reflect such changes complicates their usefulness for social science research.

The use of these standard-based measures influences quantitative studies on human rights effectiveness, including by scholars who have top-notch methods skills and the desire to make their mark with some counterintuitive findings. Take, for example, the previously mentioned articles suggesting that ratifying the Convention against Torture (CAT) is associated with an increase in the use of torture. More plausibly, when a state ratifies the CAT, the obligations of the Convention provide an opportunity for the international community to monitor that state more closely in order to see if it is complying with its newly accepted obligations under human rights law. This closer monitoring of torture then produces more awareness of torture, not more torture itself.

To be clear, I am not a data skeptic, rejecting quantitative data because it is less nuanced than case study work. I have used both CIRI and PTS in my research and I value them as data sources. However, I believe both scholars and activists should be aware of how and why human rights data may be biased and, therefore, careful in their use. Scholars need to be more informed users of these data and human rights practitioners need to be aware that sometimes their increased skill in information politics could be used to claim that they are not having any positive effect. Most importantly, the data should not be treated as the objective measure of human rights; it should be used with great care when supporting a claim that a human rights situation has not improved. As my colleague Malcolm Sparrow reminds us, what is important to remember about invisible harms is that many measures we design to try to reveal them are not actually measures of the problem, but "composite measures that combine some information of the scope of the problem with the proportion of incidents that are reported."[100] Despite problems with measurement, however, we must continue to measure, and to do so in different and creative ways.

After my article with Ann Marie Clark was published, Chris Fariss, a gifted methods scholar, produced a sophisticated and persuasive article making related arguments and providing modeling solutions. Fariss demonstrated that a new technique called latent variable modeling can be used to combine standard-based measures, like CIRI and PTS, with events data, which include actual lists of events related to human rights, to correct for the changing standard of accountability. Using this new model, Fariss then showed that the ratification of the CAT is associated with improvement in human rights, not a decline.[101]

Not all human rights data is subject to information effects. Events-based data are less susceptible than standard-based measures like CIRI and PTS, for example.[102] As we saw earlier in this chapter, some human rights issues, like the right to education and the right to health, can be measured in more straightforward ways— literacy rates, the percentage of school-age children in primary schools, the percentage of children who receive immunizations, the infant and child mortality rates, etc. Events-based data that has been collected for a long time (such as literacy rates or infant mortality) will be more reliable for discerning trends than data that we have started collecting more recently and which have expanding definitions, such as data about violence against women and rape. Similarly, data about illegal practices that governments or individuals are trying to hide will be harder to obtain and will be more likely to display information effects than data about more technical issues such as infant mortality, or more visible and centralized practices, such as the use of the death penalty.[103]

Scholars such as Patrick Ball have devoted their careers to developing better data and warning scholars and activists about bad data.[104] Some data is better than no data, but not all sources of data are equal. Both activists and researchers need to develop more nuanced understandings of human rights information in order to measure change more accurately.

Conclusion

Although the information paradox may appear to be a technical issue, the stakes of this debate are high. Understanding whether and where human rights activism and laws are having an effect is an important, yet difficult task because much of the data we use to measure effectiveness is created by human rights movements and institutions. We know that human rights activists have been effective in using information politics in creating new issues, putting those issues on the agenda, and constructing a changing standard of accountability for what constitutes a human rights violation. At the same time, because we are increasingly inundated with dire human rights information and because it is difficult to measure progress in this area, the common belief is that core physical integrity rights in the world are getting worse.

What are the implications of this argument for activists and scholars? First, I think it is incumbent on both activists and scholars to be aware of the issues discussed here: cognitive heuristics and biases, comparison to the ideal, changing standards of accountability, and the information paradox. Second, we need to be aware that we are not alone in thinking about these problems and trying to cope with them. Scholars in other disciplines have been grappling with such issues for many years and have developed concepts and solutions that may be of use to human rights scholars and activists, concepts such as invisible harms and the availability heuristic. A colleague from the school of public health told me that public health research has been grappling for a while with what they call "surveillance bias" or detection bias, where they recognized that the closer they look at some health issue, the more likely they are to find problems.[105]

The human rights movement is essentially a movement seeking to make invisible harms visible. It does so by shining a light on the dark corners of the state. Amnesty International uses the symbol of a candle to show how they bring light to bear on previously invisible problems. Yet somehow the human rights movement and human rights scholarship have not always realized the repercussions of making invisible harms visible. One of those repercussions is that the harder we look for human rights violations, the more we find. In other words, our field too suffers from surveillance bias. We need to look to our colleagues in other disciplines who have been grappling with these issues for a more extended period of time for new means of research and analysis.

Activists also need to be aware of the possible unintended negative consequences of their work. In an even more complex way, such people need to know that their work can simultaneously have both positive intended effects and negative unintended effects. The positive intended effect of changing standards of accountability is that more rights are recognized; the negative unintended effect is that some people may use this as evidence that the world is getting worse and, therefore, become discouraged. Keeping this in mind, perhaps human rights activists should rely less on information politics, less on so-called "naming and shaming," and more on what we might call "effectiveness politics"—identifying techniques and campaigns that have been effective at improving human rights. The human rights movement should explore new tactics in human rights rather than assume that producing another report is the best approach to every human rights problem.[106] For example, activists in Serbia trying to secure the release of their detained colleagues found that it was more effective to hold an outdoor rock concert outside the gates of the jail focused on getting the prisoners released than to write another report or do a press release. Likewise, human rights activists might work less on constantly pressing to raise the standard of accountability and more on making sure that existing standards of accountability are not flouted.

Human rights progress is not inevitable, but rather contingent on continued commitment and effort. Without the belief and untiring activity of activists, change often will not occur. But if activists and their supporters come to believe that their efforts on behalf of human rights are suspect or even counterproductive and thus retreat to inactivity, human rights progress could indeed stall or move backwards. Some expectation of hope sustains human rights work. Although hope in itself is insufficient, work sustained by reasoned, well-informed hope is not.

CHAPTER SIX

What Does and Doesn't Work to Promote Human Rights?

NADIA MURAD BASEE TAHA was nineteen years old when Islamic State insurgents (ISIL) attacked her village in August of 2015.[1] She lived in Kocho, a village in the remote northeast of Iraq, near Mt. Sinjar, and she belongs to the Yazidi people, an independent religious community and one of Iraq's oldest minorities. ISIL killed the men in the village and kidnapped the girls, women, and boys. Nadia witnessed the deaths and kidnapping of her family members. The boys from the village were sent to training camps, forced to convert to the creed of ISIL, and trained to become ISIL fighters. Nadia herself, like many young women, was abducted and sold into sexual slavery, passed from one ISIL member to another.[2] The UN estimates that around 3,000 persons, mainly Yazidis, remain in ISIL captivity as of March 2016. According to the UN, ISIL's attacks on the Yazidi population "pointed to the intent of ISIL to destroy the Yazidis as a group," which "strongly suggests" that ISIL has perpetrated genocide.[3]

Nadia eventually managed to escape. She fled Iraq and began speaking out about the persecution of the Yazidis in order to draw the attention of the world to the plight of those who are still in captivity. I had the fortune of having her speak to my human security class at the Harvard Kennedy School as part of a discussion on genocide. Nadia spoke softly but clearly in a colloquial Arabic about her ordeal and the challenges facing her community. She was joined by Murad Ismael, the co-founder and Executive Director of Yazda, an NGO set up to help the Yazidi people.[4] Murad was there both to translate and to tell his part of the story. Nadia told us that, before the attack, she had finished eleventh grade and advanced to the twelfth. She liked studying history, she said, but her dream was to work in a beauty salon in her village. Murad had been a student too. At the time of the attacks he was studying geophysics at the University of Houston, receiving phone calls from panicked family members as ISIL attacked their villages and forced them out of their homes. He looked around the classroom at my students, silent for moment. His voice caught and he lowered his head. Did our classroom remind him of the time when all he had to worry about were papers and exams, when the survival of his community did not rest on his shoulders?[5]

As a brief introduction to the topic of genocide, I had shared with my students the definition of genocide and a chart detailing the rise and fall of genocide and politicide in the late twentieth century (see Figure 5.2 in chapter 5). When we looked at the Yazidi case, we found that the definition of genocide fit their situation. In the chaos and violence of the civil war in Iraq, ISIL had attacked the Yazidis with the intent of destroying them, accusing them of being infidels and devil worshippers.[6] Part of the plan for the course was to listen to the voices of victims and be attentive to data so that we could map the prevalence, causes, and possible tools to prevent and respond to massive violence. I thought perhaps it would give some glimmer of hope both to my students and to Nadia and Murad to show that the trend in genocide had fallen. I was wrong. Both Murad and Nadia pointed out, movingly and correctly, that genocide is much more than numbers. It is every person, a whole community, many dead, others spread to the winds. "A genocide destroys a society as a whole, not only by killing," Murad said.[7] Nadia and Murad were still without news of whether many of their family members were alive or dead. Nadia's nephew, on the other hand, had managed to text her from an ISIL training camp, saying he had converted—he now believed the Yazidis were infidels. Multiply these individual experi-

ences of horror by hundreds and thousands and that is the after-
math of genocide.

How do we listen with full hearts and open minds to victims of
human rights violations, never converting them to a number, to a
trend line on a graph, and yet at the same time not lose track of the
evidence of change? For every country in the database on genocide,
there are people like Murad and Nadia, survivors who travel from
one place to another to tell their stories, to get their issues on the
agenda of policymakers. When Nadia and Murad heard they had
"only" two speaking events at the Kennedy School, they said it was
easy compared to most days. When they described the government
officials they had met, they spoke of a sense of being just one more
agenda item on busy schedules. Nadia and Murad's success depends
on people hearing their story, magnifying it, and figuring out how
to bring pressure to bear. But theirs is just one story among what
would seem to be a clamor of misery and abuse.

That genocide appears to be declining in the world offers no
comfort to Nadia or Murad. But such data is important for those of
us who wish to understand human rights trends in the world and
who try to use these trends to figure out how to improve human
rights. How do we account for the decline in genocide and politicide? How can we use that knowledge to try to prevent genocide and
other human rights violations in the future? This chapter explores
what is known about the causes and prevention of genocide and
other human rights violations and how that knowledge can inform
our policies and our attitudes. Because of the problems with comparisons to the ideal, which I discussed in chapter 2, in this chapter
I will focus on research that relies on empirical comparisons of
human rights change, both quantitative and qualitative.

This book bears the subtitle *Making Human Rights Work in the
21st Century*. To that end, this chapter turns to the main processes
for promoting human rights. I will use literature on the causes of
human rights violations and on explanations for compliance with
human rights law to suggest six policy tools that have been and can
be used to address human rights violations: 1) diminish war and
seek nonviolent solutions to conflict; 2) promote democracy and
enhance the quality of existing democracies; 3) guard against dehumanizing and exclusionary ideologies, whether about race, religion,

gender, class, or any other status; 4) encourage states to ratify existing human rights treaties and work to enforce human rights laws and norms through nonviolent means; 5) end impunity, by supporting domestic and international accountability that can deter future crimes; and 6) support, expand, and protect domestic and transnational mobilization on behalf of human rights.

Each of these policy recommendations is extremely difficult to implement and will take decades, perhaps centuries to bear fruit. Yet evidence in this chapter demonstrates that the world is already moving in these directions in terms of the decline in war, increase in democracy, and increase in individual criminal accountability for human rights violations. Before moving to an in-depth discussion of each of these policy recommendations I discuss how we study the risk factors for human rights violations.

How Do We Study the Causes or Risk Factors of Human Rights Violations?

Understanding why and how governments and insurgents use violence is a prerequisite to developing effective protections against human rights violations. While there is no single, unified theory to explain repression, research has identified some important political, economic, ideological, and psychological factors associated with systematic human rights abuses such as genocide. Below I discuss each of these factors and what we know about their contributions to repression.[8] I focus mainly on violations of personal integrity rights because that is where the literature is the strongest, but I will also discuss the literature on violations of economic, social, and cultural rights.

There are roughly two schools of thought as to why political authorities violate the rights of their citizens: those who think repression is rational and those who see it as the result of ideological or psychological factors. The best answer is a combination of these ideas; any effort to end human rights violations in the world will have to be attentive both to the costs and benefits of repression as well as to the psychological and ideological factors that drive it.

State repression (mass killing, torture, disappearance, and political imprisonment) is committed mainly by state security forces and by militaries, and sometimes also by armed insurgents. The people directing these forces often calculate the costs and benefits of using repression to achieve their goals.[9] According to the rational choice approach, those in power choose to repress dissent when the costs of doing so are lower than the costs of institutionalizing liberal democracy.[10] Some people think this is too mechanical an explanation for terrible abuses, but the theory of rationality is confirmed by many case studies of human rights violations. The literature on the Rwandan genocide and on ethnic cleansing in the former Yugoslavia, for example, shows how state elites, facing threats to their power both on the battlefield and at the negotiation table, deliberately chose to use mass murder as a means of maintaining their power.[11] Research thus suggests that it is not ethnic diversity or factionalization in itself that drives violence and repression, but rather the choices made by leaders to manipulate factionalization to pursue their own political ends.[12] In the case of Rwanda and elsewhere, research has also stressed the failure of international actors to raise the perceived costs of violence.[13] Leaders in oppressive states as different as Argentina during the Juntas and Sudan under Bashir benefitted greatly from repression, since it allowed them to punish their political opponents, stay in power, and reap the economic and political rewards of such power.

Prior to the 1970s, there were virtually no costs for leaders who repressed their populations; they had almost total impunity. Under these circumstances, it should not come as a surprise that repression figured into the calculations of authoritarian leaders. Even when they eventually lost power, past dictators could count on a comfortable retirement in exile, often drawing on considerable wealth squirreled away in international accounts. For these reasons, it is useful to think about authoritarian leaders as rational actors choosing repression from an array of possible policies.

Leaders also can be motivated by less rational concerns. They care about their prestige and the esteem they receive from their followers and from other world leaders. Leaders may also sincerely believe in the ideas they use to inflame racial, ethnic, or religious hatred. To understand the roots of repression we need to understand leaders as rational and ideological, capable of strong belief as well as of manipulation to fuel their self-interest.

It is important to understand what both domestic and international actors can do to make it more costly to choose repression and more rewarding to protect and promote human rights. Since many repressive leaders are rational actors, they may be deterred from further human rights violations if the costs of committing such violations are clear and likely to be implemented. Likewise, such leaders may choose to respect human rights if the rewards for doing so are straightforward and appealing. In exchange for membership in the European Union, for example, countries throughout Eastern Europe made substantial changes to their human rights policies and practices.[14]

Two core findings have received repeated and consistent confirmation across studies of repression. First, real or imagined threats to their regime, such as wars, coup attempts, terrorism, or revolutions, motivate leaders to choose repression.[15] Second, when there are no restrictions on the power of authorities, especially in authoritarian regimes without checks and balances, leaders are more likely to violate the rights of their citizens. If there are fewer constraints on power, there are fewer costs to repression, since there is low risk of being removed from office. In the parts of the chapter that follow we will explore the most promising policy options to discourage repression and to promote human rights that emerge from existing research.

Diminish War and Seek Nonviolent Solutions to Conflict

Statistical analyses confirm that the presence of war, especially civil war, is the factor most strongly correlated with repression.[16] More specifically, civil war is one of the most important risk factors for genocide.[17] Other threats to the survival of a government, including the existence of separatist movements and insurgent or terrorist groups, are also positively correlated with repression.[18]

The good news for human rights is that international war and international conflicts short of war have been declining for years. By war, coders mean a conflict with at least 1,000 battle deaths a year; by conflict, they mean any conflict with at least twenty-five battle deaths a year. The bad news for human rights is that civil wars and conflicts, what researchers call "intrastate conflict," are on the rise, after having declined from 1990 to 2012. Figure 6.1 shows

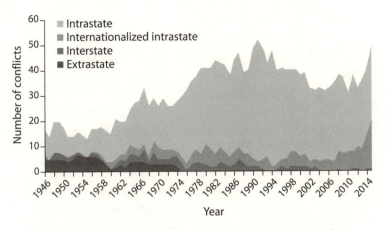

FIG. 6.1. Armed conflict by type, 1946–2015. *Source*: Erik Melander,
Therése Pettersson, and Lotta Themnér, "Organized Violence, 1989–2015,"
Journal of Peace Research 53, no. 5 (2016): 727–742.
Uppsala Conflict Data Program One-Sided Dataset.

trends for four types of conflicts: international war, or interstate conflict; intrastate conflict; internationalized intrastate conflict, such as the current conflict in Syria, where international actors are deeply involved; and so-called extrastate conflict, or colonial wars, which, as we see from the chart, ended in the mid-1970s.[19]

The number of international wars is small, and the main problem in the world today continues to be intrastate conflict, or civil wars. Another crucial issue tied to this is the number of people killed in conflict. People believe there is greater violence and suffering now than in the past because they believe there is more death in war and conflict than there used to be. Yet Figure 6.2, which gives the number of annual battle-related deaths in the combined conflicts since 1947, shows that battle deaths have declined more significantly than the number of conflicts. The chart ends in 2007—if it went up to 2016, we would see an uptick that would indicate new battle deaths in Syria and elsewhere in the Middle East. Still, that alone would not change the general trend. The new battle deaths in 2015 bring the total number of battle deaths back up to 100,000, somewhat above the levels of the peaks in 1990 and 2000, but not up to the level of the 1980s.[20]

Tanisha Fazal has pointed out that the decline of deaths in war is due in part to improvements in military medicine. Fazal argues that all research on the decline of conflict relies directly or indirectly

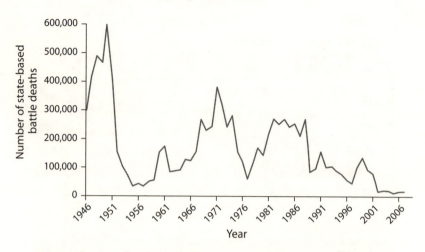

FIG. 6.2. Number of battle deaths from state-based armed conflicts, 1946–2007. *Source*: Human Security Report Project, accessed January 28, 2017, http://www .hsrgroup.org/our-work/security-stats/State-Based-Armed-Conflicts-By-Type.aspx. The original data source is the UCDP/PRIO Armed Conflict Dataset v. 4, 2008.

on the decrease in battle deaths since war and conflict are defined by battle-death thresholds. The decrease in battle-related deaths is in turn the result of improvements in military medicine, in addition to the decline in conflict. She incorporates both battle deaths and non-fatal battle casualties into her analysis to address this issue. Fazal concludes that "even accounting for the battle wounded and notwithstanding improvements in medical care in conflict zones, the number of casualties of war still fell." Fazal's research thus "tempers, but does not negate," empirical claims about the decline in war more generally. She also goes on to note that the rise in improved military medicine is in itself an aspect of the humanitarian ideals that some authors argue have contributed to the decline in war.[21]

My policy recommendation of seeking nonviolent solutions to human rights crises is complicated because military intervention is often proposed as one of the key solutions to repression. Since people are both concerned with human rights *and* pessimistic about the effectiveness of the ordinary legal and policy tools, they often demand the use of military force to prevent mass atrocities. This has led to some unwarranted conflation between human rights and what is called the "Responsibility to Protect," or R2P, a three-part doctrine that essentially redefines sovereignty as a responsibility of governments to protect their own populations and of the international community to assist governments in their efforts to protect their populations. The very last sentence of this statement says that, if the state fails to protect its population from genocide, crimes against humanity, and war crimes, the international community must be prepared to take stronger measures, "including the collective use of force through the UN Security Council."[22] Although collective force is characterized as an option to be implemented only as a last resort, for careless users of the term, R2P has become synonymous with military intervention to promote human rights and, for some, military intervention and human rights promotion are seen as two sides to the same coin.[23]

Not a single human rights treaty says states are encouraged or even permitted to use military invasions to enforce human rights. The Genocide Convention, for example, calls upon state parties to "undertake to prevent and punish" genocide, but never specifies that they should use military intervention to do so. The bulk of the treaty is concerned with legal punishment. One article says that state parties may "call upon the competent organs of the United Nations" to take action for the prevention and suppression of genocide, but this is still far from authorizing or even encouraging military intervention. The preamble to the Rome Statute of the ICC says explicitly, "nothing in this Statute shall be taken as authorizing any State Party to intervene in an armed conflict or in the internal affairs of any State." The use of military force for the purposes of international peace and security is part of the UN Charter, and not found in human rights treaties. The Security Council has always had the authority to order military intervention and more recently has started to interpret its mission of promoting international peace and security as being about human rights.[24] But that is very different from saying that human rights and R2P are the same thing. Indeed, the ICC has been seen and should be seen as an alternative to the use of military force, not as a complement to it.

Many human rights activists around the world are opposed to the use of military force to promote human rights; this is particularly true in Latin America and many parts of the Global South. Although a few powerful voices, especially from the United States, support military force to promote human rights, this should not be seen as reason to associate human rights with military intervention more generally.[25]

As the single most important factor correlated with human rights violations, war will always be risky as a tool to diminish human rights violations.[26] Not only war itself but also occupation after war can have negative consequences. According to recent research on terrorism, suicide bombers are most likely to appear in places suffering foreign military occupation.[27] How could we urge more military occupation and involvement to stop ISIL, for example, when it seems likely that the original Iraq invasion and occupation contributed to the rise of ISIL in the first place?

But it is not just powerful governments that need to renounce war as a tool to promote human rights. Many insurgent groups are enamored with violence as a tool for justice, and the existence of separatist movements and insurgent or terrorist groups also positively correlates with repression. Thus, the use of an armed insurgency to promote human rights risks provoking more repression. Erica Chenoweth and Maria Stephan show that, between 1900 and 2006, campaigns of nonviolent resistance were more than twice as effective as their violent counterparts. Chenoweth and Stephan attribute this primarily to the greater ability of nonviolent campaigns to attract widespread support, thus separating regimes from their main sources of power.[28] Another reason that nonviolent resistance is more effective may be that it does not provoke more repression in the way that violent resistance does.

Another problem is that many victims of human rights violations and other affected people advocate violence as a solution. When Murad thought about how the ISIL siege of the Yazidis on Mt. Sinjar had been broken, he remembered that US airstrikes had allowed many Yazidis to escape. How could he not place his hopes in military forces when that was the one response that brought immediate freedom and relief? Then again, Murad realized the dangers. The airstrikes of the ISIL training camps had an unintended negative consequence: they killed the young Yazidi boys who had been taken to the camps as forced recruits.[29]

What do we say to Murad and others like him, including many suffering in Syria today, when they urge a military solution? While victims and affected people need to play a privileged role in helping set the human rights agenda, there are challenges in uniting personal experience with activism and research.[30] Policymakers and academics need to listen with full hearts to affected people and also use research to recommend policy. Research is starting to come down on the side of choosing nonviolent means to pursue human rights and that is the response I recommend.

The lesson many take from Rwanda is that the international community must be prepared to intervene militarily more quickly and more frequently to prevent mass atrocities. I question this conclusion. Military intervention is a blunt instrument that carries with it more potential to inflame mass atrocity than to calm it. Some research suggests that historically the US use of military force has contributed to democratization in some cases, such as Japan and Germany after World War II.[31] However, a more recent quantitative study of the subject demonstrates that "military intervention contributes to the rise of state repression by enhancing the state's coercive power and encouraging more repressive behavior."[32] Earlier studies found that military intervention neither improved human rights in target countries nor contributed to their democratization.[33] The US invasion of Iraq, sometimes justified by the Bush administration using the language of human rights, is an example where the use of illegal, unilateral military force exacerbated human rights abuses rather than preventing further violations. Many human rights scholars and activists who advocated the war in Iraq now recognize it as the human rights disaster it was. Michael Ignatieff, for example, now regrets his support for the war in Iraq, though he continues to recommend military intervention to promote human rights in Syria.[34] The desire to prevent mass atrocity by means of military intervention comes from a desire to help and to protect, which is good. But over twenty years after the Rwandan genocide, it appears that the mass atrocities of our age—Iraq, Afghanistan, and now Syria—have been exacerbated rather than constrained by military intervention.

I admit some exceptions to my skepticism about using war to prevent human rights violations. The UN should have expanded the number of peacekeepers on the ground in Rwanda before and during the genocide there; they should have also enlarged their mandate to include protection of civilians. In general, research suggests that use of UN peacekeepers can make important contributions to peace. In addition, limited and focused military missions, like the airstrikes that helped the Yazidis escape from the ISIL siege, could be used in extreme situations. More forceful military implementation of ICC arrest warrants could and should also be used in some circumstances. Still, the general policy recommendation remains— the world needs to find alternative, nonviolent means to promote human rights.

Although I don't rule out military means to prevent genocide as a last resort, I do argue that it distorts the idea of the international protection of human rights to concentrate mainly on military intervention. The UN Security Council is an imperfect institution, allowing as it does the five permanent members to veto any actions against themselves or their close allies. So why would I prefer military intervention authorized by the Security Council to unilateral military intervention? First, because it is so difficult, almost impossible, to get a vote on military intervention without a veto by at least one permanent member, such intervention will be limited to very extreme situations where large-scale global consensus exists. This protects against the willful manipulation of information and argument to serve patently self-interested interventions, such as we saw in the unilateral interventions of Russia in Crimea in 2014 or the United States in Iraq in 2003. Second, Security Council-mandated intervention is legal under the UN Charter and thus often perceived as more legitimate by most actors, even actors that oppose it.

I would much rather see the great powers use military might to forcefully execute arrest warrants from an international tribunal than see a full-fledged unilateral military intervention to address mass atrocity. In the former Yugoslavia, for example, all the indicted war criminals were eventually turned over to the ICTY because the powers with troops in the region finally started to use their military to execute arrest warrants.[35] This had the effect of preempting war crimes or at least making war criminals go into hiding where they could do less harm. If countries took seriously the outstanding arrest warrants of the ICC, mass atrocities might be prevented; moreover, it would send a strong deterrent signal to potential future perpetrators.

With regard to Syria, the debate often narrows to whether we should intervene militarily. I argue that a better understanding of what has contributed to human rights effectiveness will temper the tendency to think we can improve human rights by military means. It is also important to note that trust in social activism may be low in countries that have histories of invasive management by more powerful countries (either through colonization or through post-colonial mandates), even when such activism is locally organized and begins with a human rights agenda. These societies often see local activism as a tool of foreign powers trying to push an otherwise peaceful society into civil war.[36]

Promote Democracies and Enhance Their Quality

One of the most important nonviolent means to protect human rights is the promotion and support of democracies. Multiple studies have found that democratic regimes are less likely to engage in repression than nondemocratic governments.[37] Elections offer opportunities to remove authorities from office, thus raising the costs of oppression. Democratic institutions also provide established, nonviolent mechanisms to address grievances and reinforce values of deliberation and peaceful contestation. While most agree that democratic political institutions reduce repressive behavior in general, research indicates that democratic institutions mainly contribute to decreased repression only after a certain high democracy threshold is reached. Moreover, some institutions or configurations of a democratic regime have greater effects on repression levels than others.[38]

A full-fledged democracy with high levels of participation, a system with electoral competition between multiple parties, and constraints on the use of executive power is necessary to discourage repression.[39] In other words, merely holding elections is not enough to make a democracy. Policies need to encourage high levels of citizen participation in politics, including but not limited to voting in elections. There also need to be multiple political parties competing with one another in elections. A single-party system is not able to create the level of competition necessary for democracy.[40] Finally, the necessary rights to make both participation and competition meaningful need to be in place. If the government threatens citizens for simply speaking their minds, for example—denying them freedom of speech—the conditions for serious elections are not in place.

Some scholars worry that countries making the transition to democracy or semi-democratic countries are actually more prone to human rights violations than authoritarian ones. This concern has led some to conclude, for example, that there is "more murder in the middle," that is, more human rights violations in countries attempting to move from authoritarianism to democracy.[41] While it is true that semi-democracies do not deliver the same level of human rights protection as full democracies, it has not been persuasively demonstrated that semi-democracies are more prone to human rights violations than are autocracies. In fact, democratizing countries have significantly lower odds of genocide than autocracies.[42]

The good news for human rights is that the number of democracies in the world increased to an all-time high in the mid-2000s. In spite of this, there exists the perception of a "recession" in democracy—that more and more countries are retreating from democracy to semi-democracy or even to authoritarianism. This is what my colleague Steven Levitsky, writing with Lucan Way, calls the "myth of democratic recession."[43] Just like the literature on human rights, there is serious pessimism behind perceptions of democratic rollback, with some authors claiming that freedom has "plummeted" or that we might be seeing the "beginning of the end of democracy."[44] The reality contradicts this pessimism. By around mid-1990, the number of democracies in the world overtook the number of autocracies (see Figure 6.3). There have been some recessions in democracy, such as in Thailand, Turkey, and Venezuela, while other countries have improved their levels of democracy, such as Ghana, Peru, Senegal, and Serbia. According to Freedom House, in the last decade, though more countries have had a decline in the democracy scores than have improved, the number of democracies is still significantly larger than the number of fully authoritarian regimes and, despite backsliding in some countries, the trend in Figure 6.3 has not been reversed.[45]

Among many governments, as well as among some scholars and activists, doubt remains about whether democracy is essential for human rights improvements. Some claim that to speak in favor of democracy is an ideological statement, maybe even a religious one.[46] But the numerous studies on the causes of human rights violations have made it clear that democracy is essential for human

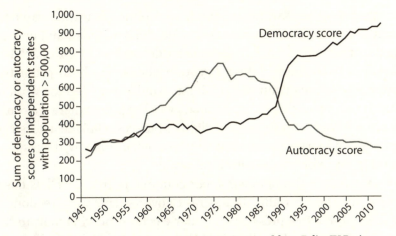

FIG. 6.3. Democracy and autocracy, 1946–2015. Source of data: Polity IV Project, Center for Systemic Peace, accessed January 28, 2017, http://www.systemicpeace .org/polityproject.html. This chart reflects updated data sent by the Center for Systemic Peace.

rights to succeed, but not sufficient.[47] While many democracies do not have robust human rights practices, there are not any countries with robust human rights practices that are not democracies.

It is difficult to promote democracy from abroad and, at a minimum, international actors need to avoid undermining democracy. In chapter 4, I showed how the United States subverted democracy during the Cold War in places such as Guatemala, Iran, the Congo, Brazil, and Chile. A main foreign policy puzzle for countries concerned with human rights is how to prevent coups and support fragile democracies. Because democracy is essential for the promotion of human rights and because it is difficult to reconstruct a democracy after it has been overthrown by a coup, a cardinal rule in human rights policy should be to thwart coups whenever possible. Although it takes a high-level democracy to produce real human rights benefits, even a flawed democracy is preferable to an authoritarian regime because a flawed democracy can transition into a high-quality democracy more easily.

Constructing and sustaining a democracy is a difficult and time-consuming process. This is consistent with a major theme in this book: human rights change takes time. You cannot construct a democracy from the outside, and you certainly cannot construct one overnight. As we saw in chapter 4, promoting democracy can be a matter of decades. A reformer in the field of democracy and human rights must have a "high tolerance for delayed gratification."[48] For example, had the fledgling Egyptian democracy been protected from the military coup in 2013, it still would have been the work of many years to reform that democracy to the point where we could have confidence in its human rights practices. Outside actors can provide support for democratic reforms but, ultimately, the responsibility for reform rests with local people.

Democracy can help enhance economic rights as well as basic physical integrity rights. Democratic governments with freedom of association, a free press, and regular elections provide tools to the population to work on behalf of their economic rights and to vote for governments more committed to the economic well-being of their citizens. A correlation between democracy and economic well-being has also been confirmed by other quantitative studies looking at economic and social rights.[49]

Promote Economic Growth and Equality

Studies routinely show a link between poverty and human rights violations of various types.[50] Research also points out that inequality, especially income inequality, is associated with abuses to core physical integrity rights as well as economic rights.[51] More specifically, one study looked at the impact of income and land inequality on physical integrity rights and found a robust relationship between income inequality and personal integrity rights abuse; the effects of land inequality were less substantial than those of income inequality.[52]

Economic equality also matters for the protection of women's rights. Amartya Sen brought the world's attention to the millions of missing women in the world, the result of a range of violent practices against girls and women. Poverty alone cannot explain which countries have the most missing women; economic inequalities between men and women also play a role. Countries and regions where women are engaged in gainful employment and make economic contributions to the household have few or no missing women. Gainful employment can either be paid work outside of the home, or work that is not paid but provides income for the family, such as

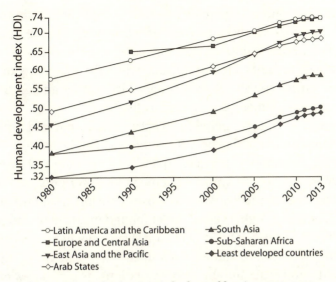

FIG 6.4. Human development index by world region, 1980–2013.
Max Roser, *Human Development Index by World Region 1946–2013.*
https://ourworldindata.org/human-development-index/. The author,
Max Roser, licensed this visualization under the CC BY-SA license.
Data source: United Nations Development Program.

farming. For example, countries in sub-Saharan Africa, where women produce much of the food consumed by the household, are much less likely to have missing women than other countries where women are not viewed as making similar economic contributions to the household.[53]

Just as in the areas of human rights and democracy, there is significant pessimism today about human development, which involves economic growth and focuses on improving opportunities and choices for all people while enhancing their well-being. With regard to human development, as with human rights and democracy, the situation on the ground is more positive than one might expect listening to the news. The Human Development Index (see Figure 6.4), a combined measure of GDP, literacy, and life expectancy, reveals that all regions of the world have experienced improvements in human development since 1980 and some, especially East Asia, have experienced significant improvements in human development, while other regions, especially sub-Saharan Africa, have progressed more slowly.[54]

Data on economic inequality is more complicated than that on human development because there are various ways to measure it.[55] Inequality *among countries* has decreased, due in particular to the dramatic growth of China and India, while the inequality of *individuals* within countries, including within China and India, has increased, sometimes quite dramatically.[56]

There is no simple recipe for what international and domestic actors can do to diminish poverty and inequality. Defenders of economic globalization claim that expanding free trade and capitalist investment will lead to improvements in human rights conditions, while others either arrive at the opposite conclusion or find no correlation between high levels of direct foreign investment and political and civil rights.[57] This is why I am skeptical when I hear people speaking with great confidence about the "root causes" of poverty, inequality, and other human rights violations, as if we knew exactly what they were.

The increasingly well-supported view is that trade openness is associated with better physical integrity rights as well as with improvements in some economic and social rights.[58] Still, certain neoliberal policies exacerbate inequality and negatively impact basic human rights. For example, structural adjustment programs imposed by the International Monetary Fund (IMF) that call on governments to liberalize and privatize their economies in the context of strict budget discipline are associated with worsening physical integrity rights, economic rights, and social rights, especially workers' rights.[59] This was certainly the case in the authoritarian neoliberal dictatorships in Argentina and Chile, which carried out structural adjustment programs in the context of widespread rights abuses. The most promising policies for diminishing inequality within countries appear instead to be more progressive taxation, including a proposal for a global tax on capital, and policies to equalize meaningful access to education.[60]

The debate about policies for growth and equality has a long history in Latin America where intellectuals were the originators of developmentalism and dependency theory. When working on my dissertation and first book, I was interested in human rights issues, but in the ethos of the time—still heavily influenced by Marxism—I was told that if I was interested in human rights, I should study political economy.[61] In the 1950s and 1960s, Latin American economists had developed their own critique of capitalism, arguing that less developed countries faced declining terms of trade for primary products and thus could not develop more rapidly without using trade and investment barriers to encourage domestic industry, a model called import substituting industrialization (ISI). The Latin American economist Raúl Prebisch led two international institutions calling for a more equitable economic order, the Economic Commission for Latin America and the Caribbean (ECLAC) and the UN Conference on Trade and Development (UNCTAD). ECLAC and UNCTAD were among the important voices working with developing countries to call for a New International Economic Order (NIEO), a set of proposals for improving the terms of trade for primary products, increasing development assistance, and reducing tariffs in developed countries. But by the 1980s, after decades of experimenting with ISI, some progressive Latin American economists began drawing attention to the fact that no Latin American country had managed to attain the goal of growth *with* equity.[62] Meanwhile, other less developed countries in East Asia, using a different economic model of export promotion and high investments in education, were experiencing more dramatic growth and higher levels of equity. The success of the so-called "Asian tigers" created impetus in Latin America for more open trade and investment.[63] Unfortunately, these policies were first implemented under repressive authoritarian regimes.

Democratic regimes with relatively open trade and investment policies can adopt social policies that have positive effects on both poverty and inequality. Under democratically elected governments of the left and center-left, Brazil, Argentina, Chile, and Uruguay continued economic policies of relatively open trade and investment post-dictatorships. These policies delivered economic growth, but risked increasing already high levels of inequality in the region. To counter that, the governments used inclusive social policies, including social security policies and education policy, to decrease poverty and inequality. For example, under the leftist government of the Frente Amplio (Broad Front), Uruguay has been one of the fastest growing economies in Latin America while decreasing poverty and inequality. It had an annual average growth rate of 4.8 percent between 2006 and 2015; moderate poverty went from 32.5 percent in 2006 to 9.7 percent in 2015, extreme poverty went down from 2.5

percent to 0.3 percent in the same period, and income levels among the poorest 40 percent of the Uruguayan population increased much faster than the average growth rate of income levels for the entire population. The inclusive social policies that made the greatest impact in Uruguay involved expanding the coverage of existing social programs; for example, around 87 percent of the over-65 population is now covered by the pension system.[64] In addition, the government has provided a laptop computer to every schoolchild.[65] Writing about former president José Mujica, an ex-Tupamaro guerrilla, Jonathan Gilbert says, "his government opted for a middle ground, favoring private sector projects to spur economic growth and modest interventions to distribute wealth."[66]

From Uruguay we learn that countries can decrease poverty and inequality with inclusive social policies funded by better tax policy. All this is more realistic in the context of economic growth, which is more likely in countries with more open trade policies. Yet inequality cannot be quickly eliminated. One reason Uruguay has better levels of equality today is that it has been a fairly equal country since reformers first introduced innovative social policy in the early twentieth century. As with many small countries, Uruguay has flourished under open trade and investment policies, which in turn provide resources for social policy. Of course, social policy is still a matter of political will—will that exists in Uruguay, but not in many other countries. If we are concerned about improving equality, ending poverty, and enhancing economic and social rights, we need to focus on how to enhance and encourage inclusive social policies. In other words, contrary to what I was told back in the early 1980s, if you want to study human rights, it is important to study government and politics, not only the economy. In particular, we need to understand how to enhance inclusive social and tax policies. Such policies are compatible with open economies, as we see in Uruguay and in the social democracies of Western Europe.

Guard against Dehumanizing and Exclusionary Ideologies

The literature on the psychological and ideological explanations for human rights violations points to the role of dehumanizing ideologies, as well as the related concept of "the exclusion of the victim from the universe of obligation."[67] Dehumanizing language and other exclusionary practices can portray individuals and groups as unworthy of the ordinary protections offered to humans and thus encourage and justify the abuse of human rights.

Ideologies that exclude and dehumanize certain people are one of the most important risk factors for genocide.[68] The Yazidi case reveals the pervasiveness of dehumanizing ideology in the context of genocide. Murad recalls that when he was young, another boy asked to see Murad's "tail." Murad replied, of course, that he had no tail, but never forgot the comment.[69] This was dehumanization in practice; the Yazidis, in this example, were characterized as animals. Other examples of dehumanizing language include calling humans cockroaches (as occurred in Rwanda) or naming them as cancers that need to be cut away from the flesh of the society to cure it.

Exclusionary ideologies are belief systems that identify some purpose or principle that is so important that it is used to justify persecution or elimination of groups of people who are defined as contrary to some desired end.[70] These ideologies, which may differ dramatically from one another, all share a characteristic line of thought: the ends justify the means. They target certain national, religious, or racial groups, and justify human rights violations as necessary in targeting those groups. This overriding purpose, combined with the use of brutal means to achieve that purpose, has led to a surprising connection between utopianism and genocide. In his comparative study of four genocides—the Soviet Union under Stalin, Nazi Germany, Cambodia under the Khmer Rouge, and the former Yugoslavia—Eric Weitz argues that ideational factors and, in particular, quests for utopia, are central to the explanation of genocide.[71]

These exclusionary ideologies sometimes target political groups of the left, such as the national security doctrine in Latin America that justified killing supposed communists, and sometimes groups of the right, such as when the Pol Pot regime in Cambodia used Marxist ideology to justify killing the bourgeoisie. Today we often hear dehumanizing and exclusionary language being used against suspected terrorists, as when presidential candidate Donald Trump said that the country needed to be able to use torture to "beat ISIS" and "beat the savages."[72] In exclusionary ideologies, targeted groups are scapegoats for a broad array of a country's problems; for example, immigrants are blamed for a country's economic difficulties. In the case of the Yazidis, the exclusionary ideology of ISIL is ostensibly a religious one. ISIL saw their religious ends furthered by killing the people they called infidels. In the Darfur region of Sudan, researchers have shown how the state mobilized racial ideologies to dehumanize groups, contributing to genocide there.[73]

If we combine dehumanization with another psychological predisposition associated with repression—the tendency to obey authority—it can lead to severe human rights violations. The famous Milgram experiments showed that large percentages of ordinary citizens in New Haven were prepared to give electrical shocks to other individuals when ordered to do so by an authority figure, even when they could hear the victims' cries and even when the victim stopped responding, apparently unconscious or dead.[74] Humans in groups, however, add a need for conformity with group opinion to their strong need to be obedient to authority. The presence of a single dissenter can often alter the tendency of individuals to conform. In the Milgram experiments, for example, when the experimenters planted an individual in the scenario who refused to comply with the command to give electric shocks, the overall compliance rate fell dramatically.[75] Our psychological dispositions can thus both contribute to human rights violations and be a tool to fight against them.

One way to think about human rights movements is as equivalent to the dissenters in the Milgram experiment. By standing up to authority, these movements provide an example of non-compliance and thus diminish the feeling individuals have that they are compelled to obey authority and to comply with unethical or illegal orders. This explains in part why the presence of more human rights organizations within a country improves the human rights situation there.[76]

Psychological explanations for human rights violations often complement rather than compete with political and economic explanations. As we saw in the case of the Yazidis, although the context of war created conditions for human rights violations, the beliefs and dehumanizing language and practices of ISIL were the proximate cause of the abuses. Almost all situations of mass human rights violations combine features like war and authoritarianism with psychological mechanisms like dehumanization and the human need for conformity and obedience to authority.

Ratify Human Rights Treaties and Work to Enforce Human Rights Law

For many years, one of the main demands and accomplishments of the human rights movement was to produce more complete human rights declarations and treaties on a wide variety of issues. A large number of treaties now protect and promote a diverse set of rights (see Figures 6.5 and 6.6). An examination of the rate of ratification of some of the core treaties listed below reveals a steep climb in the number of states that have committed to the treaties.

There has been a heated academic debate about the effectiveness of human rights treaties. For reasons discussed in chapter 5, problematic findings have arisen concerning compliance.[77] Some early

American Declaration of the Rights and Duties of Man (1948)
Universal Declaration of Human Rights, UDHR (1948)
Genocide Convention (1951)
European Convention on Human Rights (1953)
Refugee Convention (1954)
Convention on the Elimination of All Forms of Racial Discrimination, CERD (1969)
International Covenant on Civil and Political Rights, ICCPR (1976)
International Covenant on Economic, Social and Cultural Rights, ICESCR (1976)
American Convention on Human Rights (1978)
Convention on the Elimination of All Forms of Discrimination against Women, CEDAW (1981)
Convention against Torture and Other Cruel, Inhuman or Degrading Treatment or Punishment, CAT (1987)
Convention on the Rights of the Child, CRC (1990)
Convention for the Protection of All Persons from Enforced Disappearance, CED (2010)
Rome Statute of the International Criminal Court (2002)
African Charter on Human and Peoples' Rights (2005)
Convention on the Rights of Persons with Disabilities, Disabilities Convention (2008)
Declaration on the Rights of Indigenous Peoples (2007)

Fig. 6.5. Key International Human Rights Declarations and Treaties

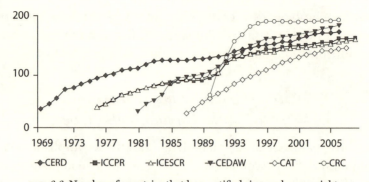

FIG. 6.6. Number of countries that have ratified six core human rights treaties: The Convention on the Elimination of All Forms of Racial Discrimination (CERD); the International Covenant on Civil and Political Rights (ICCPR); the International Covenant on Economic, Social and Cultural Rights (ICESCR); the Convention on the Elimination of All Forms of Discrimination against Women (CEDAW); the Convention against Torture (CAT); and the Convention on the Rights of the Child (CRC). Source: United Nations.

research suggested that human rights treaties did not lead to improvements and, in some cases, were counterproductive.[78] A second wave of studies has called into question some of the findings in this earlier work. Beth Simmons has made crucial contributions to this debate. Her work demonstrated that human rights laws and institutions have a positive impact on a variety of human rights under certain conditions, specifically when countries are undergoing political transition toward greater democracy.[79] Simmons reasoned that, in these countries, citizens had the motivation to pursue human rights change because they had been subject to widespread violations under the previous authoritarian regime. Moreover, those citizens had the means to pursue such change because their societies were sufficiently open for them to use international law to mobilize.[80]

In countries that are already fully democratic, citizens might not feel the benefits of the ratification of a treaty. They likely have multiple channels to pursue protections of their rights already, including domestic courts, ombudsmen, and civil society organizations. Citizens in fully democratic countries are thus more likely to rely on resources other than international law. Fully authoritarian regimes, on the other hand, often ratified human rights treaties for show and had no intention of complying with them. For example, the government of General Augusto Pinochet, dictator of Chile from 1973 to 1990, ratified the CAT in 1988. Around the same time, Pinochet put forward a plebiscite that would have allowed him to stay in power for another eight years. Perhaps he thought that ratifying the CAT would improve his image with voters. Even after ratifying the treaty, the Pinochet regime continued to engage in torture.[81]

Some scholars argue that research showing that human rights law has the greatest impact in transitional countries is evidence that the human rights movement has been effective only in "easy" cases, where it is less needed. Hafner-Burton and Ron argue, for example, "By some calculations, just over fifty states have begun a democratic transition since the 1960s. This suggests that only one quarter of the world's countries could have been helped by international human rights laws and treaties."[82] There are a number of responses to this claim. First, if human rights law has helped in fifty countries, then that would be an important indicator of progress. What other tool of social change can say with some confidence that it has helped one quarter of the world's countries? But this claim actually under-counts the number of transitions since 1960 and it neglects the fact that new political openings were created in dozens and dozens of cases once considered tough—like Poland, South Korea, El Salvador, and Nigeria. Human rights activism contributed directly to many of these political transitions.[83]

There is no doubt that, after the third wave of democracy, the remaining countries are "hard cases" for the human rights move-ment—countries with entrenched authoritarian or semi-authoritarian regimes such as those in China, Sudan, Syria, and Russia. Some of these countries, like Russia and Azerbaijan, have learned how to manipulate the system and give the appearance of democracy at the same time as they solidify a semi-authoritarian rule. Other countries, such as Hungary, have used democratic means to craft increasingly authoritarian policies. Venezuela became adept at creating a democratic façade for authoritarian rule, thus forestall-ing criticism.[84] These leaders "learned how to manage competitive elections, coopt rivals and independent media, control the private sector, and starve civic and opposition groups of resources without resorting to the kind of naked repression or fraud that could trigger a domestic legitimacy crisis and international isolation."[85]

That many hard cases remain does not mean that the human rights movement has only succeeded in "easy cases" and thus is insignificant because it is only relevant where it is needed less. First, what is an "easy case" or a "hard case" is often constructed ex post facto. In the 1980s, many countries that were once considered hard cases became transitional countries. For example, at the time *no one* expected the USSR or the states of Eastern Europe to begin transitioning to democracy. For analysts to say that the human rights movement only succeeds in the easy cases and to include all of Eastern Europe in that camp is disingenuous and ahistorical. As long as there are no definitions ahead of time as to what constitutes a hard case and an easy case, and the definition of an easy case seems to be any country that transitions to democracy and improves human rights, I don't take this critique very seriously.

Recent research on compliance with human rights treaties shows that treaty ratification is a useful tool that should be encouraged and pursued by states. No one, however, should be under the illusion that treaty ratification in and of itself will lead to human rights change. Treaties are only one tool and their ability to lead to human rights progress depends on whether actors in treaty bodies, at the UN, in courts, and, most importantly, in domestic civil society are working to convert treaty commitments into state practice.

While we are coming to learn that international human rights law does influence state practice, what remains unclear are the mechanisms that link treaties to positive improvements in human rights conditions. One possibility is that the change comes from above; that is, through socialization in international institutions, leaders begin to slowly alter their practices.[86] However, a common complaint from critics of international institutions like the UN is that they allow abusive states like Ethiopia, Russia, or Saudi Arabia to become members, which diminishes the influence of such institutions.[87] The states with the worst human rights records often make strong diplomatic efforts to get elected to the Human Rights Council with the intention of blocking condemnations of their domestic human rights practices. When these repressive states band together to protect one another, they create some of the Council's most hypocritical moments. At the same time, research by Ann Marie Clark has shown that the criticism of state practice in the Council can have a positive impact on human rights in the country criticized, at least with respect to countries that have ratified the relevant treaties.[88] Clark's research is the first to show that even the most political of the human rights institutions, the Council, can bring about positive change under certain conditions.

A second and more convincing possible explanation for how treaties can positively affect human rights is that the power of international law is defined by its ability to influence change from below, that is, from within the states themselves.[89] For example, in *Activists beyond Borders*, Margaret Keck and I argued that domestic social movements in repressive societies often were the first to organize and that they used the legal tools at their disposal, including international law, both to try to protect themselves and to initiate change. These domestic NGOs and social movements also relied on transnational allies and international support to carry out their work. The reality is probably a combination of both explanations—groups do not work strictly from above or below, but often combine bottom-up and top-down tactics to promote human rights.

Beth Simmons developed a related domestic politics theory of treaty compliance. According to this theory, groups emboldened by state commitment to human rights agreements use those agreements to change national policy agendas, to litigate in domestic courts to enforce protection of their newly guaranteed rights, and to engage in acts of social mobilization. Litigation and mobilization are such important mechanisms for promoting human rights that I devote the remainder of this chapter to them.

End Impunity through Domestic and International Prosecutions

The power of accountability has been the focus of research I have conducted with a series of co-authors and collaborators for over a decade.[90] The link between accountability and human rights has been shown to be so strong that I believe impunity itself is a cause of human rights violations. Accountability can be thought of as the accommodation between the needs of power and the claims of justice.[91] Accountability mechanisms permit those affected by the actions of the powerful to demand that the powerful explain their actions and be sanctioned if what they do is illegal. The failure to secure accountability for legitimate claims of justice erodes public trust. Some authors discuss two types of accountability: soft (making power-holders explain their actions) and hard (punishing poor or criminal performance).[92] Other scholars list a range of ways to respond to the abuse of power in international politics, including legal, market, peer, and reputational.[93] No single method is sufficient to solve all problems of impunity. Instead, multiple accountability mechanisms are necessary to address different kinds of impunity issues and to reinforce one another.

Recent analysis of a National Science Foundation-supported database by our team of researchers has demonstrated that individual criminal accountability needs to be a central part of my policy recommendations to improve core human rights practices.[94] My quantitative research with Hun Joon Kim on domestic human rights prosecutions, for example, shows that countries using such trials see improvements in levels of repression compared to countries that do not use trials.[95] Most of the recommendations I discussed previously, such as reducing poverty and inequality or ending conflict, involve deep structural changes in societies that take a long time and great resources. Ending impunity, though not fast or easy, as we have seen in the case of Guatemala's search for accountability for genocide in chapter 4, can be a concrete, focused, and relatively inexpensive policy compared to some of the massive structural changes advocated in this chapter.

In most cases, countries should, and often do, use domestic courts to enforce both domestic and international law. For example, when Argentina ratified the Convention on the Rights of the Child, domestic courts used provisions of that Convention to help families locate the children of the disappeared. In the United States, our federal courts have all the tools at their disposal to prosecute Bush administration officials for use of torture, if the executive and legislative branches would let them do their work.

Accountability is important because it can help build rule of law, thus strengthening democracy. There are many definitions of rule of law, but all stress the need for an independent judiciary. Another key element of rule of law is that no one should be above the law, including the leaders of a country. Human rights prosecutions of powerful state officials can underscore that no one is above the law, which builds confidence in the rule of law. Some scholars even argue that creating rule of law must occur before a country can take on the task of accountability.[96] In this model, the creation of an independent judiciary must precede any attempts at accountability. Yet this rigid sequencing is not how change usually takes place. An independent judiciary is created when judges and courts work to exercise and expand their autonomy. In some countries, human rights prosecutions have been the means through which judges and courts build law and the public discovers that law can be a tool for social change. Catalina Smulovitz, for example, has argued that the trials of the juntas in Argentina contributed to the "discovery of law" in that country.[97]

Studies have repeatedly found that strong domestic courts, at times boosted by regional and international legal networking, serve to enhance the effect of international commitments.[98] Some theorists have gone as far as to contend that the barriers between international and domestic sources of law are starting to erode.[99] Geoff Dancy and I have shown that ratification of treaties with individual accountability provisions is empirically associated with a higher number of human rights prosecutions.[100] These human rights prosecutions—including both high-profile trials of leaders like Peru's Alberto Fujimori and of lower-level security forces—then lead to improvements in human rights practices through a combination of deterrence and normative communication.[101]

The 1990s were the decade of what I have called the justice cascade.[102] This was the period when, for the first time in history, countries began to hold state officials and non-state groups criminally accountable for past human rights violations. The good news for human rights worldwide is that accountability is becoming more common and impunity is decreasing. Figures 6.7, 6.8, and 6.9 reveal increases in both domestic and international human rights prosecutions over time, as well as the increase in truth commissions, which can also be tools for ending impunity if they are of high quality.[103]

The justice cascade has led human rights victims throughout the world to call for justice. For example, Murad and Nadia wanted the Yazidi case referred to the International Criminal Court (ICC). There were, they knew, some barriers. Since Iraq had not ratified

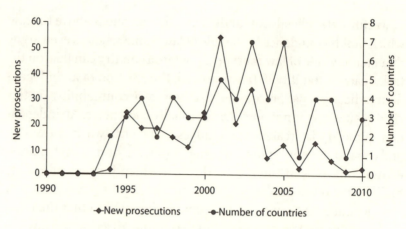

FIG. 6.7. International prosecutions (all countries). *Source*: Adapted from Geoffrey Dancy's chart for the Transitional Justice Research Collaborative website (https://www.transitionaljusticedata.com) using data from the NSF-funded Transitional Justice Collaborative.

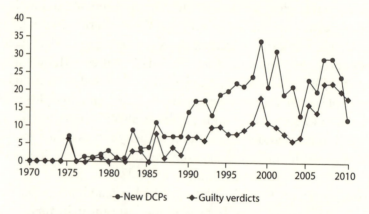

FIG. 6.8. Transitional domestic criminal prosecutions (DCPs) and guilty verdicts. *Source*: Adapted from Geoffrey Dancy's chart for the Transitional Justice Research Collaborative website (https://www.transitionaljusticedata.com) using data from the NSF-funded Transitional Justice Collaborative.

the Rome Statute of the ICC, the only way that the Yazidi case as a whole could come to the Court was if the Security Council referred it. Murad and Nadia had been asked to talk to members of the Security Council in a special briefing on trafficking arranged by Samantha Power, the US Permanent Representative to the UN at the time. They had spoken with the French ambassador, who said he would be prepared to present their case the very next day to the

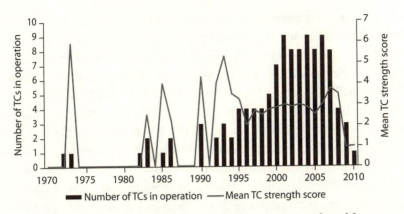

FIG. 6.9. Number and strength of truth commissions. *Source*: Adapted from Geoffrey Dancy's chart for the Transitional Justice Research Collaborative website (https://www.transitionaljusticedata.com) using data from the NSF-funded Transitional Justice Collaborative.

Security Council, if he believed that he could garner support. Russia, however, was likely to veto and China would perhaps do the same. The United States also, though in favor of justice, has long opposed the ICC and thus found it difficult to support a referral. The United States preferred creating a special hybrid international tribunal for the situation in Iraq, and potentially in Syria too. Yet Nadia and Murad felt that they could not depend on the domestic judicial system in Iraq and it was to the ICC that they turned. Although no trial could return their dead family members to them, they hope that their call for justice will deter future atrocities.

Support, Expand, and Protect
Human Rights Mobilization

Committed domestic human rights organizations are the first and most important bulwark against human rights violations. The organizations have the knowledge and the legitimacy to intervene effectively in domestic politics. But these domestic groups do not function in isolation. Often, such organizations turn to allies in transnational advocacy networks and use transnational legal processes to bring about positive human rights change while also protecting themselves, especially in societies where domestic social movements still face repression.[104] By "transnational" I do not mean to say that international groups or pressures from above alone make the difference. Transnational is not a synonym for international; instead it refers to relations that cross borders and link together national efforts in different places. With various co-authors, I have used the terms "boomerang model" and "spiral model" to describe how domestic groups go outside their societies to pressure their governments from above. In the boomerang metaphor, the organization throws a boomerang outside of the country in the hope that it will come back and hit its government. The spiral model is an extended boomerang—it takes into account that such campaigns involve iterated attempts of domestic and international pressure. These models are neither fully top-down nor fully bottom-up; instead, they show how domestic groups often initiate change, and then build transnational coalitions to help carry out their plans.[105]

Since the late 1990s, much research on the advocacy work of NGOs has focused on the pejoratively termed act of "naming and shaming." I have never liked this term and did not use it at all in *Activists beyond Borders*. Instead, Margaret Keck and I said the main way that transnational networks work is through "information politics"—creating politically relevant information and moving it to where it is likely to have the greatest effect. The purpose of information politics is not necessarily to shame, but rather to shine a light on practices that governments or non-state actors need to improve. Nevertheless, the term "naming and shaming" has taken off and most academic studies of information politics use it. Whatever you call it, it often works. But mere shaming is not enough. Improvements in human rights practices occur when naming and shaming is done by networks with connections to domestic human rights NGOs within the target states.[106]

Some scholars have provided useful and sophisticated tests of the arguments put forward in earlier qualitative work on advocacy. For example, the extensive work of Amanda Murdie addresses, among other themes, the impact of global civil society actors, especially international nongovernmental organizations (INGOs) and their tactics.[107] Murdie finds positive effects of targeted information campaigns, particularly when there are domestic groups within target states that also pressure for human rights change.[108] She also finds some "neighborhood effects" where active INGOs in neighboring states can make an impact across borders. Information campaigns, from domestic and international NGOs, have both improved practices and changed the standard by which we judge rights-abusive countries.

Human rights organizations also have to learn to be more effective actors. Information politics and naming and shaming may not always be the most effective ways to bring about change. One way for NGOs to be more effective is to consider who actually makes the decisions about compliance with human rights law and focus their activism on those decision makers. To get a state to comply with an obligation to avoid discrimination against women, for example, is different than figuring out how to get ISIL to stop committing genocide against the Yazidi people. Each warrants a nuanced approach.

Traditionally, we have thought about the state as the source of all compliance decisions, but this is legal fiction. Diverse actors are responsible for abusing or fulfilling rights. For example, insurgent groups can violate rights, such as the genocide against the Yazidis by a non-state actor, ISIL. Sometimes, transnational corporations, or even families, may be the places where human rights compliance decisions need to be taken. The appropriate mechanism to induce compliance depends upon the nature of the actors. Even when the decisions appear to be made by the state, the actual compliance decisions may be more or less centralized. The decision to stop using the death penalty is quite centralized, for example. Torture, on the other hand, can be decentralized, spread through many police stations or military barracks.[109] The location of many compliance decisions about economic rights may even rest in the private sector.[110] Although states have a duty to protect women against employment discrimination, the location of the compliance decision is different for public sector employment than for private sector employment. The state can only directly implement non-discrimination in the public sector and must use carrots and sticks to discourage discrimination in the private sector. This is the reason why, when Simmons tests the impact of the Women's Convention (CEDAW) on women's employment, she uses data on women's employment from the public sector rather than the private.[111] It is simply more realistic to expect a human rights treaty ratified by a state to have an impact within the state's apparatus.

Likewise, while punishment through trials can make an impact on state officials carrying out repression, this does not mean that punishment or deterrence works for all human rights change.[112] Effectiveness depends on the location of the compliance decision and the kinds of individuals making choices about whether to violate rights. Different kinds of actors may be influenced by different mechanisms. Take, for instance, female genital cutting, practiced mainly in small villages with the permission of the families, who believe they are doing the best thing for their daughters by enabling them to be marriageable. It makes little sense to try to stop the practice by shaming or punishing governments that have already prohibited the practice. Tactics focused on local responses through family and community education and ceremonies are far more effective in diminishing the frequency of this practice.[113]

Attention to the location of the compliance decision can help us develop more effective tactics to bring about human rights change. Although "naming and shaming" has become the most common and most scrutinized tactic among many human rights activists, it is not and should not be the only, or even the main, tactic used. NGOs are aware of the need for innovation and are developing programs, such as the "New Tactics in Human Rights," that look for new approaches to human rights work and then encourage activists to write up their methods and train other activists. Likewise, tactical mapping is a technique that helps activists strategize about the location of the compliance decision and then design more effective interventions, that is, actions aimed at the individuals involved in human rights violations.[114]

Human rights activism is only one of the many factors that can contribute to human rights progress; others include economic development, political democracy, and the absence of civil and international war. Multiple studies, using a wealth of the best data on the topic, have shown that we can be cautiously optimistic about the impact of the work of human rights INGOs, but that for the greatest success, information politics need to be combined with efforts to build strong domestic advocacy sectors within states, while also bringing pressure to bear from outside.

Human rights organizations are using new technology to create increasingly diverse forms of information politics. Information politics provokes backlash from repressive governments, who in turn try to hide invisible harms and to persecute and delegitimize human rights NGOs. Relying upon more sophisticated technology, including satellite imagery, digital platforms, and forensic science, allows the human rights movement to continue information politics in the face of government intransigence. Human rights organizations have turned to reconnaissance satellite images to identify mass graves and other warning signs of mass atrocity in regions that may be too dangerous to access through traditional field investigations. Organizations also use digital platforms to collect data about human rights violations in war zones, such as the work of Syria Tracker which uses crowd-sourced material to create a live map of the conflict.[115]

Widespread peaceful resistance is more effective in contributing to the downfall of dictatorships than is armed resistance.[116] Processes of peaceful resistance, therefore, have the potential to alter human rights outcomes. The question for human rights researchers is what role rights advocacy has played in encouraging and supporting effective pockets of resistance for social movements. Skeptics argue that the human rights movement is removed from the masses and that its legalism crowds out other forms of activism.[117] However, initial evidence suggests that peaceful social movements articulating rights-based claims have been relatively successful in pushing authoritarian governments toward democratic transition, a precondition for the improvement of human rights outcomes.[118]

One of the favorite claims of human rights skeptics, and of social scientists in general, is that well-meaning actions will increase the probability of "negative unintended consequences."[119] Social scientists have done valuable work demonstrating that pro-violation constituencies exist, and that they will react negatively against efforts to protect the human rights of certain individuals.[120] Yet, as Hirschman pointed out, although we should be attentive to the possibility of unintended consequences, we should not assume such consequences will only be negative.[121] Both negative and positive unintended consequences of human rights actions are possible. Human rights gains are always made through struggle and virtually always provoke backlash. In some cases, an unexpected negative consequence may be worth the risk.[122]

No political scientist or human rights advocate should be naïve about the amount of time and struggle it will take to bring about human rights change. For example, to have expected Egypt to move seamlessly from authoritarianism to democracy in 2011 would have been unrealistic. But it is counterfactual speculation to believe that the attempt by Egyptian activists to demand democracy or human rights was too early and, therefore, produced the backlash and that a more gradualist strategy would have succeeded. Without the demands, there would have been no chance for political transformation in the first place.

Another key issue in the discussion of human rights activism is foreign funding. Ethically and politically, should we be concerned that the bulk of funding for human rights organizations in the Global South comes from foreign foundations and from foreign governments? In many countries of the Global South there may be less of a tradition of charitable giving and the existing donations tend to focus on traditional institutions such as churches or mosques.[123] Before the 1980s, Western governments and foundations almost exclusively funded governments and government institutions, even repressive governments. Human rights activists criticized wealthy Western countries for supporting human rights violators, urging them to cut off funding to oppressive governments.[124] From the perspective of taxpayers in countries of the Global North, we might prefer that our foreign aid budgets fund civil society organizations instead of repressive states. Instead of seeing foreign funding as illegitimate, we might see it as compensation for prior wrongs.

Even recognizing that foreign funding of civil society human rights groups might be necessary and legitimate, such funding remains problematic for NGOs and they need to address the issue. Even well intentioned foreign funders can distort the priorities of domestic NGOs by undermining their independence or controlling their agendas. In the worse scenarios, foreign aid also promotes "briefcase NGOs," or "fake groups that exist only on paper and provide few services. In one recent study, surveyors discovered that some 75% of registered NGOs in Uganda's capital, Kampala, did not really exist."[125] Mexican human rights activist Sergio Aguayo also noticed this trend when he spoke of the new "pretender" human rights NGOs that had sprung up in Mexico; they had "corrupted the concept of NGOs and human rights." Such pretender human rights NGOs may not only fail to provide services, but actually give cover for groups that oppose human rights ideas.[126]

Yet, even in relation to genuine human rights organizations, foreign funders have institutional requirements about reporting and handling finances that can contribute to a two-class system between NGOs in the North and South. Organizations based in the Global North still receive the bulk of the funds from human rights foundations and "they continue to have disproportionate power when it comes to setting the international agenda . . . rather than through collaborative process with NGOs of the of Global South."[127]

Colombian based scholar-activist César Rodríguez-Garavito, a founder and current Executive Director of Dejusticia, one of the region's most important human rights organizations, is committed to building bridges in the global human rights community, between activists and academics, between law and social science, between North and South, and among countries within the Global South. Rodríguez-Garavito and his Human Rights Lab at the University of los Andes, in an analysis of the critiques of human rights law, institutions, and movements, reached somewhat optimistic conclusions. Yet, when asked which of the many critiques most resonate with his own experience with Dejusticia, a Bogotá-based NGO, he singles out the "vertical and top down relations between northern organizations and southern organizations." He finds it "incongruent with human rights values." Rodríguez-Garavito cannot believe, for instance, that the human rights field does not have a standard practice of co-authoring reports. But what he cares most about is that "there is a lot of energy and possibilities for being more efficacious that get lost and wasted because of the model of non-collaboration."[128]

Around the world, larger and more professional NGOs tend to receive the bulk of foreign funding because they have the institutional capacity to handle such funds. In Turkey, for example, European Union funding of NGOs has enhanced the autonomy and capacity of NGOs, but also has led to "over-professionalization" and a decline in volunteerism.[129] This could swell the ranks of a professional NGO class divorced from grassroots social movements. In some cases, these fears may be exaggerated; rather than a divorce between NGOs and social movements, we sometimes see an effective division of labor between the two, some of it conscious and some of it unintended.[130] A Mexican colleague, Karina Ansolabehere, calls this "multi-directionality" between elites and grassroots actors and suggests that we are likely to see more of it in the near future.[131]

Lucia Nader has discussed these issues in Brazil. She recalled that, when she and her co-workers looked down from their NGO offices at street protests which they had not helped to organize and which they did not even anticipate, she felt a chasm open up between her reality and that of the protesters on the streets. A journalist covering the protests reassured her: "You people are the before and the after of the streets." He meant that protests are episodic, while human rights organizations work continuously to put into practice some of the ideas from the street. But that did not assuage Nader's concern that NGOs have had to become too professionalized and "solid." Such solidity may put them at a disadvantage in what Nader refers to as the more "liquid world" of street protests and social media. She argues that it is a daily struggle to navigate how human rights organizations can "be solid enough to persist and have the desired impact and yet 'liquid' enough to adapt, take risks and take advantage of the opportunities that contemporary society provides."[132] These problems do not exist only in the Global South; they can be found in the difference between professional NGOs and grassroots movements in the United States and Europe as well, but foreign funding can exacerbate the problem by generating a nationalist reaction from groups of both the left and right who fear that domestic priorities will be distorted.

Despite their problematic nature, few activists or scholars argue that foreign funds should be discontinued.[133] Instead, what most commentators envision is a diversified response where some organizations make moves to localize funding, while others continue to accept external support. Any NGO obliged to seek local funding is required to be more engaged in building a domestic constituency for its work and, therefore, be more in touch with the needs and concerns of local audiences. Human rights movements need to build stronger domestic constituencies. This should be a priority especially for domestic human rights organizations in societies that have more democratic governments and are not operating in situations of fear and uncertainty.

Conclusions

This chapter has provided recommendations for making human rights work in the twenty-first century based on a survey of social science research on the causes of human rights violations. Although I have focused primarily on the risk factors for repression and genocide, many of the factors I discuss—war, authoritarianism, poverty, economic inequality, and exclusionary ideologies—are also risk factors for a wider range of rights violations, including violations of economic and social rights.

I used what we know about these risk factors to make policy recommendations about the most promising methods to promote human rights. I also provided trend information on developments in the area of crucial risk factors, including data on the global decline in conflict, the rise in democracy, the decrease in impunity, and the rise in human rights NGOs and social movements. Improvements in these areas suggest a connection between the risk factors and the diminishing of some human rights violations.

The recommendations here may seem daunting—building democracy, diminishing conflict, and enhancing growth and equality are some of the biggest challenges we face today. Yet, as the trend data shows, we are not starting from scratch. Many of these processes are well on their way and the challenge is not constructing so much as sustaining existing trends. But what to do first? Some scholars believe that it is important to carry out some of these tasks in a special sequence—e.g., first we need economic growth and then we can work on democracy, or first we need rule of law and then we can have accountability. Scott Straus's book on Rwanda, for example, shows that elections held in an atmosphere of intense ethnic conflict and without well-developed judicial institutions and the rule of law led to greater conflict, not democracy.[134] Based on this example, actions establishing rule of law must precede democratic elections. Nevertheless, social science research on a wide variety of countries has not revealed any privileged order for achieving democracy, development, rule of law, peace, and human rights. Moreover, the idea that a country must develop rule of law and end ethnic conflict before it can have elections sounds like a convenient recipe for autocrats to avoid change. We could be critical of the policy, sometimes attributed to the United States, of promoting elections no matter what the circumstances. But in practice I can't point to a specific example where US insistence on promoting elections really created problems. Could we say that the United States insisted too much on promoting elections in Egypt, for example? Actually, it would appear that Egyptians in the street insisted on elections. The problem with policy is usually too little commitment to democracy, not too much. A bigger problem in Egypt eventually appeared to be too thin a commitment to democracy, both on the part of the Egyptian public that supported the coup against Morsi and of foreign powers that failed to do more to prevent it.

Albert Hirschman's concept of possibilism appears particularly relevant here. Hirschman developed possibilism in the context of rigid economic theory that posited a sequenced model of development. He opposed the notion that there was a necessary sequence towards development that had to be adopted and instead proposed that forward and backward linkages were useful.[135] A similar possibilist approach is necessary for improving efforts to promote human rights. We know that democracy, peace, development, and human rights are all correlated with one another and that they can produce a virtuous circle, each contributing to the next. But, as far as I can tell, political scientists and economists have not determined what needs to come first, much less the remaining order of the sequence. Hirschman's genius would have us look for unexpected ways that each step can contribute to one another. Catalina Smulovitz's argument that human rights prosecutions contributed to building rule of law in Argentina would be one such Hirschmanian insight.

As we look at human rights in the twenty-first century, there are two particularly worrisome trends: the rise in inequality and the continuation of serious conflict. Although international conflict is declining worldwide, prominent conflicts in the Middle East are generating exactly the kinds of human rights violations we would expect—killings, rape, displacement, and a massive flow of refugees. Meanwhile, in both the developing and the developed worlds, inequality among individuals continues to increase. These issues will require more attention from human rights advocates around the world, using all the skills and strategies they have honed in their other struggles. This is a chapter about which policies work and which do not in the promotion of human rights. The first and most important insight is that we need to continue to pursue the difficult, slow, and mainly nonviolent changes and processes that have contributed to many positive trends in the world.

PART IV

Making Human Rights Work in the Twenty-First Century

CHAPTER SEVEN

Conclusions

EVIDENCE FOR HOPE
WITHOUT COMPLACENCY

LESS THAN ONE WEEK after the election of Donald Trump as the new president of the United States in November of 2016, Amnesty International USA (AI USA) held its annual conference for the Northeast and New England. Amnesty volunteer members and activists from the region gathered in Boston to participate in workshops and plan their work for the coming year. A friend of mine and long-time AI organizer and leader, Jack Rendler, attended the conference and led a workshop on human rights in North Korea. He estimated the average age of the conference's participants at about twenty-five.[1] This surprised me—I had come to think of AI as made up primarily of older human rights activists, like Rendler, who got involved in the heyday of human rights activism in the 1970s.

The conference started with a performance by a local indigenous band, the Eastern Medicine Singers. They said that they wanted to teach everyone a song and a dance and that the performance would act as a blessing for the work ahead. Pretty soon 200 to 300 young people were dancing around the auditorium. Evan Mawarire then spoke, a Zimbabwean pastor who had used social media (#ThisFlag) to organize a huge protest in Zimbabwe in July 2016 against government corruption and the denial of basic services. The authorities arrested and imprisoned Mawarire, charging him with inciting violence and later with subversion and attempting to overthrow the government, i.e., with treason. If convicted of the treason charge, he would have faced up to twenty years in jail. Mawarire was the subject of a global AI Urgent Action appeal and AI's deputy director for southern Africa, Muleya Mwananyanda, said, "Mawarire's arrest was a calculated move by the embattled Zimbabwean government to intimidate activists who spoke out against President Robert Mugabe."[2] AI wasn't the only group supporting Mawarire; about one hundred lawyers from the group Zimbabwe Lawyers for Human Rights showed up in court to offer legal assistance; members of the general public also crowded the courtroom. The judge eventually dismissed the case for procedural irregularities.[3] AI later helped Mawarire leave Zimbabwe. When speaking to the AI conference in Boston, Mawarire said he had felt absolutely hopeless when was charged with treason and he thanked and credited AI members for helping get him released.

After the opening sessions, the AI conference participants in Boston could choose to attend a diverse series of workshops with topics ranging from "Keeping Yourself Safe During a Protest," to "The America I Believe in: How to Organize against Fear, Hate, and Bigotry," to "Stopping Unlawful Use of Deadly Force by Police," to "Strategies to Stop Corporate Human Rights Abuses." The workshops did not focus solely on reporting human rights violations; they also talked about designing strategies for action and gave training in specific tactics. The conference ended with a candlelight vigil and a reading of the Universal Declaration of Human Rights.

In the context of the US election, Rendler said that many people "came into the conference angry and hopeless," but that, as he watched the conference progress, "what I saw unfolding before my eyes was these young people moving from hopelessness to action. They realized that there were action options and they became more energized." Then, with his wry sense of humor, he added, "Actually I prefer them sad and hopeless because once they are energized, it is just a wall of noise."[4]

The organizers of the AI conference knew how to incorporate the ideas stressed by Saul Alinsky, which I discussed in the introduction to this book: that social change requires anger, hope, and the belief that we can make a difference. My survey of literature on human rights and my conversations with activists on the front lines suggest that we may have too much critique and despair at the moment and not enough hope, resilience, or belief that we can make a difference. Of course, we need to have humility, especially when we are aware of how little we know and how we often fail. In fact, one source of resilience is the ability to learn from failure and overcome obstacles.[5] The organizers of the AI conference and the young people who attended found the right balance of anger and hope, as well as the training to learn how to make a difference. The conference offered, in that first week after the US elections, a glimpse of a way forward, one that is entirely consistent with the history I tell in this book.

This book is my response to critiques of human rights law, institutions, and movements, in particular those that have questioned the legitimacy and effectiveness of human rights. Legitimacy is related to effectiveness, linking the two parts of the book together. Beliefs about effectiveness can strengthen or weaken perceptions of legitimacy and an initial commitment to legitimacy can predispose people to see effectiveness.[6] In this concluding chapter, I examine first effectiveness and then legitimacy to stress what I believe is the evidence for hope.

The Effectiveness of Human Rights Law, Institutions, and Movements

Throughout this book, I have measured human rights progress in relation to the human rights listed in the Covenant on Civil and Political Rights and the Covenant on Economic, Social and Cultural Rights. I have argued that, to evaluate progress, we must have a basic methodological agreement and the method that I have endorsed is one of empirical comparison, where we look at how state and non-state behavior has changed in comparison to earlier practices or to situations in different countries or regions. In order to do this, we must look at human rights issue by issue since it is impossible to make accurate general statements about all human rights. We also have to look at change over time, sometimes decades or more, because human rights change takes time. Within an issue area, I envision compliance on a continuum that moves from none to complete. Movement along that continuum from less to more compliance constitutes human rights progress on that issue, even if current practice falls short of full compliance. Using this method, it is completely possible and indeed common that we will also witness movement backwards on the continuum, as we have seen in Egypt with regard to basic integrity rights, in the United States on its policy of torture and secret detention, and in the Middle East with the increase in refugees fleeing the wars in Syria, Afghanistan, and Iraq.

We must continue to push states and non-state actors towards full compliance by stressing the ongoing gap between their behavior and full compliance. But, as I discussed in chapters 1 and 2, we cannot use only comparison to the ideal as our method for measuring progress; under this method it would be almost impossible to say that improvements ever had occurred. Virtually all of what I call "human rights progress" or improvements in human rights practices exists in a context where further improvements need to be made; the gap between behavior and full compliance still exists and has the potential to expand. Human rights progress is always a process and never an endpoint. Moreover, it is a process that can be reversed, that has often been reversed. Vigilance is necessary to sustain human rights progress and prevent retrogression.

Two characteristics intrinsic to human rights issues complicate our efforts to measure effectiveness. First, many human rights violations are invisible harms and thus difficult to measure. Human rights movements are devoted to shining light on invisible harms and bringing them to global attention. In doing so, however, the movements may lead people to think that human rights situations are worsening when in reality we just know more and care more about them. Paradoxically, the very success of the human rights movement in increasing information and awareness can be used as evidence that human rights law and activism do not work, an argument based on the high level of continuing abuses in the world. Second, human rights movements are dedicated to raising the bar of what constitutes a human rights violation, thus creating a changing standard of accountability. Human rights is thus a moving target, with its definition constantly being expanded through the ongoing work of activists and institutions. This is one of the most impressive aspects of rights, yet also causes the greatest measurement problems when one is trying to talk about progress. Understanding the information paradox and the changing standard of accountability shouldn't make us complacent, but it can make us despair less and be more informed users of data measuring rights violations.

Thoughtful work evaluating the progress and effectiveness of human rights will need to take into account these obstacles to accurate measurement in order to develop solutions to address them. In doing so, human rights researchers can seek guidance or inspiration from other fields that have been coping with similar issues of measurement for a longer time. Public health researchers, for example, are aware of a phenomenon similar to the information paradox that they call "surveillance bias," where the closer they look at something, an illness for example, the more they find it, and they are taking actions to try to address the surveillance bias in their research. My colleague Malcolm Sparrow, whose book *The Character of Harms* addresses invisible harms from the perspective of public management, said that one of his main motivations for writing his book was that he had observed "multiple fields all discovering by themselves, and somewhat in isolation, certain basic truths about the harm-reduction business that were in fact quite generic."[7] Sparrow told me that, if the relatively new field of human rights "appeared to be exploring these measurement issues without knowledge of or reference to the many analogues in other areas, the result could be to make the emerging field appear embarrassingly isolated, or 'siloed.'" Sparrow pointed out that there is much that human rights scholars "can learn quite quickly and easily from others, to minimize the amount of fumbling around in the dark they need to do!"[8] Human rights researchers are already moving to address measurement issues in sophisticated ways, as evidenced by the innovative methodological work of scholars like Christopher Fariss, Will Moore, and Patrick Ball and his team at the Human Rights Data Analysis Group.[9] But the great majority of human rights activists, the general public, and most academics who work on human rights either don't understand or don't accept the idea that our field suffers from an information paradox that may influence our understandings of effectiveness. There is still work to be done.

Having established the value of empirical comparisons and of the careful use of data, I went issue by issue to evaluate where there are improvements in human rights and where there has been retrogression, especially in chapters 2, 5, and 6. My hope is that I have convinced the reader that the general perception that human rights are worsening across the board is deeply flawed. Human rights progress has not resolved all conflicts, oppressions, and inequalities, but it has not yet had the chance. We need to recognize that human rights change takes time and that we need to try to evaluate change over decades, not only years. The concept of human rights, though not infallible, has proven itself effective in the past. It should be trusted to continue to effect change in the future.

Legitimacy and Human Rights

In addition to tackling the issue of effectiveness concerning the international protection of human rights, I have addressed three main critiques that undermine this concept's legitimacy.[10] First, I have argued that the international protection of human rights did not emerge from the Global North and that the concept of human rights does not necessarily derive from or align with the geopolitical and economic interests of countries in the Global North or of global capitalism more generally. Second, I have argued that international human rights institutions, working together with human rights movements, are a key part of the solution to current problems, one that is all the more important if countries like the United States and the United Kingdom withdraw their support for human rights. Finally, I argue that there is little reason to believe that human rights are "minimal" and "powerless to address inequality."[11] I have discussed each of these issues in sections dispersed throughout the book, but here I summarize my main arguments in response to these critiques.

Human Rights Ideas and Institutions
Have More Diverse Origins

Much of the critique of human rights as being aligned with the geopolitical and economic interests of the Global North is derived from flawed histories about the origins of human rights and their evolution. For this reason, I spent much of chapters 3 and 4 discussing the origins of the ideas and institutions for the international protection of human rights. I have argued, using my own historical research on Latin America and a growing body of detailed historical research from around the world, that both countries in the Global South and campaigns originating there contributed strongly to the emergence of human rights ideas, institutions, and movements, which often arose in opposition to US policy and to neo-liberal authoritarian regimes, not hand in glove with them.

A closer look at the emergence of human rights ideas worldwide reveals that they do not come only from liberalism or Christianity, as some authors have claimed.[12] Rather, these ideas have much more diverse origins, including civic republicanism, socialism, and communitarianism. Looking closer at human rights documents from the Global South also reminds us of some forgotten aspects of the history of human rights. First, civil and political rights *and* economic and social rights coexisted in human rights law from the moment that the international protection of human rights was first endorsed by governments, with the American Declaration and the UDHR. Second, both rights and duties were stressed, not only in the American Declaration of the Rights and Duties of Man, but also in the African Charter on Human and Peoples' Rights.[13] Both the American Declaration and the African Charter stressed that individual duties could complement individual rights, not conflict with them. This idea of combining individual duties and individual rights could serve as a tool for achieving more consensus on the legitimacy of human rights norms, particularly in developing nations and those outside the Global North. The almost forgotten histories of human rights and duties from the periphery can provide a bridge to modern debates over rights, duties, and responsibilities, adapting discourses in a multipolar world where emerging powers such as Brazil, India, China, Russia, and South Africa will increasingly help determine the outcome of international human rights debates.[14]

Human rights work in the coming years of the twenty-first century may look very much like the Cold War period of 1948–1973, where the major powers were mainly in opposition to the international protection of human rights and where momentum and progress depended on the actions of smaller countries, with support from emerging NGOs and civil society. But in the twenty-first century, these small countries and activists have far more institutional resources at their disposal—the human rights law, institutions, and movements that earlier activists created in the mid- to late twentieth century. Even so, it will take all their creativity and energy to sustain human rights progress in the more hostile environment we entered after the Brexit vote and the election of Donald Trump.

Some authors and activists argue that human rights ideas don't work as mobilizing tools in the Global South because people there do not trust human rights organization and, furthermore, believe such organizations are at the service of the great powers, and the United States in particular. In this case, we have a rare opportunity to bring survey data to bear on this topic. Since legitimacy consists of what people believe, survey evidence on beliefs is a good way to explore this issue. From 2012 to 2014 James Ron and David Crow conducted surveys of 9,380 respondents in six countries in four world regions: Colombia, Ecuador, India, Mexico, Morocco, and Nigeria. They asked about attitudes toward the US government, human rights, and local and international human rights organizations in order to test some arguments made by international relations scholars. There was some interesting variation by country but, overall, Ron and Crow found that people in these six countries in three different regions of the developing world have "pretty good" levels of trust in their local human rights organizations. Such trust is not limited to one group of people, such as those with higher incomes or greater transnational connection. Rather, people with different levels of education, income, and geographic locations (urban and rural) have trust in human rights organizations, and those who report they have had contact with these human rights organizations are more likely to trust them. Finally, local human rights organizations are not perceived as handmaidens of powerful countries, and awareness that they receive foreign funding does not diminish trust in most countries.[15] This suggests that human rights organizations continue to have appeal in these countries and could be used as a mobilizing tool in campaigns.

Human Rights Movements and Human Rights Institutions Work Together

Some critics would have us believe that there is a sharp division between human rights institutions and human rights movements, as institutions have become bureaucratized and indifferent, even imperial, while human rights movements have remained pure.[16] Such a division misses the fact that human rights advocates helped create many of today's human rights institutions. Advocates of human rights instill these institutions with their hopes and expectations and continue to use and depend on them, even as they critique the institutions and push for reform. For example, human rights movements in Latin America depended upon and contributed to human rights institutions in the 1970s that diplomats had helped build in the tempestuous 1950s and 1960s; moreover, activists continue to rely on these institutions in the present. Human rights progress is greatest in those regions with strong regional human rights institutions, as well as strong social movements. These are not two opposing forces, but potentially complementary ones.

Social movements and NGO advocates are often dissatisfied with human rights institutions. They correctly critique the UN Human Rights Council as a place where hypocrisy and power politics are common, where diplomats from authoritarian regimes can be elected as members and diplomatic language obscures tragedies. But they also recognize that the Council has evolved over time in response to the demands of human rights advocates. In the 1970s, a diplomat in the UN Commission on Human Rights (the previous name of the Council) couldn't even mention a country accused of human rights violations by name; today, every country of the world must submit to a Universal Periodic Review of its human rights practices and NGOs from around the world are invited to submit their critiques of country practices. Sri Lankan human rights activists struggled long and hard to get the Council to adopt a resolution on accountability for the human rights violations during their civil war because they thought it would help their domestic advocacy.

Human rights institutions are mainly tools and arenas. Although they can be put to good use, as they were in the interaction of the UN Human Rights Council with Sri Lankan activists, these institutions can also be captured and tamed by repressive regimes. As a result of what one author has called "the Dictator's Learning Curve," many authoritarian regimes have become much more savvy about countering the maneuvers of democracy promotion campaigns and human rights movements.[17] They have learned that the resolutions of human rights institutions can help legitimize or delegitimize their regimes and thus they work hard to line up support for resolutions praising their countries. These examples serve as yet another illustration of human rights work as an ongoing struggle, where complacency and indifference can erode past progress. During the Cold War in Latin America, for example, the OAS was frequently an anticommunist club of authoritarian governments. When its organ, the Inter-American Commission on Human Rights, began to do important human rights work in spite of this, it was because specific individuals in the Commission fought to realize its potential. Today, even the Council of Europe, once considered a global bastion of human rights ideals, has come under attack from within by authoritarian regimes such as Azerbaijan. Gerald Knaus has shown how the Ilham Aliyev regime helped capture the Council of Europe and neutralize its ability to speak about political prisoners and fraudulent elections in Azerbaijan. Yet instead of simply concluding that human rights institutions are part of the problem, Knaus reminds us that "All human creations require care and attention. When the maintenance of a building is neglected, cracks appear in the ceiling. Before long falling debris will pose a threat to anyone who seeks shelter. The same is true today for the architecture of human rights protections."[18] Human rights institutions can decay if they are not maintained scrupulously by human rights defenders. A similar situation exists with the Inter-American system, so chronically underfunded by states that it must lay off staff. The Latin American states that created the Inter-American system have failed to care for and maintain it properly. In 2013, some states, spearheaded by Ecuador, even tried to eliminate the Inter-American Commission on Human Rights entirely. Only a concerted and well-organized campaign by Latin American human rights organizations managed to stave off the attack on the Commission.[19]

The division between human rights institutions and human rights movements thus proves to be disingenuous. Large human rights institutions can become bureaucratized, indifferent, and even captured, but they are not inevitably so; that happens when human rights advocates, inside and outside of institutions and governments, in both the North and the South, let down their guard, don't pay attention, or lose a crucial battle. Domestic human rights advocates around the world continue to be the most indispensable tool for making human rights work. But, at many stages of their struggle, domestic advocates require the support of international and regional human rights institutions, transnational human rights networks, and the foreign policies of democratic states, both in the North and in the South. Those who would romanticize human rights movements and demonize human rights institutions ignore that the collaboration between movements and institutions has been a central motor for human rights change.

Human Rights Law, Institutions, and Movements as Powerful Tools for Addressing Inequality

Human rights work has been the principal tool for addressing multiple forms of inequality in the world. As such, there is reason to believe that human rights is a promising discourse with the ability to address economic discrimination and inequality. Yet, Moyn says human rights are "minimal" and "have been powerless against inequality," and some human rights activists echo his claim.[20]

Let's think about the first assertion. Why would we see human rights progress as minimal? If a person had all the rights declared in the UDHR of 1948, not only would that person have protections of life, liberty, security, the freedom of thought and religion, and the right to participate in politics, they would also have access to education, social security, work (and equal pay for equal work), freedom of movement, a standard of living adequate for their health and well-being, including food, clothing, housing, and medical care as well as necessary social services. They would have equal protection under the law and be protected against discrimination "of any kind, such as race, colour, sex, language, religion, political or other opinion, national or social origin, property, birth or other status." Not to mention their right to leisure, which includes paid vacations. Since the UDHR was drafted, many new rights have been added to international human rights law. In their totality, these rights are certainly not minimal and I fear that academics like Moyn and human rights activists who echo his claims do us a disservice. I'm not even sure what part of it they find minimal. I wish deeply that every person around the world had these rights, though we are far from it. Moreover, although the UDHR does not place a ceiling on inequality, it is possible to wish and work for more economic equality within the framework of human rights and to do so without disparaging this movement's declarations and aspirations as minimal. I encourage people to reread the UDHR—as Amnesty International did at the end of its November conference—or the American Declaration. They are a great contrast to some of the genuinely minimal demands for social policy in the United States.[21]

In response to Moyn's second claim, I would argue that human rights law, institutions, and movements have made important inroads in "status" inequality around the world. *Status inequality* refers to inequality based on differences in esteem and respect, which can be connected, as the UDHR says, to "race, colour, sex, language, religion, political or other opinion, national or social origin, property, birth or other status." Status inequality is not separate from economic inequality since it refers to beliefs about cultural status, about who is "better"—and these can generate very significant material differences, as people have seen with the effects of racism in the United States for example, where the legacy of slavery and continued racism is a fundamental source of economic inequality.[22]

Looking at the history of human rights struggles, we can see that human rights has been a powerful movement, perhaps the most powerful movement for addressing multiple forms of inequality in the world, including those based on difference in race, gender, sexual orientation, and disability. Since human rights movements have been effective in addressing other kinds of inequality, why would we expect that they would be "powerless" to address economic inequality? Women's rights advocates have long known that political inclusion and economic equality for women were simply two sides of the same coin. Women needed to have political inclusion in order to pursue economic equality and economic inclusion to protect their physical integrity. Amartya Sen has made the same argument with regard to civil and political rights and economic and social rights. Civil and political rights of speech, association, and assembly are crucial tools to permit individuals to pursue their economic rights.[23] The demands for the right to work, the right for equal pay for equal work, the right to form labor unions, the right to food, heath, and social security could all contribute to more economic equality. All these rights have been pursued by human rights activists using the many tools of human rights law, with varying degrees of success. For example, the International Network for Economic, Social and Cultural Rights (ESCR-Net) connects over 280 NGOs, social movements and advocates across more than seventy-five countries to build a global movement for human rights and social justice, working on corporate accountability and economic policy in order to "challenge unjust structures and policies, and promote alternative models of development."[24] Treaties like the Women's Convention (CEDAW) and the Convention on the Elimination of All Forms of Racial Discrimination (CERD) are as much about economic equality in education and the workplace as they are about political inclusion.

Today, human rights NGOs, especially those based in the Global South, are working to address the serious shortcomings of a neoliberal order that ignores human rights. César Rodríguez-Garavito, one of the most innovative scholar/activists of human rights, has written a series of books outlining the important work that activists from the Global South are doing to promote a wide range of economic and social rights, indigenous rights, and environmental concerns.[25] For example, the Treatment Action Campaign in South Africa, connected to a global network that included rights-based development groups such as Oxfam, called attention to the conflict between the intellectual property rights of large pharmaceutical companies and the right to health and to basic medicines. Their campaigns were successful in pressuring companies to provide antiretroviral drugs to African countries at lower prices. In the end, a solution was reached recognizing that a country's control over crucial public health crises can take precedence over intellectual property rights.[26]

The issue of business in human rights has been a rapidly growing area of human rights activism and scholarship, bringing together people from the Global North and the Global South to address economic disparities and use new tactics to hold corporations accountable. [27] For example, the issue of tobacco involves corporations, public health, and human rights. The global spread of tobacco implicates the lives of over one billion people in the developing world. Smoking today is taken up by the most vulnerable populations in the world: children, the poor, and the mentally ill. Uruguay recently won a major case against Phillip Morris, protecting Uruguay's ability to label cigarettes in ways that protect its population. This victory is not the product of a single NGO or a single country, but involved transnational networks and multi-stakeholder alliances. In the case of Uruguay, the Frente Amplio government put the packaging law in place. When sued by Phillip Morris, the government hired a law firm in Washington, D.C., Michael Bloomberg decided to help pay the legal costs, and Harold Koh, former Dean of the Yale Law School and former Legal Adviser for the US State Department, offered pro bono legal assistance to the Uruguay legal team. Koh argued that tobacco is a human rights issue, affecting the right to health of millions of people around the globe. Uruguay and the countries campaigning to protect the right to health acquired no less an ally than comedian John Oliver, whose send-up of Phillip Morris's obvious greed and cynicism was as hilarious as it was well researched.[28]

Stressing duties as useful complements to human rights can be an essential tool to address global public policy challenges, including economic inequality. To confront global inequality, it is necessary to stress both the economic rights of individuals to an adequate standard of living and also the duties of corporations and individuals to pay taxes so that governments can address poverty and inequality at home and abroad.[29] It may be equally important to stress the duties of countries to close down their tax havens and prevent money laundering.[30] In the words of economist Gabriel Zucman, Assistant Professor of Economics at the University of California, Berkeley:

> Each country has the right to choose its forms of taxation. But when . . . the British Virgin Islands enables money launderers to create anonymous companies for a penny or when Switzerland keeps the wealth of corrupt elites out of sight in its coffers, they all steal the revenue of foreign nations. . . . In the end, the taxes that are evaded have to be compensated for by higher taxes on the law-abiding, often middle class households in the US, Europe, and developing countries. Nothing in the logic of free exchange justifies this theft.[31]

Organizations campaigning for economic and social rights have increasingly pointed to tax havens as a large part of the reason why states don't have the available resources to provide adequate economic and social rights. More forcefully addressing the tax haven issue may be one of the key ways to get developing countries the resources they need to reduce hunger. The Center for Economic and Social Rights (CESR) works on tax avoidance and evasion, which it sees as a systemic drain on government revenues needed for the fulfillment of human rights. They are one of a number of human rights organizations that have started to grapple with what it might mean to have a tax policy for human rights, including efforts to shut down tax havens. CESR argues that, "Taxation is a crucial instrument for the realization of human rights, not just because it is necessary for ensuring sufficient resources, but also because tax policy plays a fundamental role in redressing inequalities and in shaping how accountable governments are to their people."[32]

The contributions that human rights can make to economic equality have been recognized by people working in humanitarian and development organizations. Institutions such as Oxfam have been at the forefront of efforts to make humanitarian and development organizations think about rights-based development. After working on issues of poverty and inequality for many years, these organizations realized that poverty and inequality were not primarily about a lack of resources, but rather about exclusion from politics and the economy. In some places that exclusion is overt and legal, as in South Africa under apartheid. In other places the exclusion is less visible but still has an impact, as Oxfam USA has found working with workers (mostly immigrants) in the food processing industry. By focusing on exclusion, Oxfam has shown how a rights-based model can be useful in addressing issues of poverty and inequality. The idea of rights-based development has helped activists raise key issues with companies, points that they could not easily have raised outside of the framework of rights.[33]

Despite these efforts, economic inequality continues to rise. I believe that even more vigorous human rights campaigns could help address inequality, including tax evasion, corruption, and a lack of broad educational access. We need more human rights activism on issues surrounding economic inequality. Then again, human rights movements don't have to be the only tools for fighting inequality. The concept is compatible with other visions of justice. Social justice and human rights, for example, complement one another; as both

Amartya Sen and Mathias Risse have argued, human rights can help promote and realize justice.[34] Some theorists believe in "crowding out," where one discourse, such as human rights, somehow silences or narrows the range of emancipatory options available to us.[35] I have seen little evidence of such crowding out. The influence of Marxism, for instance, declined on its own accord as a result of developments in the former USSR and Eastern Europe; human rights may have provided an alternative discourse, but it did not crowd out Marxism. I have not found evidence of this happening with other emancipatory discourses either.

What the Legitimacy of Human Rights Means Going Forward

The human rights movement has proven itself capable of innovation, including in campaigns for the protections of economic and social rights. Structural changes in the world are creating new conditions for human rights activism. César Rodríguez-Garavito has argued that the rise of emerging powers such as Brazil, Russia, India, China, and South Africa, the expansion of the range of actors and the types of legal and political strategies, and the availability of new information and communication technologies represent a transition—an opportunity for creativity and innovation. He believes that these structural transformations "point towards a much more diverse, decentralized, and network-like human rights field than in previous decades."[36] But much depends on how human rights advocates adjust to change as they move ahead.

Since the international protection of human rights did not come from the Global North, we should not design solutions in which powerful governments like the United States will necessarily be the leaders. I don't believe in an elite club of "stewards" of human rights as proposed by Emilie Hafner-Burton. Although Hafner-Burton doesn't tell us who the stewards will be, there is an implication that the United States and Western Europe will need to take the lead.[37] I believe that the leaders will be from a more diverse set of states than Hafner-Burton suggests. Just as the UN Charter and the UDHR reflected the beliefs of a wide coalition of states and non-state actors, so too will the champions of ongoing human rights struggles be a diverse group, a mosaic of countries from around the world that will take the lead on different human rights issues at different times. This is not just wishful thinking. States, activists, and institutions in the Global South have made wide-ranging contributions to justice, including in the areas of economic and social rights. Brazil and South Africa, for example, took the lead on LGBT rights in the UN Human Rights Council. Brazil and Mexico have contributed to the diffusion of effective social policies involving cash transfers.[38] Colombia has adopted the most far-reaching and innovative reparations program of any country in the world and is in the process of setting a new model for peace agreements that incorporates provisions for justice and reparations.[39] The Constitutional Court of South Africa has issued a series of path-breaking decisions on the rights to health and housing, while India's Supreme Court has reaffirmed a constitutional right to food and ordered a massive investment in school lunch programs to help implement it.[40] Small countries can make a difference—witness the roles that Jordan, Costa Rica, and Liechtenstein have played as the chairs of States Parties for the ICC, shepherding the ICC through its first difficult decade of life. Countries will move in and out of leadership in human rights, depending on what political parties are in power and other pressing issues.

Most of the countries around the world that have at times supported a human rights agenda have also experienced periods of retrogression. I wish neither to homogenize nor romanticize the human rights protagonism of countries in the Global South. Brazil played an important role in 1948 when it called for an Inter-American Court of Human Rights, but, in 2011, halted its financial contribution to the OAS to protest a ruling from the Inter-American Commission on Human Rights (IACHR). The IACHR had called on the Brazilian government to suspend construction of the Belo Monte dam because it had not consulted with local indigenous people about the project. Around the same time, Brazil sponsored a resolution at the Human Rights Council in favor of LGBT rights.[41] Brazil can take, and has taken, a leadership role in the area of human rights, but it has also worked to undermine rights, at times doing both simultaneously. The apparent dissonance is not unique. The anti-apartheid struggle was one of the world's earliest and most extensive global human rights campaigns. The ANC government under Mandela later provided leadership for the creation of the International Criminal Court and ratified the Statute in 2000, yet by 2016 South Africa was in the process of withdrawing from the Court. As we have seen in the historical chapters of this book, India played a key role advocating human rights in the UN. The Indian Supreme Court has also made path-breaking decisions on some economic and social rights, most importantly, the right to food. Then, in 2014, Indians elected Narendra Modi as their Prime Minister. The leader of the right-wing Hindu nationalist BJP Party, Modi was the Chief Minister of Gujarat state at a time when violence amounting to ethnic cleansing against Muslims was carried out with the complicity of the state government. These examples demonstrate that countries in the Global South have politics as changeable and complex as those in the United States. Their ability to contribute to the global human rights agenda will, understandably, vary.

There is no reason to believe that either China or Russia will promote the international protection of human rights in the near future. The rise in the power and influence of China is in fact worrisome for the agenda on the international protection of human rights, though, at the same time, China's rapid economic development has done more to lift large numbers of people out of poverty than any other recent trend. China has a policy of indifference to the internal human rights practices of other states and this lack of attention to democracy and human rights is attractive to neighboring governments and trading partners. As they seek to grow with China, neighboring states will be sensitive and accommodating to China's interests and ideals. These countries are likely to gravitate away from the United States and towards China.[42] Nevertheless, China's continued problems with soft power make it unlikely to be able to persuade large swaths of the world to embrace its policy alternatives to human rights and democracy promotion.[43] Iain Johnston argues that the fear that China may be undermining democracy and human rights in the world may be overblown. There is not evidence, for example, that China's policy of aid or arms transfer in Africa is actively supporting authoritarian countries or those that violate human rights.[44]

The United States should be a vital part of the coalition to protect and promote human rights internationally. Right now, however, the United States is hampered in its ability to play a more central role in this movement. Even prior to the election of Donald Trump, the United States was not doing its part to protect human rights—the Bush administration carried out a policy of torture and rendition and failed to seek any accountability for it, invaded Iraq, and, more generally, flaunted international law. The Obama administration failed to seek accountability for Bush administration torture and to end indefinite imprisonment at Guantánamo, and even expanded the use of targeted killing. In the end, the United States must lead by example, not by giving advice to others that it does not intend to follow.

Women's rights and the rights of people with disabilities are instances where the United States has led by example. Much is made of the US failure to ratify the Women's Convention (CEDAW) and the Convention on the Rights of Persons with Disabilities, yet, in these two areas, US domestic legislation has led the way and our practice tends to be more in compliance with the treaties than many of the other countries that have ratified them—what Harold Koh calls compliance without ratification.[45] However, concerning the area of torture, rendition, and political prisoners, the very core of the human rights agenda, the United States has backslid terribly and this has damaged our ability to speak on behalf of core rights. Before Trump's election, in an earlier draft of this chapter, I wrote:

> ... the single most important thing the United States can do to exercise human rights leadership is to close Guantánamo and end the practice of arbitrary and indefinite detention practices there. Second, the United States must hold the Bush administration officials who were responsible for practices of kidnapping, arbitrary detention, and torture criminally accountable for these acts. They are contrary to our constitution, our domestic statutes, and our international law obligations. Nothing would go further to reestablishing US legitimacy to act in the field of human rights than holding individuals accountable for these crimes.

After the election of Trump, all this feels outdated and impossible. Our main task today is to prevent the Trump administration from returning to policies of torture and rendition.

We live in dangerous times. Never has it been so important that domestic and international human rights advocates and scholars collaborate. We must take action guided by past successes in promoting human rights and based on our best history and social science. I disagree with those who argue that we should only engage in domestic politics and abandon international human rights norms and law.[46] On the contrary, we will need even stronger domestic movements that look both internally and internationally in order to protect vulnerable populations from hate and discrimination and to mobilize groups harmed by globalization. Human rights will continue to be a discourse that can mobilize both domestic and international publics.

Due to the current political context, this book appears all the more necessary, as it provides a history of past struggles in which the US and UK governments were often on the wrong side of human rights. It discusses how oppressed people have long used human rights ideas to improve their lots, while elites, and often US elites, sat on the sidelines. We have seen how newly decolonized states propelled the human rights agenda while the United States was engulfed in racial discrimination in the 1960s. Oppressed groups brought pressure from above on a US government trying to win the hearts and minds of the developing world during the Cold War. At the same time, international pressures worked together with domestic social movements to end formal racial segregation in the United States. This demonstrates how strong domestic social movements can benefit from the support of transnational networks and international institutions.

More recently, international pushback on the Bush administration's torture and rendition policy worked together with domestic opposition to the policy to shut down abuses by the US government. Bush, Cheney, and Rumsfeld were not persuaded by arguments about international norms and law, but they eventually understood that they were unable to pursue their interests because of the resistance they faced, including the possibility of criminal accountability for US officials. International norms and law inspired other countries to take a firm stand against US torture, which in turn limited the government's ability to pursue its perceived interests. In a recent *Foreign Affairs* article, Douglas Johnson, Alberto Mora, and Averell

Schmidt document the strategic costs of the torture and rendition policy to long-term US interests, arguing that the policy hurt America because other institutions and countries believed in and enforced international human rights law.[47]

Human rights change is a long-term process that has experienced and will continue to experience dramatic setbacks, of which the Trump administration's stated indifference to international human rights law is the latest example. But this is far from the first time that the US government has opposed human rights movements. Concerted domestic efforts *in collaboration with* international pressures from foreign governments and human rights movements and institutions will be essential in mitigating the potential for the Trump administration to commit human rights violations. A closer look at the history of human rights ideas provides models of collaboration between domestic movements and international pressures, models that offer hope and guidance in this difficult moment. Rather than putting the idea of human rights aside, we need it now more than ever.

Making Human Rights Work

Patience and the knowledge that human rights and democracy are won by means of long, drawn-out effort should be the important takeaways of this book. The process of demanding and securing human rights has never been easy or without contestation. On the contrary, struggle and conflict are at the heart of this book as they are at the heart of the human rights movement. Starting in Bogotá with the American Declaration of the Rights and Duties of Man, I have followed the convoluted twists of human rights support through the Cold War and into the twenty-first century. Human rights progress was never spontaneous, nor was it the result of the natural evolution of law or global culture in the countries; moreover, it did not flow smoothly from the West and its Enlightenment tradition to the rest of the world. At each step, delay has been the rule, not the exception. Only with a long-term view can the trend towards progress be discerned. I believe that, in time, scholars too will look back at this period as a watershed in the path towards protecting human rights.

The first lessons for making human rights work are that our "so-lutions" cannot exacerbate those very conditions that we know are causes of human rights violations in the first place, especially war, authoritarianism, impunity, and dehumanizing or exclusionary ide-ologies. I have argued that war should not be seen as an important tool to promote human rights because research suggests that mili-tary intervention has no major effects on human rights and, at worst, it contributes to state repression.[48] Given the huge expense and suffering provoked by any war, such research underscores my belief that military intervention should be avoided in all but the most extreme situations, and then only used when authorized by the UN Security Council.

As regards dehumanization, we need to be aware of how we de-humanize other people and cultures and to guard against those practices. Today, some people in the United States and Western Eu-rope demonize Islamic fundamentalists in a way not very different from how the United States and many Latin American leaders spoke of communists, including elected communists, during the Cold War. Ideologies that dehumanize opponents are associated with more repression and with a logic of the ends justifying the means. Human rights progress requires a different approach. Human rights do not let the ends justify the means because the means are also the ends. In other words, if the well-being and rights of individual humans are the ends we seek, abusing those rights cannot be the means to that end. Finally, human rights do not lend themselves to dehuman-ization because they insist that every human has the same rights by virtue of being human.

When the concept of human rights works, it does so by support-ing people's aspirations and movements for rights, not by imposing rights from the outside. You cannot bomb a country into protecting rights. In the same way, you cannot destroy democracy in order to save it. The means are the ends and whatever change happens has to be consistent with rule of law. Some have called this argument "minimalist" in the sense that it focuses on procedural guarantees. If the national security ideology and violent revolutionary discourse are examples of maximalism, I welcome the contributions of mini-malism. To call them minimalist misses the essence of human rights, which is that the ultimate goals of human rights are as maximalist as any worldview, but there are limited means that can be used to reach those goals.

Conclusion

This book has focused on the legitimacy and effectiveness of human rights law, institutions, and movements. I have argued that both concepts—legitimacy and effectiveness—always involve comparison and so the crucial issue we have to engage is this question: "Compared to what?" Compared to other existing emancipatory norms, institutions, and practices, I argue human rights movements have been the most legitimate and most effective in promoting human well-being. Yet, because human rights tactics are mainly deliberative and nonviolent, the change human rights promotes comes slowly and only as a result of concerted struggles.

The future I foresee is one that involves continued struggles in the context of ongoing human rights violations. Effective movements can adapt the law and discourse of human rights to their advantage with innovative tactics, thus translating rights-based ideals into local and international practices. Where they succeed in leading to more democracy and to increasing the costs of repression for powerful leaders, conditions will improve—slowly, and with fits and starts.

My survey of past and current human rights research suggests that we are not at all in "the endtimes of human rights" or "the twilight of human rights law." On the contrary, we are in a period of vibrant dynamism in human rights movements, laws, and institutions. Recent developments around the world and in the United States have led some to despair, but by looking more carefully at the history of human rights and at current trends we can find hope for progress in spite of struggles and backlash. The two biggest factors correlated with human rights violations in the world are war and authoritarianism and we have seen both of these factors declining globally. Still, after a number of years of decline, the number of intrastate conflicts increased again in 2014 and 2015 and the number of democracies has not increased since 2000, which means more needs to be done to decrease war and enhance democracy in order to continue to provide human rights payoffs. Impunity for past human rights violations is another trigger for future violations. Although we are still awash in impunity, the rise of domestic and international processes and effective truth commissions has gradually begun to combat this as well.

Human rights processes are one set of tools that have contributed to improvements in some human rights outcomes around the world. Compared to other existing tools, such as the use of military intervention or an increase in foreign aid, the expenditures in time and money on human rights are not enormous; they are moderate and acceptable in relation to the outcomes we document. Within our imperfect world, it appears that human rights processes have promising results and should be further developed, enhanced, and diversified to continue successfully.

Shortly after the Trump election, a human rights activist ironically tweeted, "If only there was a set of universal ideals & values that humanity could unite around to counter xenophobic populism . . ."[49] We have such a set of universal ideals and values, embodied in international institutions, painstakingly constructed over decades through deliberation and struggle by a diverse set of actors, including leaders and activists from the Global South. These ideals were not imposed, but were consented to after endless hours of debate and through the legal ratification of dozens of international human rights treaties now endorsed by most countries of the world. They have been embodied in human rights institutions and used by activists worldwide to mobilize people and generate positive change. We need those ideals and institutions more than ever. We need our anger about injustices and about human rights violations. But we also need hope, resilience, and the belief that we can make a difference, and it is just that which I hope this book provides.

ACKNOWLEDGMENTS

SINCE I DEDICATED THIS BOOK to some of my mentors, I want to begin by acknowledging their influence on my work. Raymond (Bud) Duvall first introduced me to international relations theory, to dependency theory, and, most importantly, to what it meant to think rigorously when I was an undergraduate student at the University of Minnesota. Later, as his colleague for many years, I continued to benefit from his probing mind and generous spirit. My interest in human rights dates to my time as an exchange student in Uruguay and my work with a human rights organization after I finished my undergraduate degree. David Weissbrodt helped me secure that first job in human rights, and later, as my colleague and friend, taught me much of what I know about human rights law. The theoretical and philosophical origins of this book go back to graduate school days and, in particular, to my encounters with the work of Albert Hirschman. As a student in the early 1980s with a background in human rights activism, I initially felt the only choice I had was to embrace the economic determinism of the left if I wanted to confront the neo-realist structuralism that dominated international relations debates at the time. But I doubted the possibility and the efficacy of the economic, if not political, revolution that dependency theory called for. The more nuanced and hopeful work of Hirschman seemed to chart a different course—one where ideas and agency mattered and where change occurred in unexpected and gradual ways. I can't remember which of Hirschman's works I first encountered, but whether reading his critique of the economic determinants of democracy, his celebration of the work of reformmongers, or his condemnation of applying foreign and inappropriate models to Latin American development, his words resonated with my own lived experiences and prior research. Albert Hirschman later became a mentor and we discovered that we not only shared an interest in economic development in Latin America, but also in human rights.

Around the same time, John Ruggie was introducing me to ideas that he would later call constructivism and that dovetailed with possibilism; he provided a theoretical language to address these issues with an international relations (IR) audience. Ruggie also encouraged me to put together my interest in IR theory with my love for research in Latin America, something I have continued in this book. When I arrived in Argentina for research, Elizabeth Jelin first introduced me to social movement theory, showed how one could both be close to social movements and maintain a critical edge, and modeled what it meant to be a strong senior woman scholar (note that I learned this in Argentina and Brazil, where the research institutes at which I worked had many more senior women than the political science department at Columbia University). Robert Keohane furthered my understanding of systematic thinking and is a model of what it means to be a mentor and friend. He also demonstrated how to take risks and not be pigeonholed into doing only one kind of international relations. Each of the mentors I mention here has been a "trespasser," in the words of Albert Hirschman, moving from one discipline to another and across subfields in our disciplines.

I am grateful to the Radcliffe Institute for Advanced Study and the Harvard Kennedy School for nominating and appointing me as a Radcliffe Professor, with the great privilege of two years of research leave at Radcliffe. This book is a product of that privilege. Just walking through the Radcliffe Yard and into Byerly Hall each morning was an invitation into the life of the mind, while my work and teaching at that beehive we call the Kennedy School and at its Carr Center for Human Rights Policy meant that I always kept one foot in current debates over politics and policy. I recognize two generous families who supported the endowed chairs I held while writing this book, the Ryan family and the Pforzheimer family. I thank my very interdisciplinary Radcliffe human rights reading group— novelist V.V. Ganeshananthan, historians Tyrell Haberkorn and Irmtrud Wojak, legal scholar Carol Steiker, and philosopher John Tasioulas—for their thoughtful comments on an early chapter. I also thank Dean Lizabeth Cohen and Judith Vichniac, Associate Dean of the Radcliffe Fellowship Program, for their support. I'm particularly grateful to Radcliffe for helping me meet and hire the individual who most helped with all aspects of this book over three years, one of my Radcliffe undergraduate research partners, Jessica Tueller. Jessica joined my team of research partners at Radcliffe in 2014 and, together with Giovanna Robledo and Grayson Fuller, assisted with the early research on Latin American contributions to human rights. Later, I discovered Jessica was not only a great research assistant, but that she was also a helpful editor, organizer, corrector of copyedits, and producer of indices. She worked with me efficiently every step of the way, always with good humor and a can-do attitude. Carr Center Fellow Fernando Berdion del Valle helped supervise my research team at Radcliffe and later became my co-author on the topic of the history of human rights and duties. My faculty assistant, Derya Honça, also provided editorial assistance and perceptive comments and suggestions on the manuscript.

I owe an intellectual debt to a handful of co-authors who worked with me on articles where some of the ideas for this book germinated. In particular, I thank Geoffrey Dancy, a kindred intellectual spirit, who worked with me to formulate some of the arguments in chapter 6 and gave me permission to draw on some of our co-authored material. Likewise, Ann Marie Clark and I first developed some of the critique of the human rights measures I present in chapter 5, and I am grateful for her willingness to let me use some material from earlier drafts of our co-authored article. Finally, in chapter 6, I use material from a co-authored handbook chapter with Hans Peter Schmitz.

Beyond my co-authors, there are a series of scholars who influenced the manuscript in many ways. Foremost among them is César Rodríguez-Garavito; I am indebted to César for a whole series of exchanges and discussions that have spurred my thinking and writing on this book. I have benefitted greatly from reading much of what he has written, and his co-authored article on human rights critiques helped me locate the focus of this book on the two biggest challenges: legitimacy and effectiveness. I'm grateful to Liliana Obregón not only for her research on creole consciousness, but also for a tour of her hometown of Bogotá, including the sites where the American Declaration of the Rights and Duties of Man was drafted. We joked that we were the only two people who seemed to care that the first intergovernmental declaration of human rights had been written in those very buildings in Bogotá. One day I hope that the city of Bogotá will place a plaque on the Gimnasio Moderno building, recognizing that it was the place where the American Declaration of the Rights and Duties of Man was drafted.

My foray into the forgotten histories of human rights from the Global South has been such a longstanding intellectual obsession that I barely know how to thank all the people who influenced or helped me. I wrote my first article on the topic in 1997, stressing Latin American contributions to ideas of human rights and democracy promotion. My research has been informed at every stage by other scholars working in this area, ranging from Jan Herman Burgers, whose 1992 article "The Road to San Francisco," first got me started thinking, to Steven Jensen's 2016 book, *The Making of International Human Rights: The 1960s, Decolonization, and the Reconstruction of Global Values*, that fortunately came out just in time for his research to be included in this manuscript. The list of authors I have learned from on this topic is too great to mention all of them here, but their names and scholarship can be found in the text of the book, in my endnotes, and in the suggested further reading section.

My editors, Eric Weitz and Brigitta van Rheinberg, made multiple contributions to the book. They heard me out and supported me when I said I needed to write a rather different book than the one I had originally pitched to them about Latin American history. For their support, their excellent and detailed comments on the book proposal and the entire manuscript, and their marshaling of the most useful group of reviewers I can imagine, I am deeply appreciative. I am particularly grateful to Eric Weitz, not only for his own important work on the history of human rights, but also for suggesting that I incorporate some findings from research by a new set of historians of human rights in the context of decolonization and the Cold War more generally.

It is always difficult to thank anonymous reviewers, but I have rarely received more well-informed and thoughtful comments and suggestions than those provided by the reviewers for this book. Considering myself fortunate for such reviews, I tried to respond to almost all of their suggestions for revisions.

I want to thank Luis Moreno Ocampo for reminding me at various times to keep my focus on the real opponents of human rights:

the governments who repress their citizens and harass human rights NGOs, or that use human rights hypocritically to justify military interventions they wish to carry out for other reasons. I also want to thank the hundreds of people from the human rights institutions and movements I have interviewed over many years, including those I interviewed specifically for this book, in particular Heba Morayef, Lucia Nader, Sergio Aguayo, Doutje Lettinga, Tawakkol Karman, Jack Rendler, César Rodríguez-Garavito, Navi Pillay, Gaston Chillier, Paula Romo, Carolyn Patty Blum and Miguel Pulido. I also wish to thank all of the participants in two workshops organized by the Human Rights Lab at the University of los Andes in Colombia and the Open Society Foundations on the topic of "A Human Rights Crisis? A Proposal to Reflect, Reassess, and Retool" for their feedback on the draft of what became chapter 5 of this book. Special thanks to Holly Cartner for her careful read and supportive comments. I also wish to thank all the participants at a workshop organized at Brown University in 2015 on "Transnational Advocacy Networks: Reflecting on 15 years of Evolving Theory and Practice" for their comments and suggestions on a draft chapter of this book, and in particular Peter Evans, César Rodríguez-Garavito, Doutje Lettinga, Harsh Mander, Margaret Keck, Amanda Murdie, Louis Bickford, Cecelia Santos, Enrique Peruzzotti, Kathryn Hochstetler, Maritza Paredes, Daniela Ikawa, and Patrick Heller. Participants in a Workshop entitled "How Do We Know What We Know? Charting the Future for Human Rights Documentation and Analysis" at Arizona State University in 2015 gave me helpful comments on my paper and shared their own insights on issues related to chapter 5. I'm particularly grateful to organizers Reed Wood and Daniel Rothenberg and to participants Patrick Ball, Scott Edwards, Christopher Fariss, David Gartner, Milli Lake, and Will Moore.

I'm appreciative of comments and suggestions from colleagues at three workshops held at the Harvard Kennedy School, in Bogotá, Colombia, and at the Munk School at the University of Toronto, on teaching for a more strategic and outcome-oriented human rights practice. Thanks to members of the Harvard Human Rights Colloquium who commented either in writing or in person on chapter 1, including Mathias Risse, Beth Simmons, Jacqueline Bhabha, Gerald Neuman, Tyler Giannini, Phuong Pham, Patrick Vinck, Douglas

Johnson, Steven Pinker, Zachary Kaufman, Sam Moyn, and Sushma Raman. Thanks to my colleagues at the Harvard Kennedy School who attended and gave comments in response to a faculty research lunch talk, especially Malcolm Sparrow, Robert Putnam, Jane Mansbridge, and Archon Fung. Thanks to Katherine Marino, for her close read of and suggestions on chapter 3 and for permission to cite to her forthcoming book manuscript. In addition, for diverse forms of comments, assistance, and support, I would like to thank Charlie Clements, Brooke Coe, Shamila Daluwatte, Alastair Iain Johnston, Bridget Marchesi, Joseph Nye, Tamya Rebelo, Alejandro Chehtman, Fidelis Magalhaes, Maria Beatriz Bonna Nogueira, Stephen Northfield, Michelle Morais de Sa e Silva, Raymond Offenheiser, Richard Price, and Averell Schmidt.

I also want to recognize the collegiality of some scholars I refer to as the "critics" in this book. Some of critics I know well—James Ron, Jack Snyder, Leslie Vinjamuri, and Samuel Moyn. They have always been open to debate and have invited me to engage with them in diverse formats. I appreciate the genuine intellectual disagreements and stimulating exchanges we have had.

My husband, Douglas Johnson, has been both my inspiration and my best support for everything I have ever written. We have discussed virtually every argument in this book. I thank my parents for their lifetime of love and support, for their commitment to human rights, and for my mother's reading aloud my last book to my father as he grew blind. They motivated me to write another book that they might want to read aloud.

Chapter 1. Introduction: Anger, Hope, and the Belief You Can Make a Difference

1. In my thinking about this pessimism and critique, I am very much indebted to the survey of the literature organized by César Rodríguez-Garavito and his Human Rights Lab at the University of los Andes in Bogotá, Colombia, although I have organized my own categories and responses in a somewhat different way. César Rodríguez-Garavito and Sean Luna, of the Human Rights Lab at the University of los Andes, "A Human Rights Crisis? Unpacking the Debate on the Future of the Human Rights Field," in *The Future of Human Rights: Critique, Response, and Likely Scenarios* (unpublished manuscript). This article was originally a paper prepared for discussion at the Open Society Foundations & Human Rights Lab's workshop. For the paper see César Rodríguez-Garavito and Sean Luna, of the Human Rights Lab at the University of los Andes, "A Human Rights Crisis? Unpacking the Debate on the Future of the Human Rights Field," paper prepared for discussion at the Open Society Foundations & Human Rights Lab's workshop on the Future of Human Rights, Rio de Janeiro, March 8, 2016, https://static1.squarespace.com/static/557f5fe4e4b0a17c309a0dcd/t/58a8908c29687f223ffbe21e/148744207549.

2. Heba Morayef, interview with author, March 9, 2016, Rio de Janeiro, Brazil. All subsequent information on Morayef comes from this interview.

3. Heba Morayef, interview with author, March 9, 2016, Rio de Janeiro, Brazil.

4. Heba Morayef, interview with author, March 9, 2016, Rio de Janeiro, Brazil.

5. Sergio Aguayo, interview with author, May 26, 2016, Cambridge, MA. All statements by Aguayo in this paragraph come from this interview.

6. Kendra Dupuy, James Ron, and Aseem Prakash, "Foreign Aid to Local NGOs: Good Intentions, Bad Policy," *openDemocracy*, November 15, 2012, http://www.opendemocracy.net/kendra-dupuy-james-ron-aseem-prakash/foreign-aid-to-local-ngos-good-intentions-bad-policy.

7. Kendra Dupuy, James Ron, and Aseem Prakash, "What Drives the Crackdown on NGOs, and How Can It Be Stopped?," *openDemocracy*, April 22, 2016, https://www.opendemocracy.net/openglobalrights/kendra-dupuy-james-ron-aseem-prakash/what-drives-crackdown-on-ngos-and-how-can-it-b.

8. Harsh Mander, "India's Equivocal Engagement with Transnational Advocacy" (paper presented at Transnational Advocacy Networks: Reflecting on 15 years of Evolving Theory and Practice, Brown University, Providence, RI, April 30, 2015).

9. Jenna Johnson, "Trump Says 'Torture Works,' Backs Waterboarding and 'Much Worse,'" *Washington Post*, February 17, 2016, https://www.washingtonpost.com

/politics/trump-says-torture-works-backs-waterboarding-and-much-worse/2016/02
/17/4c9277be-d59c-11e5-b195-2e29a4e13425_story.html.

10. See "Full Executive Order Text: Trump's Actions Limiting Refugees into the U.S." *New York Times,* January 27, 2017, https://www.nytimes.com/2017/01/27/us /politics/refugee-muslim-executive-order-trump.html. In the first months of his presidency, Trump met with Egyptian President Abdel Fattah el-Sisi and Turkish President Recep Tayyip Erdogan. Tillerson's speech, "Remarks to US Department of State Employees," on May 3, 2017, can be found at the US Department of State Website: https:// www.state.gov/secretary/remarks/2017/05/270620.htm. For reactions, see an op-ed by John McCain, "Why We Must Support Human Rights," *New York Times,* May 8, 2017, https://www.nytimes.com/2017/05/08/opinion/john-mccain-rex-tillerson- human-rights.html.

11. Ban Ki-moon, "Opening Remarks at Press Conference with President Erdogan of Turkey at the World Humanitarian Summit" (speech, Istanbul, Turkey, May 24, 2016), http://www.un.org/apps/news/infocus/sgspeeches/print_full.asp?statID=3053.

12. Will Dahlgreen, "Chinese people are most likely to feel the world is getting better," YouGov UK, January 5, 2016, https://yougov.co.uk/news/2016/01/05/chinese -people-are-most-optimistic-world/.

13. Stephen Hopgood, *The Endtimes of Human Rights* (Ithaca, NY: Cornell University Press, 2013); Eric A. Posner, *The Twilight of Human Rights Law* (New York: Oxford University Press, 2014); Sebastian Strangio, "Welcome to the Post-Human Rights World: Geopolitical Alignments and the Rise of Populist Nationalism Have Unleashed a Global Backlash against Human Rights," argument, *Foreign Policy,* March 7, 2017, http://foreignpolicy.com/2017/03/07/welcome-to-the-post-human-rights -world/.

14. Posner, *The Twilight of Human Rights Law.*

15. Eric A. Posner, "Have Human Rights Treaties Failed?: Human Rights Law Is Too Ambitious and Ambiguous," opinion, *New York Times,* December 28, 2014, http:// www.nytimes.com/roomfordebate/2014/12/28/have-human-rights-treaties-failed.

16. See Jens David Ohlin, *The Assault on International Law* (New York: Oxford University Press, 2015).

17. Email sent to section members from the Section Chair of the ISA Human Rights Section, July 3, 2015.

18. Michael Ignatieff has called human rights the "lingua franca of global moral thought." Michael Ignatieff, *Human Rights as Politics and Idolatry,* University Center for Human Values Series (Princeton, NJ: Princeton University Press, 2001), 53.

19. For a comprehensive summary of the critical literature and some responses, see Rodríguez-Garavito and Luna, "A Human Rights Crisis?" The authors reviewed more than 250 academic articles, books, and blog posts from diverse disciplines, including political science, anthropology, sociology, and law.

20. The definition used by Mark Suchman from organizational theory focuses on an organization being desirable or appropriate. Mark Suchman, "Managing Legitimacy: Strategic and Institutional Approaches," *The Academy of Management Review* 20, no. 3 (1995): 574. I add the part about authenticity, which is drawn from discus-

sions of legitimacy and authenticity in language studies, because I believe authenticity is one key part of legitimacy in the human rights field. See Claire Kramsch, "Authenticity and Legitimacy in Multilingual Second Language Acquisition" (unpublished paper), http://cms.arizona.edu/index.php/multilingual/article/viewFile/9/20. I want to thank Sushma Raman for drawing my attention to authenticity as an aspect of legitimacy.

21. "Venezuela Must Uphold Rights of 'Even Those Who Disagree with State Policies' – UN Human Rights Chief," *UN News Centre*, November 12, 2015, http://www.un.org/apps/news/story.asp?NewsID=52537#.WFbJJIUnJUt.

22. In 1993/94, when I was granted tenure at the University of Minnesota, only 19% of full-time political science faculty were women. By 2014, a large survey of American Political Science Association members shows women accounted for 39% of full-time faculty. Lisa Brandes, et al., "The Status of Women in Political Science: Female Participation in the Professoriate and the Study of Women and Politics in the Discipline," *PS: Political Science & Politics*, June 1, 2001, http://www.apsanet.org/portals/54/Files/Status%20of%20Women/200106WmnReport.pdf. Also, *Pipeline to Tenure: Institutional Practices for Hiring, Mentoring, and Advancing Women in Academia: Report prepared by the APSA Committee for the Status of Women in the Profession (CSWP)*, accessed December 8, 2016, http://web.apsanet.org/cswp/wp-content/uploads/sites/4/2016/01/FINAL-Pipeline-Report-May2016.pdf.

23. The variation among countries does not necessarily follow the division between the developed and less developed world. In Japan, for example, women make up just 12.7% of the academics at the country's top-rated universities, while in Turkey, 47.5% of staff at the top five universities are female. Jack Grove, "Global Gender Index, 2013," *Times Higher Education (THE)*, May 2, 2013, https://www.timeshighereducation.com/features/global-gender-index-2013/2003517.article.

24. Eric Cameron, "Marriage Equality Takes Effect in Uruguay," *Human Rights Campaign*, August 5, 2013, http://www.hrc.org/blog/marriage-equality-takes-effect-in-uruguay/.

25. "Revolutionary Truth: Tunisian Victims Make History on First Night of Public Hearings for TDC," *International Center for Transitional Justice (ICTJ)*, November 17, 2016, https://www.ictj.org/news/tunisia-truth-dignity-public-hearings-live.

26. Kishore Mahbubani and Lawrence H. Summers, "The Fusion of Civilizations: The Case for Global Optimism," *Foreign Affairs* 95, no. 3 (2016): 127.

27. Hopgood, *The Endtimes of Human Rights*.

28. See Steven L. B. Jensen, *The Making of International Human Rights: The 1960s, Decolonization, and the Reconstruction of Global Values*, Human Rights in History (Cambridge: Cambridge University Press, 2016); Roland Burke, *Decolonization and the Evolution of International Human Rights* (Philadelphia: University of Pennsylvania Press, 2010).

29. I take the term "contentious history" from the title of a book by Christopher Roberts, *The Contentious History of the International Bill of Human Rights* (Cambridge: Cambridge University Press, 2015).

30. Navi Pillay, interview by author, May 5, 2016, Cambridge, MA.

31. Hopgood, *The Endtimes of Human Rights*; Posner, *The Twilight of Human Rights Law*; Mark Osiel, "The Demise of International Criminal Law," *Humanity Journal*, June 10, 2014, http://humanityjournal.org/blog/the-demise-of-international-criminal-law/.

32. Stephen Hopgood, "The Endtimes of Human Rights," in *Debating The Endtimes of Human Rights: Activism and Institutions in a Neo-Westphalian World*, Strategic Studies Project, ed. Doutje Lettinga and Lars Van Troost (Amnesty International Netherlands, 2014), https://www.amnesty.nl/sites/default/files/public/debating_the _endtimes_of_human_rights.pdf.

33. Hopgood, *The Endtimes of Human Rights*, xii.

34. Maria Brant, "Besides Human Rights, I Don't See a Solution for Serving the Victims," *Sur International Journal on Human Rights, English Ed.* 11, no. 20 (December 2014): 90–95.

35. Raquel Rolnik, "UN Special Procedures System Is 'Designed to Be Ineffective,'" *Sur International Journal on Human Rights, English Ed.* 11, no. 20 (December 2014): 80–88.

36. I draw on a co-authored article with Ann Marie Clark. Ann Marie Clark and Kathryn Sikkink, "Information Effects and Human Rights Data: Is the Good News about Increased Human Rights Information Bad News for Human Rights Measures?" *Human Rights Quarterly* 35, no. 3 (2013): 539–568.

37. Albert O. Hirschman, *A Bias for Hope: Essays on Development and Latin America* (New Haven: Yale University Press, 1971).

38. Albert Hirschman explains that one reason why it is hard for social scientists to talk about ethics is that modern social science arose "in the process of *emancipating* itself from traditional moral teachings." Albert O. Hirschman, "Morality and the Social Sciences: A Durable Tension," in *Essays in Trespassing: Economics to Politics and beyond* (Cambridge: Cambridge University Press, 1981), 294–306.

39. I am grateful to Richard Price because, under his prodding, I first tried to outline an explicit approach to the ethics of human rights that combines attention to normative issues and to empirical research findings.

40. Hirschman, "Morality and the Social Sciences," 305–6.

41. Amartya Sen, "Rights and Agency," in *Consequentialism and Its Critics*, ed. Samuel Scheffler, Oxford Readings in Philosophy (Oxford: Oxford University Press, 1988), 187–223; Martha C. Nussbaum, *Women and Human Development: The Capabilities Approach* (Cambridge: Cambridge University Press, 2000); John Tasioulas, "Human Rights, Legitimacy, and International Law," *American Journal of Jurisprudence* 58 (2013): 1–25; Charles R. Beitz, *The Idea of Human Rights* (Oxford: Oxford University Press, 2009); Mathias Risse, *On Global Justice* (Princeton, NJ: Princeton University Press, 2012).

42. I thank Erin Kelly for this categorization of "practical" or "functional" philosophers of human rights. Erin Kelly, " 'Practical' Philosophical Theories of Human Rights" (memo, Radcliffe Exploratory Seminar on Human Rights Studies Today, Harvard University, Cambridge, September 2015).

43. Jack Donnelly, *Universal Human Rights in Theory and Practice*, 2nd ed. (Ithaca, NY: Cornell University Press, 2003), 40.

44. Richard M. Price, ed., *Moral Limit and Possibility in World Politics*, Cambridge Studies in International Relations 107 (Cambridge: Cambridge University Press, 2008). Similar points have been made by Joseph S. Nye, *Nuclear Ethics* (New York: Free Press, 1986); J. L. Holzgrefe and Robert O. Keohane, *Humanitarian Intervention: Ethical, Legal, and Political Dilemmas* (Cambridge: Cambridge University Press, 2003), 50–51.

45. See, e.g., Dursun Peksen, "Does Foreign Military Intervention Help Human Rights?," *Political Research Quarterly* 65, no. 3 (2012): 558–571; James David Meernik, Steven C. Poe, and Erum Shaikh, "The Use of Military Force to Promote Human Rights," in *Conflict Prevention and Peacebuilding in Post-War Societies: Sustaining the Peace*, ed. T. David Mason and James David Meernik, Contemporary Security Studies (London: Routledge, 2006), 160–76.

46. Here I use categories developed in some of my earlier work, especially, Kathryn Sikkink, "The Role of Consequences, Comparison, and Counterfactuals in Constructivist Ethical Thought," in *Moral Limit and Possibility in World Politics*, ed. Richard M. Price, Cambridge Studies in International Relations 107 (Cambridge: Cambridge University Press, 2008), 83–111.

47. This devaluing of democracy is significant because one of the most important explanations for the rise and fall of democracy in Latin America is whether political groups believe in it. The fact that fewer and fewer groups expressed belief in and support for democracy contributed to the downfall of democratic regimes. Scott Mainwaring, *Democracies and Dictatorships in Latin America: Emergence, Survival, and Fall* (Cambridge: Cambridge University Press, 2013).

48. Hirschman, *A Bias for Hope*; Albert O. Hirschman, *Journeys toward Progress: Studies of Economic Policy-Making in Latin America* (New York: Greenwood Press, 1968); Philipp H. Lepenies, "Possibilism: An Approach to Problem-Solving Derived from the Life and Work of Albert O. Hirschman," *Development and Change* 39, no. 3 (2008): 437–459.

49. Lepenies, "Possibilism," 448.

50. Jeremy Adelman, *Worldly Philosopher: The Odyssey of Albert O. Hirschman* (Princeton, NJ: Princeton University Press, 2013), 453; Hirschman, *A Bias for Hope*; Hirschman, *Journeys toward Progress*.

51. Albert O. Hirschman, "The Search for Paradigms as a Hindrance to Understanding," *World Politics: A Quarterly Journal of International Relations* 22, no. 3 (1970): 329–343. Also, see Hirschman's introduction to the book by David P. Ellerman, *Helping People Help Themselves: From the World Bank to an Alternative Philosophy of Development Assistance*, Evolving Values for a Capitalist World (Ann Arbor: University of Michigan Press, 2005), xvii–xviii.

52. Hirschman, *Journeys toward Progress*.

53. Some of this appears in Saul D. Alinsky's most famous book, *Rules for Radicals: A Practical Primer for Realistic Radicals* (New York: Random House, 1971), but John-

son recalls this particular formulation from a training course he did with Alinsky in Chicago in the late 1960s.

Chapter 2. Response to the Critics: How to Evaluate the Legitimacy and Effectiveness of Human Rights

1. Doutje Lettinga, telephone interview by author, January 25, 2016.

2. Stephen Hopgood, "The Endtimes of Human Rights."

3. Samuel Moyn, "Human Rights and the Age of Inequality," in *Can Human Rights Bring Social Justice?: Twelve Essays*, ed. Doutje Lettinga and Lars van Troost (Amnesty International Netherlands, 2015), 13–18, https://www.amnesty.nl/content/uploads /2015/10/can_human_rights_bring_social_justice.pdf.

4. Doutje Lettinga and Lars van Troost, "Introduction," in *Can Human Rights Bring Social Justice?: Twelve Essays*, ed. Doutje Lettinga and Lars van Troost (Amnesty International Netherlands, 2015), 9, https://www.amnesty.nl/sites/default/files /public/can_human_rights_bring_social_justice.pdf.

5. Doutje Lettinga, "How Revolutionary Are Global Human Rights?," *Open Global Rights*, May 13, 2015, https://www.opendemocracy.net/openglobalrights/doutje-lettinga/how-revolutionary-are-global-human-rights.

6. David Kennedy, "International Human Rights Movement: Part of the Problem?" *Harvard Human Rights Journal* 15 (2002): 24.

7. Patrick Corrigan, "G8 Must Put Rights at Heart of Decisions," *Amnesty International UK*, June 17, 2013, https://www.amnesty.org.uk/blogs/belfast-and-beyond/g8 -must-put-rights-heart-decisions.

8. Rodríguez-Garavito and Luna, "A Human Rights Crisis?"

9. Martha Finnemore, "Legitimacy, Hypocrisy, and the Social Structure of Unipolarity: Why Being a Unipole Isn't All It's Cracked Up to Be," *World Politics* 61, no. 1 (2009): 58–85 at 61; Ian Hurd, "Legitimacy and Authority in International Politics," *International Organization* 53, no. 2 (1999): 379–98 at 381.

10. Linz proposes and uses this definition to think about the legitimacy of governments, but it is useful also when thinking about other institutions, including international institutions. Juan J. Linz, *The Breakdown of Democratic Regimes: Crisis, Breakdown, & Reequilibration* (Baltimore: Johns Hopkins University Press, 1978).

11. Linz, *The Breakdown of Democratic Regimes*.

12. Mark Suchman, "Managing Legitimacy," 574.

13. Paulo Sérgio Pinheiro in interview with Maria Brant, as quoted in "Besides Human Rights, I Don't See a Solution for Serving the Victims," *Sur International Journal on Human Rights, English Ed.* 11, no. 20 (December 2014): 90–95.

14. Stephen Hopgood, *The Endtimes of Human Rights*; David Kennedy, "Boundaries in the Field of Human Rights: The International Human Rights Movement: Part of the Problem?," *Harvard Human Rights Journal* 15 (2002): 99–317.

15. See, for example, Tony Evans, *US Hegemony and the Project of Universal Human Rights*, Southampton Studies in International Policy (Houndmills: Macmillan Press, 1996).

16. Samuel Moyn, *The Last Utopia: Human Rights in History* (Cambridge, MA: Belknap Press, 2010).

17. Moyn, *The Last Utopia*. The book is inconsistent in its argument at times; it recognizes that the human rights concept emerges earlier, but that the 1970s "put the concept into general circulation," (p. 125) or, "was a global human rights revolution," but more often uses the term "emergence" to refer to human rights in the 1970s (p. 116, p. 121, 217, etc.). A leading US-based human rights advocate, Aryeh Neier, has made a similar argument in his book, *The International Human Rights Movement: A History* (Princeton, NJ: Princeton University Press, 2012). Neier chooses to locate the genesis of the movement in the 1970s, the same time as the organizations he very courageously helped establish (the Helsinki Committee and Human Rights Watch).

18. Moyn, *The Last Utopia*, 181, 183, 200, 143.

19. Roland Burke, *Decolonization and the Evolution of International Human Rights*; Steven L. B. Jensen, *The Making of International Human Rights*.

20. David Kennedy, "The International Human Rights Regime: Still Part of the Problem?" in *Examining Critical Perspectives on Human Rights*, ed. Robert Dickinson et al. (Cambridge: Cambridge University Press, 2012), 19-34 at 20–21.

21. Alfred William Brian Simpson, *Human Rights and the End of Empire: Britain and the Genesis of the European Convention* (Oxford: Oxford University Press, 2004).

22. See, for example, Kathryn Sikkink, *Mixed Signals: U.S. Human Rights Policy and Latin America* (Ithaca, NY: Cornell University Press, 2004).

23. Johnson, "Trump Says 'Torture Works,' Backs Waterboarding and 'Much Worse.'"

24. Kathryn Sikkink, "From Pariah State to Global Protagonist: Argentina and the Struggle for International Human Rights," *Latin American Politics and Society* 50, no. 1 (April 1, 2008): 1–29.

25. Brooke Coe, "Regional Identities and Dynamic Normative Orders in the Global South: A Comparative Study" (Ph.D. diss., University of Minnesota, 2015), http://search.proquest.com/docview/1731233146/.

26. Here I draw on some of my earlier work, especially Sikkink, "The Role of Consequences, Comparison and Counterfactuals in Constructivist Ethical Thought."

27. On this issue, see, for example, Matthew J. Gibney, *The Ethics and Politics of Asylum: Liberal Democracy and the Response to Refugees* (Cambridge: Cambridge University Press, 2004).

28. Mathias Risse, "World Society and Pluralist Internationalism" (unpublished manuscript, August 1, 2015).

29. Amartya Sen, *The Idea of Justice* (Cambridge, MA: Belknap Press of Harvard University Press, 2009).

30. I am indebted to César Rodríguez-Garavito for drawing to my attention the similarities of my approach in this book to Sen's two concepts of justice.

31. Beth A. Simmons, "Twilight or Dark Glasses? A Reply to Eric Posner," *openDemocracy*, December 23, 2014, https://www.opendemocracy.net/openglobalrights/beth-simmons/twilight-or-dark-glasses-reply-to-eric-posner.

32. This compliance continuum elaborates further on a diagram and idea already present in Ann Marie Clark, "The Normative Context of Human Rights Criticism: Treaty Ratification and UN Mechanisms," in *The Persistent Power of Human Rights: From Commitment to Compliance*, ed. Thomas Risse, Stephen C. Ropp, and Kathryn Sikkink, Cambridge Studies in International Relations 126 (Cambridge: Cambridge University Press, 2013), 125–44. I also draw on insights from Xinyuan Dai, in her chapter in the same volume, "The 'Compliance Gap' and the Efficacy of International Human Rights Institutions," 85–102.

33. Corrigan, "G8 Must Put Rights at Heart of Decisions."

34. FAO, IFAD, and WFP, *The Multiple Dimensions of Food Security*, The State of Food Insecurity in the World (Rome: FAO, 2013).

35. World Hunger Education Service, "2016 World Hunger and Poverty Facts and Statistics," *World Hunger*, accessed December 11, 2016, http://www.worldhunger.org /2015-world-hunger-and-poverty-facts-and-statistics/.

36. The Convention on the Elimination of All Forms of Discrimination against Women (CEDAW) says in Article 11 that women have the right to, "equal remuneration, including benefits, and to equal treatment in respect of work of equal value." United Nations Entity for Gender Equality and the Empowerment of Women, *Convention on the Elimination of All Forms of Discrimination against Women*, United Nations (New York: United Nations, 1979), http://www.un.org/womenwatch/daw /cedaw/text/econvention.htm#article11.

37. "The Wage Gap Over Time," National Committee on Pay Equity, accessed March 2, 2017, http://www.pay-equity.org/info-time.html.

38. Moyn, *The Last Utopia*, 218.

39. David Kennedy, "The International Human Rights Regime: Still Part of the Problem?," in *Examining Critical Perspectives on Human Rights*, ed. Robert Dickinson et al. (Cambridge: Cambridge University Press, 2012), 19–34 at 24.

40. Samuel Moyn, "Human Rights and the Age of Inequality."

41. Doutje Lettinga and Lars van Troost, eds., *Can Human Rights Bring Social Justice?: Twelve Essays* (Amnesty International Netherlands, 2015), https://www .amnesty.nl/sites/default/files/public/can_human_rights_bring_social_justice.pdf.

42. Samuel Moyn, "Human Rights and the Age of Inequality."

43. Doutje Lettinga and Lars van Troost, eds., *Can Human Rights Bring Social Justice?*

44. Errol Black and Jim Silver, "We have a floor, now we need a ceiling: reducing Canada's income inequalities," Canadian Centre for Policy Alternatives, Manitoba Office, February 4, 2010, https://www.policyalternatives.ca/publications/commentary /fast-facts-we-have-floor-now-we-need-ceiling.

45. See the video of the event at, "History and Human Rights: A Panel Discussion," YouTube video, 2:02:39, from a panel discussion, posted by Jacqueline Bhabha, December 1, 2016, https://www.youtube.com/watch?v=LozSSje2tpc&index=1&list=PL2 SOU6wwxB0vZEgAvRotf9-INc9nA8t02.

46. Kennedy, "The International Human Rights Regime: Still Part of the Problem?," 24.

47. Moyn, "Human Rights and the Age of Inequality," 16.

48. See, for example, Moyn, "Human Rights and the Age of Inequality"; Mary Nolan, "Human Rights and Market Fundamentalism," Max Weber Lecture Series (Fiesole, Italy: European University Institute, 2014); Costas Douzinas, "Seven Theses on Human Rights: (3) Neoliberal Capitalism & Voluntary Imperialism," *Critical Legal Thinking*, May 23, 2013, http://criticallegalthinking.com/2013/05/23/seven-theses-on-human-rights-3-neoliberal-capitalism-voluntary-imperialism/; David Harvey, *A Brief History of Neoliberalism* (New York: Oxford University Press, 2005); Wendy Brown, "'The Most We Can Hope For . . .': Human Rights and the Politics of Fatalism," *The South Atlantic Quarterly* 103, no. 2 (2004): 451–463.

49. Douzinas, "Seven Theses on Human Rights." See also Moyn, "Human Rights and the Age of Inequality."

50. Nolan, "Human Rights and Market Fundamentalism," 1.

51. Jason Hickel, "A Short History of Neoliberalism (And How We Can Fix It)," *New Left Project*, April 9, 2012, http://www.newleftproject.org/index.php/site/article_comments/a_short_history_of_neoliberalism_and_how_we_can_fix_it.

52. Hickel, "A Short History of Neoliberalism (And How We Can Fix It)"; John Gerard Ruggie, "International Regimes, Transactions, and Change: Embedded Liberalism in the Postwar Economic Order," *International Organization* 36, no. 2 (1982): 379–415.

53. Jean H. Quataert, *Advocating Dignity: Human Rights Mobilizations in Global Politics*, Pennsylvania Studies in Human Rights (Philadelphia: University of Pennsylvania Press, 2009).

54. Nolan, "Human Rights and Market Fundamentalism," 4.

55. Costas Douzinas, for example, appears to cite Robert Cooper, a senior British diplomat during the Blair administration, making a reference to "voluntary imperialism" as if Cooper were a spokesperson for the human rights movement. Douzinas, "Seven Theses on Human Rights."

56. Moyn, "Human Rights and the Age of Inequality."

57. Eduardo Salvador Arenas Catalán, "Back to the Future: Human Rights Protection beyond the Rights Approach," in *Can Human Rights Bring Social Justice?: Twelve Essays*, ed. Doutje Lettinga and Lars van Troost (Amnesty International Netherlands, 2015), 41–46, https://www.amnesty.nl/sites/default/files/public/can_human_rights_bring_social_justice.pdf.

58. Hopgood, "The Endtimes of Human Rights," 14.

59. Navi Pillay, interview by author, May 5, 2016, Cambridge, MA.

60. Kathryn Sikkink, *The Justice Cascade: How Human Rights Prosecutions Are Changing World Politics* (New York: W. W. Norton & Co., 2011).

61. Hun Joon Kim and Kathryn Sikkink, "Explaining the Deterrence Effect of Human Rights Prosecutions for Transitional Countries," *International Studies Quarterly* 54, no. 4 (2010): 939–963.

62. Mark Osiel, *Mass Atrocity, Collective Memory, and the Law* (New Brunswick, NJ: Transaction Publishers, 1997).

63. Osiel, "The Demise of International Criminal Law."

64. Osiel, "The Demise of International Criminal Law."

65. See the database at Transnational Justice Research Collaborative (The National Science Foundation and the Arts and Humanities Research Council) accessed January 28, 2017, https://transitionaljusticedata.com/.

66. Osiel, "The Demise of International Criminal Law."

67. See Milli Lake, "Organizing Hypocrisy: Providing Legal Accountability for Human Rights Violations in Areas of Limited Statehood," *International Studies Quarterly* 58, no. 3 (2014): 515–526; Milli Lake, Ilot Muthaka, and Gabriella Walker, "Gendering Justice in Humanitarian Spaces: Opportunity and (Dis)empowerment Through Gender-Based Legal Development Outreach in the Eastern Democratic Republic of Congo," *Law & Society Review* 50, no. 3 (2016): 539–574. See also, Lake's forthcoming book, *UnderStating Human Rights: Gender Justice and Transnational Advocacy in the Democratic Republic of Congo and South Africa* (Cambridge: Cambridge University Press, expected 2018).

68. Sikkink, *The Justice Cascade*, chap. 7.

69. Donnelly, *Universal Human Rights in Theory and Practice*.

70. Anonymous, Skype interview by author, February 2, 2016.

71. Alex de Waal, "Writing Human Rights and Getting It Wrong," *Boston Review*, June 6, 2016, http://bostonreview.net/world/alex-de-waal-writing-human-rights.

72. De Waal, "Writing Human Rights and Getting It Wrong."

73. See, for example, "Is the United States Immune to the Justice Cascade?" in Sikkink, *The Justice Cascade*, chap. 7.

74. De Waal, "Writing Human Rights and Getting It Wrong."

75. See, for example, Julie Flint and Alex de Waal, "Case Closed: A Prosecutor without Borders," *World Affairs* (Spring 2009), http://www.worldaffairsjournal.org/article/case-closed-prosecutor-without-borders.

76. Hopgood, *The Endtimes of Human Rights*.

77. Albert O. Hirschman, *The Rhetoric of Reaction: Perversity, Futility, Jeopardy* (Cambridge, MA: Belknap Press, 1991), 153.

Chapter 3. The Diverse Political Origins of Human Rights

1. I want to thank Fernando Berdion del Valle, Grayson Fuller, Giovanna Robledo, and Jessica Tueller for research assistance for this chapter.

2. See, e.g., Hopgood, *The Endtimes of Human Rights*; Kennedy, "The International Human Rights Regime: Still Part of the Problem?."

3. Chaim Kaufmann and Robert Pape, "Explaining Costly International Moral Action: Britain's Sixty-Year Campaign against the Atlantic Slave Trade," *International Organization* 53, no. 4 (1999): 631–668.

4. Krasner has argued that these early humanitarian campaigns were undertaken only when they were initiated by powerful states. Stephen D. Krasner, *Sovereignty: Organized Hypocrisy* (Princeton, NJ: Princeton University Press, 1999).

5. Robert William Fogel, *Without Consent or Contract: The Rise and Fall of American Slavery*, 1st ed. (New York: W. W. Norton & Co., 1989), 410.

6. For the complete texts of all the international and regional treatises, agreements, and other instruments on human rights to which I refer throughout this work see Human Rights Library online from the University of Minnesota, accessed March 18, 2017, http://hrlibrary.umn.edu/treaties.htm.

7. For example, Lynn Hunt, *Inventing Human Rights: A History* (New York: W. W. Norton & Co., 2007); Mary Ann Glendon, *A World Made New: Eleanor Roosevelt and the Universal Declaration of Human Rights* (New York: Random House, 2001); Johannes Morsink, *The Universal Declaration of Human Rights: Origins, Drafting, and Intent*, Pennsylvania Studies in Human Rights (Philadelphia: University of Pennsylvania Press, 1999); Paul Gordon Lauren, *The Evolution of International Human Rights: Visions Seen* (Philadelphia: University of Pennsylvania Press, 2003), chaps. 6–7.

8. Tom J. Farer, "The Rise of the Inter-American Human Rights Regime: No Longer a Unicorn, Not Yet an Ox," *Human Rights Quarterly* 19, no. 3 (1997): 510–546.

9. The American Declaration was first approved by the Ninth International Conference of American States at Bogotá, Colombia, in April 1948. The Organization of American States (OAS) was also created at the Bogotá meeting; the America Declaration was formally adopted later by a unanimous vote of the newly-formed OAS.

10. Even Morsink, who is both meticulous in his history and fully records the Latin American contribution, mistakenly interprets the timeline, saying, "When new rights were first introduced into the earliest draft of the UDHR, in June to December 1947, the Bogota Declaration of April 1948 had not yet been drafted." Morsink, *The Universal Declaration of Human Rights*, 132. Morsink was aware of the draft produced by the Inter-American Juridical Committee, but he doesn't recognize it as the first draft of the Bogotá Declaration, though it was, just as Humphrey's Secretariat Draft was the first draft of the UDHR.

11. Kathryn Sikkink, "Reconceptualizing Sovereignty in the Americas: Historical Precursors and Current Practices," *Houston Journal of International Law* 19, no. 3 (1996–97): 705–724 at 705; Margaret E. Keck and Kathryn Sikkink, *Activists beyond Borders: Advocacy Networks in International Politics* (Ithaca, NY: Cornell University Press, 1998), 80–89; Sikkink, *Mixed Signals*, chap. 2.

12. Mary Ann Glendon, "The Forgotten Crucible: The Latin American Influence on the Universal Human Rights Idea," *Harvard Human Rights Journal* 16 (2003): 27–39; Greg Grandin, "The Liberal Traditions in the Americas: Rights, Sovereignty, and the Origins of Liberal Multilateralism," *American Historical Review* 117, no. 1 (2012): 68–91; Greg Grandin, "Human Rights and Empire's Embrace," in *Human Rights and Revolutions*, ed. Jeffrey N. Wasserstrom, 2nd ed. (Lanham, MD: Rowman & Littlefield Publishers, 2007): 191–212; Morsink, *The Universal Declaration of Human Rights*; Susan Waltz, "Universalizing Human Rights: The Role of Small States in the Construction of the Universal Declaration of Human Rights," *Human Rights Quarterly* 23 (2001): 44–72; Liliana Obregón, "The Colluding Worlds of the Lawyer, the Scholar and the Policymaker: A View of International Law from Latin America," *Wisconsin International Law Journal* 23, no. 1 (2005): 145–172; Paolo Carozza, "From

Conquest to Constitutions: Retrieving a Latin American Tradition of the Idea of Human Rights," *Human Rights Quarterly* 25, no. 2 (2003): 281–313; Jan Herman Burgers, "The Road to San Francisco: The Revival of the Human Rights Idea in the Twentieth Century," *Human Rights Quarterly* 14, no. 4 (1992): 447–478 at 450; Rainer Huhle, "Latinoamérica: Continente de la paz y los derechos humanos," *Nürnberger Menschenrechtszentrum* (2007): 1–17, http://d-nb.info/991186621/34; Rainer Huhle, "América Latina y la fundamentación del sistema internacional de protección de los derechos humanos después de la Segunda Guerra Mundial," *Memoria: Revista sobre cultura, democracia y derechos humanos* 4 (2008): 33–43; Patrick William Kelly, "On the Poverty and Possibility of Human Rights in Latin American History," *Humanity: An International Journal of Human Rights, Humanitarianism, and Development* 5, no. 3 (2014): 435–450.

13. Pamela Slotte and Miia Halme-Tuomisaari, eds., *Revisiting the Origins of Human Rights* (Cambridge: Cambridge University Press, 2015).

14. Morsink, *The Universal Declaration of Human Rights*.

15. Sikkink, "Reconceptualizing Sovereignty in the Americas."

16. Carozza, "From Conquest to Constitutions."

17. Christian Reus-Smit, *Individual Rights and the Making of the International System* (Cambridge: Cambridge University Press, 2013); Paulina Ochoa Espejo, "Paradoxes of Popular Sovereignty: A View from Spanish America," *The Journal of Politics* 74, no. 4 (2012): 1053–65.

18. Espejo, "Paradoxes of Popular Sovereignty."

19. Adam Przeworski, *Democracy and the Limits of Self-Government*, Cambridge Studies in the Theory of Democracy (Cambridge: Cambridge University Press, 2010), 50.

20. See, for example, Luis van Isschot's study of the social origins of modern human rights advocacy in Colombia based on the struggles of the early 1900s of oil workers in the Magdalena Medio region. Luis van Isschot, *The Social Origins of Human Rights* (Madison: University of Wisconsin Press, 2015).

21. Ann Van Wynen Thomas, *The Organization of American States* (Dallas: Southern Methodist University Press, 1963); G. Pope Atkins, *Latin America in the International Political System* (New York: Free Press, 1977). On the Betancourt Doctrine, see Leslie Bethell and Ian Roxborough, "Introduction: The Postwar Conjuncture in Latin America: Democracy, Labor, and the Left," in *Latin America Between the Second World War and the Cold War: Crisis and Containment, 1944-1948*, ed. Leslie Bethell and Ian Roxborough (Cambridge: Cambridge University Press, 1997), 1–32.

22. Examples include proposals by Juan Bautista Alberdi in 1844, the Tobar Doctrine in 1907, two treaties drawn up by Central American states in the early 1900s, declarations at the 1936 Inter-American Conference in Buenos Aires, and the Betancourt Doctrine in the 1950s. See Thomas, *The Organization of American States*, 214–18.

23. Jorge I. Domínguez, "International Cooperation in Latin America: The Design of Regional Institutions by Slow Accretion," ed. Amitav Acharya and Alastair I. John-

ston, *Crafting Cooperation: Regional Institutions in Comparative Perspective* (Cambridge: Cambridge University Press, 2007), 83–128.

24. See, for example, Louise Fawcett, "Between West and Non-West: Latin American Contributions to International Thought," *International History Review* 34, no. 4 (December 1, 2012): 679–704. See also Ivan I. Jaksic, *Andrés Bello: Scholarship and Nation-Building in Nineteenth-Century Latin America*, Cambridge Latin American Studies 87 (Cambridge: Cambridge University Press, 2001).

25. Domínguez, "International Cooperation in Latin America"; Donald Richard Shea, *The Calvo Clause: A Problem of Inter-American and International Law and Diplomacy* (Minneapolis: University of Minnesota Press, 1955), 140; Manuel R. García-Mora, "The Calvo Clause in Latin American Constitutions and International Law," *Marquette Law Review* 33 (1949): 205–219 at 206–8.

26. Eduardo Ricardo Pérez Calvo, *Vida y trabajos de Carlos Calvo* (Buenos Aires: Ediciones Dunken, 1996), chap. 1.

27. Espejo, "Paradoxes of Popular Sovereignty."

28. "The Mexican Constitution of 1917 with Amendments through 2015," The Constitute Project, accessed March 17, 2017, https://www.constituteproject.org/constitution/Mexico_2015?lang=en.

29. Álvarez presented his draft to the American Institute of International Law in 1917 as part of a larger project, but it is not mentioned in the final act of the Havana conference, and was not finalized and approved until 1932. René Brunet, *La garantie internationale des droits de l'homme d'après la charte de San-Francisco* (Geneva: Grasset, 1947), 87; "Final Act of the Havana Meeting of the American Institute of International Law," *The American Journal of International Law* 11, no. 2 (1917): 47–53.

30. For a discussion of the contenders, see Burgers, "The Road to San Francisco"; Dzovinar Kevonian, "André Mandelstam and the Internationalization of Human Rights," in *Revisiting the Origins of Human Rights*, ed. Pamela Slotte and Miia Halme (Cambridge: Cambridge University Press, 2015), 239–66; Huhle, "Latinoamérica"; Helmut Philipp Aust, "From Diplomat to Academic Activist: André Mandelstam and the History of Human Rights," *European Journal of International Law = Journal Europeen de Droit International* 25, no. 4 (2014): 1105–1121; Huhle, "América Latina y la fundamentación del sistema internacional de protección de los derechos humanos después de la Segunda Guerra Mundial."

31. Ricardo Joaquín Alfaro and United Nations Conference on International Organization, *Derechos y libertades fundamentales del hombre* (Panama: Imprenta Nacional, 1946), 5.

32. For example, Hopgood, *The Endtimes of Human Rights*.

33. Burgers, "The Road to San Francisco." On Mandelstam, see Kevonian, "André Mandelstam and the Internationalization of Human Rights."

34. Burgers, "The Road to San Francisco," 450–59; Jan Herman Burgers, interview by author, November 13, 1993, The Hague, Netherlands; Huhle, "Latinoamérica." On Mandelstam, also see Aust, "From Diplomat to Academic Activist."

35. Eric D. Weitz, "From the Vienna to the Paris System: International Politics and

the Entangled Histories of Human Rights, Forced Deportations, and Civilizing Missions," *The American Historical Review* 113, no. 5 (2008): 1313–1343.

36. Weitz, "From the Vienna to the Paris System."

37. A. Dirk Moses, "Raphael Lemkin, Culture, and the Concept of Genocide," in *The Oxford Handbook of Genocide Studies*, ed. A. Dirk Moses (Oxford: Oxford University Press, 2010), 19–41.

38. William Korey, "Raphael Lemkin: The Unofficial Man," *Midstream*, July 1989, 45–48. See also, Philippe Sands, *East West Street: On the Origins of "Genocide" and "Crimes against Humanity"* (New York: Alfred A. Knopf, 2016).

39. The Fifth International Conference for the Unification of Penal Law, held in cooperation with the First Committee of the League of Nations. Raphael Lemkin, *Axis Rule in Occupied Europe; Laws of Occupation, Analysis of Government, Proposals for Redress* (Washington, DC: Carnegie Endowment for International Peace, 1944).

40. Sands, *East West Street*.

41. Burgers, "The Road to San Francisco." Burgers surveyed European political thought in this period and was surprised by the failure of intellectuals and opinion leaders to reassert the human rights idea.

42. H.G. Wells, *The Times*, 23 October 1939, as cited in Burgers, "The Road to San Francisco," 494.

43. Hersch Lauterpacht, *An International Bill of the Rights of Man* (New York: Columbia University Press, 1945).

44. Manu Bhagavan, *India and the Quest for One World: The Peacemakers*, Palgrave Macmillan Transnational History Series (New York: Palgrave Macmillan, 2013), 3.

45. As cited in Gordon Connell-Smith, *The Inter-American System* (London: Oxford University Press, 1966), 142.

46. Eduardo Rodriguez Larreta, "Inter-American Solidarity: Safeguarding the Democratic Ideal: Note from Uruguayan Foreign Minister to Secretary of State," *Bulletin*, November 25, 1945, 865–66.

47. Simpson, *Human Rights and the End of Empire*, 39.

48. See Sikkink, *Mixed Signals*, chap. 2; Azza Salama Layton, *International Politics and Civil Rights Policies in the United States, 1941–1960* (Cambridge: Cambridge University Press, 2000); Mary L. Dudziak, *Cold War Civil Rights: Race and the Image of American Democracy*, Politics and Society in Twentieth-Century America (Princeton, NJ: Princeton University Press, 2011).

49. As cited in Lauren, *The Evolution of International Human Rights*, 165.

50. The differences between Wells and Hull on the contours of the postwar order played out in other issues in addition to human rights, including debates over development. See Eric Helleiner, *Forgotten Foundations of Bretton Woods: International Development and the Making of the Postwar Order* (Ithaca: Cornell University Press, 2014).

51. Lauren, *The Evolution of International Human Rights*, 162, 164–65, 167.

52. Jacob Robinson, *Human Rights and Fundamental Freedoms in the Charter of the United Nations: A Commentary*, From War to Peace (New York: Institute of Jewish Affairs, 1946), 17.

53. Brian Urquhart, *Ralph Bunche: An American Life*, 1st ed. (New York: W. W. Norton & Co., 1993), 113.

54. M. Glen Johnson, "The Contributions of Eleanor and Franklin Roosevelt to the Development of International Protection for Human Rights," *Human Rights Quarterly* 9 (1987): 19–48 at 24.

55. Lauren, *The Evolution of International Human Rights*, 174–179; Sumner Welles, *Where Are We Heading?* (New York: Harper & Brothers, 1946), 34.

56. Inter-American Juridical Committee, *The Dumbarton Oaks Proposals: Preliminary Comments and Recommendations of the Inter-American Juridical Committee* (Washington, DC: Pan American Union, 1944), 2, 5–7.

57. "Inter-American Conference on Problems of War and Peace, Final Act," in *Report of the Delegation of the United States of America to the Inter-American Conference on Problems of War and Peace, Mexico, February 21–March 8, 1945* (Washington, DC: U.S. Government Printing Office, 1946).

58. *Report of the Delegation of the United States of America to the Inter-American Conference on Problems of War and Peace, Mexico, February 21–March 8, 1945* (Washington, DC: U.S. Government Printing Office, 1946); Morsink, *The Universal Declaration of Human Rights*, 130–1.

59. Inter-American Juridical Committee, *Draft Declaration of the International Rights and Duties of Man and Accompanying Report* (Washington, DC: Pan American Union, 1946), 57–58.

60. Specifically, Moyn argues, "In my recent work on these matters, my general thesis has been that through this lost and misremembered transwar era, it is best to see human rights as a project of the Christian right for the most part, not the secular left." Samuel Moyn, "Christian Human Rights: An Introduction," *The Immanent Frame: Secularism, Religion, and the Public Sphere* (blog) 2015, http://blogs.ssrc.org /tif/2015/05/29/christian-human-rights-an-introduction/.

61. Katherine Marino, "The Vanguard of Feminist Demands" in *The Vanguard for Women's Rights: Pan-American Feminism and the Origins of Human Rights* (Chapel Hill: University of North Carolina Press, forthcoming), chapter 8.

62. This includes twelve countries from Western Europe, the United States, Canada, New Zealand, and Australia. Another six came from the USSR and Eastern Europe (including three states representing the USSR itself—the Ukrainian Soviet Socialist Republic, the Byelorussian Soviet Socialist Republic, and the USSR).

63. South Africa (under white minority rule) is not included in either group. India was there in an observer capacity since it had not yet achieved full independence. *Documents of the United Nations Conference on International Organization, San Francisco, 1945* (New York: UN Information Organizations, 1945), volume 3.

64. See for example, Sikkink, "Reconceptualizing Sovereignty in the Americas"; Morsink, *The Universal Declaration of Human Rights*; Glendon, "Forgotten Crucible."

65. Morsink, *The Universal Declaration of Human Rights*, 130.

66. Lauren, *The Evolution of International Human Rights*, 337, footnote 86.

67. Urquhart, *Ralph Bunche*, 118.

68. Urquhart, *Ralph Bunche*.

69. "Charter of the United Nations," United Nations, accessed March 18, 2017, http://www.un.org/en/charter-united-nations/.

70. Urquhart, *Ralph Bunche*, 122.

71. The term critical juncture comes from the literature on historical institutionalism. See, for example, Giovanni Capoccia and R. Daniel Kelemen, "The Study of Critical Junctures: Theory, Narrative, and Counterfactuals in Historical Institutionalism," *World Politics* 59, no. 3 (2007): 341–369.

72. "New Uruguayan Proposals on the Dumbarton Oaks Proposals," in *Documents of the United Nations Conference on International Organization, San Francisco, 1945*, 3:34.

73. "Statement of Uruguayan Delegation of Its Position with Reference to Chapters I and II of the Charter as Considered by Committee I/1," in *Documents of the United Nations Conference on International Organization, San Francisco, 1945* (New York: UN Information Organizations, 1945), 6:628–33.

74. "Report of Rapporteur, Subcommittee I/1/A (Farid Zeineddine, Syria), to Committee I/1," in *Documents of the United Nations Conference on International Organization, San Francisco, 1945*, 6:705.

75. Fabian Klose, *Human Rights in the Shadow of Colonial Violence*, trans. Dona Geyer (Philadelphia: University of Pennsylvania Press, 2013), 35–36.

76. *Documents of the United Nations Conference on International Organization, San Francisco, 1945*, 3:293 (emphasis added).

77. Bhagavan, *India and the Quest for One World*.

78. "Charter of the United Nations," United Nations, accessed March 18, 2017, http://www.un.org/en/charter-united-nations/.

79. As cited in Bhagavan, *India and the Quest for One World*, 68.

80. The American republics were ahead because they had requested a draft declaration of rights from the Inter-American Juridical Committee at the Mexico City conference in 1945—before the San Francisco Conference. The American Declaration process thus had a head start on the process of drafting; the UDHR had to wait to get started until after the San Francisco meeting and ratifications of the UN Charter. Huhle, "Latinoamérica."

81. The UN Nuclear Preparatory Committee held its first meetings in April and May 1946. Inter-American Juridical Committee, *Draft Declaration of the International Rights and Duties of Man and Accompanying Report*; Morsink, *The Universal Declaration of Human Rights*, 4.

82. See Fernando Berdion del Valle and Kathryn Sikkink, "(Re)discovering Duties: Individual Responsibilities in the Age of Rights," *Minnesota Journal of International Law* 26, no. 1 (2017): 189–245.

83. Carozza, "From Conquest to Constitutions," 12.

84. This entire section on rights and duties draws on co-authored work with Fernando Berdion del Valle, and I thank him for permission to use some of it here. See Berdion del Valle and Sikkink, "(Re)discovering Duties: Individual Responsibilities in the Age of Rights."

85. Carozza, "From Conquest to Constitutions," 12.

86. "American Declaration of the Rights and Duties of Man, 1948," Inter-American Commission on Human Rights, accessed March 18, 2017, http://www.cidh.oas.org /Basicos/English/Basic2.american%20Declaration.htm.

87. Jorge Contesse, "Inter-American Constitutionalism: The Interaction between Human Rights and Progressive Constitutional Law in Latin America," in *Law and Society in Latin America: A New Map*, ed. César Rodríguez-Garavito, Law, Development, and Globalization (New York: Routledge, 2015), 220–34.

88. Alan Watson, *Legal Transplants: An Approach to Comparative Law*, Virginia Legal Studies (Charlottesville: University Press of Virginia, 1974).

89. Dardo Regules, *La lucha por la justicia y por el derecho; apuntes sobre la IX Conferencia Panamericana reunida en Bogotá durante el mes de abril de 1948* (Montevideo: Barreiro y Ramos, 1949), 97.

90. Morsink, *The Universal Declaration of Human Rights*, 130.

91. John P. Humphrey, *Human Rights & the United Nations: A Great Adventure* (Dobbs Ferry, NY: Transnational Publishers, 1984), 31–32.

92. The Panamanian draft was prepared by the American Law Institute and the Chilean draft was prepared by the Inter-American Juridical Committee of the OAS. Morsink, *The Universal Declaration of Human Rights*, 131.

93. Morsink, *The Universal Declaration of Human Rights*.

94. Glendon, *A World Made New*; Morsink, *The Universal Declaration of Human Rights*; Humphrey, *Human Rights & the United Nations*.

95. All citations and information in this paragraph come from Morsink, *The Universal Declaration of Human Rights*, 245–46.

96. All the citations in this paragraph are from Morsink, *The Universal Declaration of Human Rights*, 247, 249.

97. Morsink, *The Universal Declaration of Human Rights*.

98. Klose, *Human Rights in the Shadow of Colonial Violence*, 39.

99. Bhagavan, *India and the Quest for One World*, 71–74.

100. UNDAW 2003 as cited in Glendon, "Forgotten Crucible."

101. Marino, "The Vanguard of Feminist Demands."

102. Marino, "The Vanguard of Feminist Demands."

103. Marino, "The Vanguard of Feminist Demands."

104. "Charter of the United Nations," United Nations, accessed March 18, 2017, http://www.un.org/en/charter-united-nations/.

105. This history has been meticulously documented in new work by Katherine Marino and by Torild Skard, and confirmed both in the memoires of US delegate Virginia Gildersleeve and in a short memo Lutz wrote about her work and that of other women at the San Francisco Conference. See Marino, "The Vanguard of Feminist Demands"; Torild Skard, "Getting Our History Right: How Were the Equal Rights of Women and Men Included in the Charter of the United Nations?," *Forum for Development Studies* 35, no. 1 (June 1, 2008): 37–60; Bertha Lutz, "Women at the Conference in San Francisco," trans. Victoria Junqueira (Museu Virtual of Brazil, n.d.), http://lhs.unb.br/bertha/wp-content/uploads/2013/02/San-Francisco-Conference -Report.pdf.

106. Marino, "The Vanguard of Feminist Demands."

107. Lutz, Notes on the San Francisco Conference, as seen by Bertha Lutz, Pleni-potentiary Brazilian Delegate (0780) ABFPF, as quoted in Marino, "The Vanguard of Feminist Demands."

108. Lutz, Notes on the San Francisco Conference, as seen by Bertha Lutz, Pleni-potentiary Brazilian Delegate (0780) ABFPF as quoted in Marino, "The Vanguard of Feminist Demands"; Lutz to Catt, May 21, 1945, Reel 12, NAWSA Papers as quoted in Marino, "The Vanguard of Feminist Demands."

109. Lutz, "Women at the Conference in San Francisco."

110. Lutz, "Women at the Conference in San Francisco."

111. Lutz, "Women at the Conference in San Francisco."

112. Bhagavan, *India and the Quest for One World*, 69–70.

113. Morsink, *The Universal Declaration of Human Rights*, 118.

114. Morsink, *The Universal Declaration of Human Rights*, 118.

115. The general public and human rights scholars do not know of Lutz and Ber-nardino, but a number of historians of women and feminism have acknowledged their work for some time. See, in particular, Leila J. Rupp, *Worlds of Women: The Making of an International Women's Movement* (Princeton, NJ: Princeton University Press, 1997); Glenda Sluga, *Internationalism in the Age of Nationalism* (Philadelphia: University of Pennsylvania Press, Inc, 2013); Rachel Soihet, *O feminismo tático de Bertha Lutz*, Série Feministas (Florianópolis, SC: Editora Mulheres, 2006); Ellen DuBois and Lauren Derby, "The Strange Case of Minerva Bernardino: Pan American and United Nations Women's Right Activist," *Women's Studies International Forum* 32, no. 1 (2009): 43–50.

116. The virtual museum was created by Teresa Cristina de Novaes Marques. It can be found at http://lhs.unb.br/bertha/.

117. In *A World Made New: Eleanor Roosevelt and the Universal Declaration of Human Rights*, Mary Ann Glendon not only details the work of Roosevelt, but also stresses the rich roles played by other important actors in the drafting the UDHR: Charles Malik of Lebanon, Peng-chun Chang of China, René Cassin of France, Hernán Santa Cruz of Chile, Carlos Romulo of the Philippines, Hansa Mehta of India, and Alexei Pavlov of the USSR. I give less attention here to the crucial roles of Charles Malik, Peng-chun Chang, and René Cassin because Glendon, Morsink, and others have discussed them at length.

118. This relates to what Louise Fawcett has argued when she says that Latin America is neither fully "Western" nor "non-Western." Fawcett, "Between West and Non-West."

119. Liliana Obregón, email interview by author, September 18, 2014. Cambridge, MA.

120. The most well-known definition of "creole" is a European descendant born in the Americas. Liliana Obregón, "Between Civilization and Barbarism: Creole Interventions in International Law," *Third World Quarterly* 27, no. 5 (2006): 815–832 at 817.

121. Arnulf Becker Lorca, "Writing the History of International Law," Paper pre-

sented at the First SJD Association Workshop, Harvard Law School, Cambridge, MA, May 9, 2015.

122. Glendon, *A World Made New*, 69–70.

123. Bonny Ibhawoh, *Imperialism and Human Rights: Colonial Discourses of Rights and Liberties in African History*, SUNY Series in Human Rights (Albany: State University of New York Press, 2007), 143–44.

124. A similar point has been made about Latin American human rights activists in the 1970s by Patrick William Kelly in his forthcoming book, *Salvation in Small Steps: Latin America and the Making of Global Human Rights Politics* (unpublished manuscript, n.d.).

125. On transnational advocacy networks, see Keck and Sikkink, *Activists beyond Borders*.

126. Eric Pace, "Carlos P. Romulo of Philippines Dies," *The New York Times*, December 16, 1985, http://www.nytimes.com/1985/12/16/world/carlos-p-romulo-of-philippines-dies.html?pagewanted=all.

127. Carlos P. Romulo, "The Philippine Pattern," *Far Eastern Survey* 13, no. 14 (1944): 125–129 at 129.

128. Glenn Mitoma, *Human Rights and the Negotiation of American Power* (Philadelphia: University of Pennsylvania Press, 2013), 75–76.

129. Mitoma, *Human Rights and the Negotiation of American Power*, 101.

130. Marino, "The Vanguard of Feminist Demands."

131. Rainer Huhle, when discussing the memoire of Victor Andrés Belaunde of Peru and specifically Belaunde's participation in the San Francisco Conference, for example, says, "his position is permeated by a strong Hispanic-Latin American regional pride, which led to a firm opposition to the decisions of the great powers at Dumbarton Oaks." Huhle, "Latinoamérica."

132. Gayatri Chakravorty Spivak, "Can the Subaltern Speak?," in *The Post-Colonial Studies Reader*, ed. Bill Ashcroft, Gareth Griffiths, and Helen Tiffin (London: Routledge, 1995), 24–28.

133. A more action-oriented form of subaltern studies comes from Boaventura de Sousa Santos and César Rodríguez-Garavito, who propose an approach they call "subaltern cosmopolitan legality." César Rodríguez-Garavito and Boaventura de Sousa Santos, eds., *Law and Globalization from Below: Towards a Cosmopolitan Legality*, Cambridge Studies in Law and Society (Cambridge: Cambridge University Press, 2005).

134. Rom Harré, 1993, as cited in Colin Wight, *Agents, Structures and International Relations: Politics as Ontology*, Cambridge Studies in International Relations 101 (Cambridge: Cambridge University Press, 2006), 210.

135. Katherine Marino reminded me that, although Bertha Lutz was in some ways an outlier in her own society, she and her feminist group deeply influenced popular political discourse in Brazil and set in motion national legislative change for women. Katherine Marino, conversation with author, April 11, 2016, Cambridge, MA.

136. Waltz, "Universalizing Human Rights."

137. Miia Halme-Tuomisaari, "Lobbying for Relevance: American Internationalist, French Civil Libertarians and the UDHR," in *Revisiting the Origins of Human Rights*, ed. Pamela Slotte and Miia Halme-Tuomisaari (Cambridge: Cambridge University Press, 2015), 330–361 at 331–32.

138. Sands, *East West Street*.

139. Regules, *La lucha por la justicia y por el derecho*, 93.

140. Mauricio García Villegas, "Ineffectiveness of the Law and the Culture of Non-compliance with Rules in Latin America," in *Law and Society in Latin America: A New Map*, ed. César Rodríguez-Garavito, Law, Development, and Globalization (New York: Routledge, 2015), 63–80.

141. Hopgood, *The Endtimes of Human Rights*, x.

142. Regules, *La lucha por la justicia y por el derecho*, 126.

Chapter 4. The Struggle for Human Rights during the Cold War

1. I am indebted to Jo-Marie Burt for helping me understand the intricacies of this case. See her reports of the ongoing legal struggles against impunity in Guatemala, "Guatemala Trials before the National Courts of Guatemala," the International Justice Monitor, last modified January 17, 2017, http://www.ijmonitor.org/category/guatemala-trials/ as well as her other work on the subject, such as Jo-Marie Burt, "Historic Verdict in Guatemala's Genocide Case Overturned by Forces of Impunity," *NACLA Report on the Americas* 46, no. 2 (2013): 1–3.

2. Comisión para el Esclarecimiento Histórico, *Guatemala: Memory of Silence = Tz'inil Na'tab'al; Report of the Commission for Historical Clarification, Conclusions and Recommendations*, 2nd ed. (Guatemala: CEH, 1998), http://www.aaas.org/sites/default/files/migrate/uploads/mos_en.pdf ; "Truth Commission: Guatemala," United States Institute of Peace, accessed June 17, 2016, http://www.usip.org/publications/truth-commission-guatemala.

3. For a discussion of the challenges to the amnesty law in Guatemala, see transitionaljusticedata.com, under 1996 amnesty law, challenges at https://transitionaljusticedata.com/browse/index/Browse.mechanism:amnesties/Browse.countryid:48. Geoff Dancy, et al., 2014 "The Transitional Justice Research Collaborative: Bridging the Qualitative-Quantitative Divide with New Data," Transitional Justice Research Collaborative, last updated 2014, https://transitionaljusticedata.com.

4. CICIG has many of the attributes of an international prosecutor, but it operates under Guatemalan law, in the Guatemalan courts, and it follows Guatemalan criminal procedure. See CICIG: The International Commission against Impunity in Guatemala, accessed June 18, 2016, http://www.cicig.org/index.php?page=about for more information.

5. King used the phrase many times, including in his speech during the march at Selma in 1965. A similar phrase was first used in an 1853 sermon by Parker. "Theodore Parker and the Moral Universe," All Things Considered, National Public Radio, September 2, 2010, http://www.npr.org/templates/story/story.php?storyId=129609461.

6. Jack Snyder and Leslie Vinjamuri, "Trials and Errors: Principle and Pragmatism in Strategies of International Justice," *International Security* 28, no. 3 (2004): 5–44.

7. Boaventura de Sousa Santos, *If God Were a Human Rights Activist*, Stanford Studies in Human Rights (Palo Alto, CA: Stanford University Press, 2015).

8. See, e.g., Moyn, "Human Rights and the Age of Inequality"; Arenas Catalán, "Back to the Future."

9. Albert O. Hirschman, "Political Economics and Possibilism," in his *A Bias for Hope: Essays on Development and Latin America* (New Haven: Yale University Press, 1971), 1–37.

10. Moyn, *The Last Utopia*.

11. My focus in this chapter will be more on diplomatic history, but there is also rich social history on human rights struggles in specific times and places throughout the region. See, for example, van Isschot, *The Social Origins of Human Rights*; Steve J. Stern, *Resistance, Rebellion, and Consciousness in the Andean Peasant World, 18th to 20th Centuries* (Madison: University of Wisconsin Press, 1987).

12. Jensen, *The Making of International Human Rights*, 46.

13. Andrew Moravcsik, "The Origins of Human Rights Regimes: Democratic Delegation in Postwar Europe," *International Organization* 54, no. 2 (2000): 217–252.

14. Jensen, *The Making of International Human Rights*.

15. Simpson, *Human Rights and the End of Empire*, 2–13.

16. The legal committee of the Council of Europe did not recommend the creation of a similar organization in Europe until over a year later, in September 1949. Moravcsik, "The Origins of Human Rights Regimes."

17. The Brazilian resolution affirmed that, "there is no properly guaranteed right without the protection of a court; and that when it comes to internationally recognized rights, judicial protection, in order to be effective, must emanate from an international organ." "Proyecto de resolución sobre la creación de una Corte Interamericana destinada a garantizar los derechos del hombre, documento publicado con la clasificación CB-125/C.VI-6," in *Actas y documentos* (Bogotá, Colombia: Novena Conferencia Internacional Americana, 1948), 6:464–65 (my translation).

18. Specifically, the Inter-American Juridical Committee said, in response to the Brazilian resolution to prepare a Statute for a new Inter-American Court of Human Rights, that "the lack of positive law on the subject is a serious obstacle to the preparation of such a Statute," and that it would be "advisable first to prepare a Convention." Inter-American Council of Jurists, *Inter-American Court to Protect the Rights of Man* (Washington, DC: Department of International Law, Pan American Union, 1953), 2.

19. Brian J. Bosch, *Balaguer and the Dominican Military: Presidential Control of the Factional Officer Corps in the 1960s and 1970s* (Jefferson, NC: McFarland & Co., 2007), 30.

20. Aníbal Luis Barbagelata and Justino Jiménez de Aréchaga, "Prólogo," in *Escritos y discursos*, Ediciones del Instituto Artigas del Servicio Exterior (Montevideo: República Oriental del Uruguay, Ministerio de Relaciones Exteriores, Instituto Artigas del Servicio Exterior, 1992), 11.

21. Piero Gleijeses, *Shattered Hope: The Guatemalan Revolution and the United States, 1944–1954* (Princeton, NJ: Princeton University Press, 1991).

22. Gleijeses, *Shattered Hope*.

23. Inter-American Conference, *Décima conferencia interamericana, Caracas, Venezuela, 10 al 28 de marzo de 1954: actas y documentos*, Conferencias y organismos 39 (Washington, DC: Unión Panamericana, 1956), 157–158.

24. Inter-American Conference, *Décima conferencia interamericana*, 265.

25. For a detailed discussion of this debate, linked to the Bricker Amendment, see Sikkink, *Mixed Signals*.

26. Organization of American States, General Secretariat, *Quinta reunión de consulta de ministros de relaciones exteriores. Santiago de Chile, 12 al 18 de agosto de 1959. Actas y documentos*, OEA/Ser.F/III.5 (Washington, DC: Unión Panamericana, 1961), 316.

27. See Sikkink, *Mixed Signals*, chap. 2; Layton, *International Politics and Civil Rights Policies in the United States, 1941–1960*; Dudziak, *Cold War Civil Rights*.

28. Inter-American Conference, *Décima conferencia interamericana*, 192.

29. In Caracas, the Guatemalan ambassador stressed that one of the goals of the revolution of 1944 was to turn Guatemala into a modern capitalist country. Inter-American Conference, *Décima conferencia interamericana*, 282.

30. Gleijeses, *Shattered Hope*, 147–148, 164.

31. Gleijeses, *Shattered Hope*, 268.

32. "Declaration of Solidarity for the Preservation of the Political Integrity of the American States Against International Communist Intervention Adopted by the Tenth Inter-American Conference," March 28, 1954, *The Avalon Project, Yale Law School* http://avalon.law.yale.edu/20th_century/intam10.asp.

33. Justino Jiménez de Aréchaga, *Escritos y discursos*, Ediciones del Instituto Artigas del Servicio Exterior (Montevideo: República Oriental del Uruguay, Ministerio de Relaciones Exteriores, Instituto Artigas del Servicio Exterior, 1992), 260–61 (my translation).

34. See, in particular, Jensen, *The Making of International Human Rights*; Burke, *Decolonization and the Evolution of International Human Rights*; Klose, *Human Rights in the Shadow of Colonial Violence*.

35. Moyn has argued that decolonization was not about human rights. Moyn, *The Last Utopia*. For an alternative interpretation, see, e.g., Burke, *Decolonization and the Evolution of International Human Rights*; Jensen, *The Making of International Human Rights*.

36. Burke, *Decolonization and the Evolution of International Human Rights*, 148.

37. Jensen, *The Making of International Human Rights*, 2.

38. Klose, *Human Rights in the Shadow of Colonial Violence*, 5.

39. Jan-Miller Muller, 2010, as cited in Jensen, *The Making of International Human Rights*, 3.

40. Frederick Cooper quoted in Jensen, *The Making of International Human Rights*, 278.

41. Burke, *Decolonization and the Evolution of International Human Rights*.

42. Eric Weitz charts how the term self-determination moved from an Enlightenment concept related to individuals having self-knowledge, and being capable of emancipation, to being about nations and collective rights. Eric D. Weitz, "Self-determination: How a German Enlightenment idea became the slogan of national liberation and a human right," *American Historical Review* 120 no. 2 (2015): 462–496.

43. Burke, *Decolonization and the Evolution of International Human Rights.*

44. G. N. Uzoigwe, "Pan-Africanism in World Politics: The Geopolitics of the Pan-African Movements, 1900–2000," in *Pan-Africanism and the Politics of African Citizenship and Identity*, ed. Toyin Falola and Kwame Essien, Routledge African Studies (New York: Routledge, 2014), 214–246 at 227. See also, Coe, "Regional Identities and Dynamic Normative Orders in the Global South."

45. Quataert, *Advocating Dignity*, 73; Klose, *Human Rights in the Shadow of Colonial Violence*, 22.

46. Uzoigwe, "Pan-Africanism in World Politics."

47. Audie Klotz, *Norms in International Relations: The Struggle against Apartheid*, Cornell Studies in Political Economy (Ithaca, NY: Cornell University Press, 1995).

48. Gary J. Bass, "The Indian Way of Humanitarian Intervention," *The Yale Journal of International Law* 40, no. 2 (2015): 227–294 at 247.

49. The UN eventually designated 1968 as International Human Rights Year.

50. Ervand Abrahamian, "The 1953 Coup in Iran," *Science & Society* 65, no. 2 (Summer 2001): 182–215 at 186.

51. Stephen Kinzer, *All the Shah's Men: An American Coup and the Roots of Middle East Terror* (Hoboken, NJ: John Wiley & Sons, 2003), 69–70.

52. Kinzer, *All the Shah's Men*, 71, 82.

53. Abrahamian, "The 1953 Coup in Iran," 186–187.

54. Shiva Balaghi, "Silenced Histories and Sanitized Autobiographies: The 1953 CIA Coup in Iran," *Biography* 36, no. 1 (2013): 71–96 at 85, 87; Mark J. Gasiorowski, "The CIA Looks Back at the 1953 Coup in Iran," *Middle East Report*, no. 216 (2000): 4–5 at 4.

55. Francis J. Gavin, "Politics, Power, and U.S. Policy in Iran, 1950–1953," *Journal of Cold War Studies* 1, no. 1 (January 1, 1999): 56–89.

56. Abrahamian, "The 1953 Coup in Iran," 204.

57. Abrahamian, "The 1953 Coup in Iran," 182, 194.

58. Gavin, "Politics, Power, and U.S. Policy in Iran, 1950–1953," 65–66.

59. Abrahamian, "The 1953 Coup in Iran," 211, 217.

60. James Risen, "New York Times Special Report: The C.I.A. in Iran," *The New York Times*, 2000, http://www.nytimes.com/library/world/mideast/041600iran-cia-index.html.

61. Balaghi, "Silenced Histories and Sanitized Autobiographies."

62. Stephen R. Weissman, "Opening the Secret Files on Lumumba's Murder," *Washington Post*, July 21, 2002, http://www.udel.edu/globalagenda/2003/student/readings/CIAlumumba.html.

63. Stephen R. Weissman, "What Really Happened in Congo," *Foreign Affairs* 93, no. 4 (2014): 14–24; Weissman, "Opening the Secret Files on Lumumba's Murder";

Edouard Bustin, "Remembrance of Sins Past: Unraveling the Murder of Patrice Lumumba," *Review of African Political Economy* 29, no. 93/94 (2002): 537–60.

64. Select Committee to Study Governmental Operations with Respect to Intelligence Activities, "Draft Assassination Report [Pages Missing]," Top Secret, Report, 1 (October 16, 1975).

65. Weissman, "What Really Happened in Congo," 14.

66. René Lemarchand, "The C.I.A. in Africa: How Central? How Intelligent?," *Journal of Modern African Studies* 14, no. 3 (1976): 401–26 at 410.

67. Lemarchand, "The C.I.A. in Africa," 404.

68. "Document 5 – Paper Prepared in the Central Intelligence Agency: CIA Position in Belgian Congo RE Political Action Operations" in *Foreign Relations of the United States, 1964–1968, Volume XXIII, Congo, 1960–1968* - Historical Documents - Office of the Historian," accessed March 20, 2016, https://history.state.gov/historical documents/frus1964-68v23/d5.

69. Christian Parenti, "In Search of Lumumba," *In These Times*, January 30, 2008, http://inthesetimes.com/article/3500/in_search_of_lumumba.

70. Parenti, "In Search of Lumumba."

71. Gary Jonathan Bass, *The Blood Telegram: Nixon, Kissinger, and a Forgotten Genocide*, 1st ed. (New York: Alfred A. Knopf, 2013), xii–xiii.

72. Syed Badrul Ahsan, "Bangladesh since 1971: How Far Has It Come?," *Asian Affairs* 36, no. 2 (July 2005): 149–57 at 152.

73. Bass, *The Blood Telegram*, 24, xiv.

74. Pratap Bhanu Mehta, as cited in Bass, "The Indian Way of Humanitarian Intervention," 229.

75. Bass, "The Indian Way of Humanitarian Intervention," 229.

76. Jensen, *The Making of International Human Rights*, 186.

77. Jensen, *The Making of International Human Rights*.

78. Burke, *Decolonization and the Evolution of International Human Rights*.

79. Burke, *Decolonization and the Evolution of International Human Rights*, 94.

80. Uzoigwe, "Pan-Africanism in World Politics," 227. This paragraph draws heavily on Jensen, *The Making of International Human Rights*, 108–117.

81. As cited in Coe, "Regional Identities and Dynamic Normative Orders in the Global South," 166.

82. See, for example, Carrie Booth Walling, *All Necessary Measures: The United Nations and Humanitarian Intervention*, 1st ed., Pennsylvania Studies in Human Rights (Philadelphia: University of Pennsylvania Press, 2013).

83. *Discurso del Excmo. Senor Raul Roa Garcia, Ministro de Relaciones Exteriores de Cuba, Pronunciado en la Sesion Plenaria Celebrada el 17 de Agosto de 1959*, Documento 93 (Santiago, Chile: Organization of American States, Fifth Meeting of Consultation of Ministers of Foreign Affairs, 1959).

84. *Discurso del Excmo. Senor Raul Roa Garcia*, 342 (my translation).

85. This was at the 1960 conference in San José, Costa Rica. Seventh Meeting of Consultation of Ministers of Foreign Affairs of American States, "XIII Preparation of the Final Act," August 22-29, 1960, http://www.oas.org/council/MEETINGS%20OF%20CONSULTATION/Actas/Acta%207.pdf at 13.

86. Seventh Meeting of Consultation of Ministers of Foreign Affairs of American States, "Appendix 5: Doc. 51: Political Stability and Underdevelopment, Draft Resolution," August 22–29, 1960, http://www.oas.org/council/MEETINGS%20OF%20 CONSULTATION/Actas/Acta%207.pdf 31–32 at 32.

87. Che Guevara, *Venceremos!: The Speeches and Writings* (New York: Macmillan, 1968), 158.

88. John Dreier, *The OAS and the Hemisphere Crisis*, Harper and Row, for the Council on Foreign Relations, New York, 1962, p. 132, as cited in Cecilia Medina Quiroga, *The Battle of Human Rights: Gross, Systematic Violations and the Inter-American System* (Dordrecht: Martinus Nijhoff Publishers, 1988), 67.

89. Medina Quiroga, *The Battle of Human Rights*, 70.

90. William Wipfler, telephone interview by author, April 29, 1996.

91. David Weissbrodt, "The Role of Intergovernmental Organizations in the Implementation of Human Rights," *Texas International Law Journal* 12, no. 2 (1977): 293–320 at 314.

92. William Wipfler, telephone interview by author, April 29, 1996.

93. Medina Quiroga, *The Battle of Human Rights*, 82, 83.

94. Genaro R. Carrió, *El sistema americano de derechos humanos*, Derechos humanos: temas y problemas 2 (Buenos Aires: Editorial Universitaria de Buenos Aires, 1987), 21–22.

95. Inter-American Commission on Human Rights, Organization of American States (OAS) Official Records, *"Third Report on the Situation of Human Rights in Chile,"* February 11, 1977, http://www.cidh.org/countryrep/Chile77eng/INDEX.htm; Inter-American Commission on Human Rights, Organization of American States (OAS) Official Records, "Report on the Situation of Human Rights in Haiti," February 9, 1995, http://www.ijdh.org/wp-content/uploads/2010/02/1995-ICHR-Report -Haiti.pdf; Inter-American Commission on Human Rights, Organization of American States (OAS) Official Records, "Report on the Situation of Human Rights in El Salvador," September 29, 1999, https://www.cidh.oas.org/annualrep/99eng/Merits /UnitedStates10.951.htm.

96. Inter-American Commission on Human Rights, Organization of American States (OAS) Official Records, "Report on the Situation of Human Rights in Argentina," April 11, 1980, http://www.cidh.org/countryrep/Argentina80eng/toc.htm.

97. Inter-American Court for Human Rights, Case of Velásquez Rodríguez v. Honduras, Inter-Am.Ct.H.R. (Ser. C) No. 4 (1988), http://www.refworld.org/docid/40279a 9e4.html.

98. Bhagavan, *India and the Quest for One World*, 109–13. Other developing countries that supported the idea of two Covenants included China, Brazil, and Venezuela.

99. United Nations, María del Carmen Almeida de Quinteros et. al. v. Uruguay, Communication No. 107/1981, U.N. Doc. CCRP/C/OP/2, July 21, 1983, https://www1 .umn.edu/humanrts/undocs/newscans/107-1981.html.

100. United Nations, "María del Carmen Almeida de Quinteros et. al. v. Uruguay."

101. United Nations, "María del Carmen Almeida de Quinteros et. al. v. Uruguay."

102. Simpson, *Human Rights and the End of Empire*, 2–13.

103. Sikkink, *The Justice Cascade*, chap. 2 on Greece and Portugal.

104. Ann Marie Clark, *Diplomacy of Conscience: Amnesty International and Changing Human Rights Norms* (Princeton, NJ: Princeton University Press, 2001).

105. European Commission of Human Rights and Council of Europe, *The Greek Case: Report of the Commission*, vol. 2 Part I, 3 vols. (Strasbourg, 1970).

106. Daniel C. Thomas, *The Helsinki Effect: International Norms, Human Rights, and the Demise of Communism* (Princeton, NJ: Princeton University Press, 2001).

107. See Sikkink, *Mixed Signals*, chap. 3.

108. This presents a different view of the role of the Carter administration than Moyn, who mistakenly interprets human rights policy in the Americas as being *mainly* about Carter. Moyn, *The Last Utopia*. See also, Sikkink, *Mixed Signals*.

109. For more information about claims of human rights' complicity with neo-liberalism, see chapter 2.

110. Hopgood, *The Endtimes of Human Rights*, xii.

111. Guillermo A. O'Donnell, *Modernization and Bureaucratic-Authoritarianism: Studies in South American Politics*, Politics of Modernization Series 9 (Berkeley: Institute of International Studies, University of California, 1979); David Collier and Fernando Henrique Cardoso, *The New Authoritarianism in Latin America* (Princeton, NJ: Princeton University Press, 1979).

112. Albert O. Hirschman, "The Turn to Authoritarianism in Latin America and the Search for Its Economic Determinants," in *The New Authoritarianism in Latin America* (Princeton, NJ: Princeton University Press, 1979), 61–98 at 61–62.

113. Mainwaring, *Democracies and Dictatorships in Latin America*.

114. Mainwaring, *Democracies and Dictatorships in Latin America*.

115. Jensen, *The Making of International Human Rights*, 280.

116. Jensen, *The Making of International Human Rights*, 197.

117. Jensen, *The Making of International Human Rights*.

118. Jane Mayer, *The Dark Side: The Inside Story of How the War on Terror Turned into a War on American Ideals* (New York: Doubleday, 2008).

119. Frank del Olmo, "A '50s Victim of the CIA Is Finally at Rest, With Honors: *Guatemala: President Jacobo Arbenz Was Toppled by a U.S.-Directed Coup; Now Even the Military Grants Him Hero Status," *Los Angeles Times*, December 11, 1995, http://articles.latimes.com/1995-12-11/local/me-12810_1_president-jacobo-arbenz.

120. For more on the Pinochet case, see Naomi Roht-Arriaza, *The Pinochet Effect: Transnational Justice in the Age of Human Rights*, Pennsylvania Studies in Human Rights (Philadelphia: University of Pennsylvania Press, 2005).

121. See, for example, Ellen L. Lutz and Caitlin Reiger, *Prosecuting Heads of State* (Cambridge: Cambridge University Press, 2009); Naomi Roht-Arriaza and Javier Mariezcurrena, *Transitional Justice in the Twenty-First Century: Beyond Truth versus Justice* (Cambridge: Cambridge University Press, 2006).

122. Ellen Lutz and Kathryn Sikkink, "The Justice Cascade: The Evolution and Impact of Foreign Human Rights Trials in Latin America," *Chicago Journal of International Law* 2, no. 1 (2001): 1–33. We borrowed the term "cascade" from legal theorist Cass Sunstein, who spoke of social norm cascades. A norm cascade, in his words, is "a rapid, dramatic shift in the legitimacy of norms and actions on behalf of those norms."

See Cass R. Sunstein, *Free Markets and Social Justice* (New York: Oxford University Press, 1997).

123. For a generous extension of this metaphor as it pertains to the Statute of the International Criminal Court, see Benjamin N. Schiff, *Building the International Criminal Court* (Cambridge: Cambridge University Press, 2008).

124. Mark A. Pollack, "The New Institutionalisms and European Integration," in *European Integration Theory*, ed. Antje Wiener and Thomas Diez, 2nd ed. (Oxford University Press, 2009), 125–43 at 127.

125. For a discussion, see David Armitage, "What's the Big Idea? Intellectual History and the Longue Durée," *History of European Ideas* 38, no. 4 (2012): 493–507.

126. Justino Jiménez de Aréchaga, *Opera minora, 1933–1979*, Colección Testimonios (Montevideo: Ediciones de la Plaza, 2001).

127. Jiménez de Aréchaga, *Opera minora, 1933–1979*.

Chapter 5. Why Is It So Hard to Measure the Effectiveness of Human Rights?

1. In this chapter, I draw on an article I co-authored with Ann Marie Clark and thank her for permission to use some of that material in this chapter. Clark and Sikkink, "Information Effects and Human Rights Data."

2. Lucia Nader, Skype interview with author, February 10, 2016.

3. Amy Joscelyne et al., "Mental Health Functioning in the Human Rights Field: Findings from an International Internet-Based Survey," *PLOS ONE* 10, no. 12 (December 23, 2015), http://journals.plos.org/plosone/article?id=10.1371/journal.pone.0145188.

4. See United Nations Human Rights, Office of the High Commissioner, "The Core International Human Rights Instruments and their monitoring bodies," accessed March 12, 2015, http://www.ohchr.org/EN/ProfessionalInterest/Pages/CoreInstruments.aspx for a description of the core international human rights instruments and their monitoring bodies.

5. See International Criminal Court, "The States Parties to the Rome Statute," accessed March 9, 2017, https://asp.icc-cpi.int/en_menus/asp/states%20parties/pages/the%20states%20parties%20to%20the%20rome%20statute.aspx.

6. In Africa, 53 countries have ratified the African Charter on Human and Peoples' Rights, but only 24 have accepted the compulsory jurisdiction of the African Court. African Commission on Human and Peoples' Rights, "Protocol to the African Charter on Human and Peoples' Rights on the Establishment of the African Court on Human and Peoples' Rights," accessed December 12, 2016, http://www.achpr.org/instruments/court-establishment/.

7. See David Luban, "The War on Terrorism and the End of Human Rights," *Philosophy & Public Policy Quarterly* 22, no. 3 (2002): 9–14, http://scholarship.law.georgetown.edu/facpub/892/; Michael Ignatieff, "Is the Human Rights Era Ending?," *The New York Times*, February 5, 2002, http://www.nytimes.com/2002/02/05/opinion/is-the-human-rights-era-ending.html.

8. "Convention on the Prevention and Punishment of the Crime of Genocide,"

United Nations Human Rights, Office of the High Commissioner, updated 2017, http://www.ohchr.org/EN/ProfessionalInterest/Pages/CrimeOfGenocide.aspx.

9. The data is drawn from the Genocide/Politicide Indicator of the Political Instability Task Force (PITF) State Failure Problem Set, 1955-2014. Center for Systemic Peace, INSCR Data Page, accessed March 1, 2017, http://www.systemicpeace.org /inscrdata.html.

10. Human Security Report Project, Security Statistics, Definitions, accessed March 1, 2017, http://www.hsrgroup.org/our-work/security-stats/Definitions.aspx.

11. Hollie Nyseth Brehm, "Conditions and Courses of Genocide" (Ph.D. diss., University of Minnesota, 2014).

12. See, for example, Helen Fein, *Genocide: A Sociological Perspective*, vol. 38, no. 1, Current Sociology (London: Sage Publications, 1990); James Waller, *Becoming Evil: How Ordinary People Commit Genocide and Mass Killing*, 2nd ed. (Oxford: Oxford University Press, 2007); Nyseth Brehm, "Conditions and Courses of Genocide"; Eric D. Weitz, *A Century of Genocide: Utopias of Race and Nation* (Princeton, NJ: Princeton University Press, 2003).

13. Sikkink, *The Justice Cascade*; Kim and Sikkink, "Explaining the Deterrence Effect of Human Rights Prosecutions for Transitional Countries."

14. I cannot say that such prosecutions have deterred genocide per se since my team has not yet had the opportunity to use our data to test the impact of prosecutions on genocide. Now that reliable data on accountability is available, we urge genocide scholars to test whether the rise of accountability is associated with the decline in genocide and politicide.

15. "Death Penalty," Amnesty International, accessed June 16, 2016, https://www .amnesty.org/en/what-we-do/death-penalty/.

16. "Death Penalty"; "The Death Penalty: An International Perspective," Death Penalty Information Center, accessed June 16, 2016, http://www.deathpenaltyinfo.org /death-penalty-international-perspective. The European Convention on Human Rights (Protocol No. 13) bans use of the death penalty at all times, even during war. The following international laws explicitly ban the death penalty, except during times of war: The Second Optional Protocol to the International Covenant on Civil and Political Rights, Protocol No. 6 to the European Convention on Human Rights, and The Protocol to the American Convention on Human Rights to Abolish the Death Penalty. For all of these treaties, see "International Human Rights Instruments," University of Minnesota Human Rights Library, accessed March 11, 2017, http://hrlibrary .umn.edu/instree/ainstls1.htm.

17. Beth A. Simmons, *Mobilizing for Human Rights: International Law in Domestic Politics* (Cambridge: Cambridge University Press, 2009).

18. Simmons, *Mobilizing for Human Rights*; Robyn Linde, *The Globalization of Childhood: The International Diffusion of Norms and Law against the Child Death Penalty* (New York: Oxford University Press, 2016).

19. Amartya Sen, *Poverty and Famines: An Essay on Entitlement and Deprivation*, Repr. with corrections (Oxford: Clarendon Press, 1982).

20. Amartya Sen, "Freedoms and Needs: An Argument for the Primacy of Political

Rights," *The New Republic* 210, no. 2–3 (1994): 31–38; Amartya Kumar Sen, "Democracy as a Universal Value," *Journal of Democracy* 10, no. 3 (1999): 3–17.

21. "Rome Declaration and Plan of Action," FAO Corporate Document Repository, November 13-17, 1996, http://www.fao.org/docrep/003/w3613e/w3613e00.HTM.

22. "Children: Reducing Mortality," World Health Organization, accessed June 18, 2016, http://www.who.int/mediacentre/factsheets/fs178/en/.

23. Kathryn Sikkink, "Codes of Conduct for Transnational Corporations: The Case of the WHO/UNICEF Code," *International Organization* 40, no. 4 (1986): 815–40.

24. Simmons, *Mobilizing for Human Rights*.

25. Simmons, *Mobilizing for Human Rights*; Daniel W. Hill, "Estimating the Effects of Human Rights Treaties on State Behavior," *The Journal of Politics* 72, no. 4 (2010): 1161–1174. Yonatan Lupu, "The Informative Power of Treaty Commitment: Using the Spatial Model to Address Selection Effects," *American Journal of Political Science*, 57 no. 4 (2013): 912–925.

26. Thomas Risse, Steve C. Ropp, and Kathryn Sikkink, *The Power of Human Rights: International Norms and Domestic Change*, Cambridge Studies in International Relations 66 (Cambridge: Cambridge University Press, 1999); Thomas Risse, Stephen C. Ropp, and Kathryn Sikkink, eds., *The Persistent Power of Human Rights: From Commitment to Compliance*, Cambridge Studies in International Relations 126 (Cambridge: Cambridge University Press, 2013).

27. See in particular chapters by Katrin Kinzelbach and Kathryn Sikkink. Katrin Kinzelbach, "Resisting the Power of Human Rights: the People's Republic of China," in *The Persistent Power of Human Rights*, 164–81. Kathryn Sikkink, "The United States and Torture: Does the Spiral Model Work?" in *The Persistent Power of Human Rights*, 145–63.

28. Oona A. Hathaway, "Do Human Rights Treaties Make a Difference?," *The Yale Law Journal* 111, no. 8 (2002): 1935–2042; James Raymond Vreeland, "Political Institutions and Human Rights: Why Dictatorships Enter into the United Nations Convention against Torture," *International Organization* 62, no. 1 (2008): 65–101.

29. Emilie M. Hafner-Burton and James Ron, "Seeing Double: Human Rights Impact through Qualitative and Quantitative Eyes," *World Politics* 61, no. 2 (2009): 360–401.

30. Malcolm K. Sparrow, *The Character of Harms: Operational Challenges in Control* (Cambridge: Cambridge University Press, 2008), 181.

31. "Violence against Women," World Health Organization, accessed March 1, 2017, http://www.who.int/mediacentre/factsheets/fs239/en/.

32. Keck and Sikkink, *Activists beyond Borders*.

33. All the material in this paragraph is drawn from two sources. Steven Livingston, "Digital Affordances and Human Rights Investigations" (unpublished paper, received March 1, 2017). Steven Livingston, "Conference Report: Technology & Human Rights in the 21st Century" (Conference report, Carr Center for Human Rights Policy, Harvard Kennedy School, Cambridge, MA), accessed March 3, 2017, http://carrcenter.hks.harvard.edu/publications/conference-report-technology-human-rights-21st-century.

34. Clark and Sikkink, "Information Effects and Human Rights Data," 540.

35. Keck and Sikkink, *Activists beyond Borders*, 194.

36. Citing Klara Selin, a sociologist at the National Council for Crime Prevention in Stockholm, in a blog posting, Martin W. Lewis, "Misleading Murder and Rape Maps, and the Sweden Rape Puzzle," *GeoCurrents* (blog), May 25, 2013, http://www .geocurrents.info/geography-of-crime-and-punishment/misleading-murder-and-rape -maps-and-the-the-sweden-rape-puzzle.

37. Sparrow, *The Character of Harms*, 181.

38. Will H. Moore, "Quantitative Data in Human Rights: What Do the Numbers Really Mean?," *openDemocracy*, May 16, 2016, https://www.opendemocracy.net/open globalrights/will-h-moore/quantitative-data-in-human-rights-what-do-numbers -really-mean.

39. Such invisible harms are so predictable that Sparrow coined yet another term for them—"Intervention-related activity measures" or IRAM. He uses the example of domestic abuse as an illustration. Experts on domestic abuse were able to anticipate that their campaigns and the resulting heightened community awareness of the problem would encourage more reporting since they promised help, protection, and services to victims who came forward. Sparrow, *The Character of Harms*, 191.

40. Steven Pinker, *The Better Angels of Our Nature: Why Violence has Declined*, Harvard Library E-Reader Collection (New York: Viking, 2011). A reprint of *The Better Angels of Our Nature* was published by Penguin books in 2011. See discussions on pp. 189–190, 193–194, 200, 203, 219, 369–70, 511–515.

41. Amos Tversky and Daniel Kahneman, "Judgment under Uncertainty: Heuristics and Biases," *Science* 185, no. 4157 (September 27, 1974): 1124–1131.

42. Amos Tversky and Daniel Kahneman, "Availability: A Heuristic for Judging Frequency and Probability," *Cognitive Psychology* 5, no. 2 (1973): 207–232.

43. Graham Allison, "The Sky Is Falling, and Other Threats," *The Boston Globe*, February 22, 2016, http://epaper.bostonglobe.com/BostonGlobe/article_popover.aspx ?guid=0555c5a0-0f1c-4394-9985-e5150e91f60f&source=prev.

44. Tversky and Kahneman, "Availability."

45. Sen, *The Idea of Justice*, 164.

46. Roy F. Baumeister et al., "Bad Is Stronger Than Good," *Review of General Psychology* 5, no. 4 (2001): 323–370.

47. Baumeister et al., "Bad Is Stronger Than Good," 323.

48. Amos Tversky and Daniel Kahneman, "Advances in Prospect Theory: Cumulative Representation of Uncertainty," *Journal of Risk and Uncertainty* 5, no. 4 (1992): 297–323.

49. Susan T. Fiske and Shelley E. Taylor, *Social Cognition*, 2nd ed. (New York: McGraw-Hill, 1991).

50. Baumeister et al., "Bad Is Stronger Than Good."

51. Felicia Pratto and Oliver P. John, "Automatic Vigilance: The Attention-Grabbing Power of Negative Social Information," *Journal of Personality and Social Psychology* 61, no. 3 (1991): 380–391. As cited in Baumeister et al., "Bad Is Stronger Than Good," 341.

52. Baumeister et al., "Bad Is Stronger Than Good."

53. Robert W. Schrauf and Julia Sanchez, "The Preponderance of Negative Emotion Words in the Emotion Lexicon: A Cross-Generational and Cross-Linguistic Study," *Journal of Multilingual and Multicultural Development* 25, no. 2–3 (2004): 266–84.

54. Alina Tugend, "Praise Is Fleeting, But Brickbats We Recall," *The New York Times*, March 24, 2012, http://www.nytimes.com/2012/03/24/your-money/why-people-remember-negative-events-more-than-positive-ones.html.

55. Professor Clifford Nass as quoted in Tugend, "Praise Is Fleeting, But Brickbats We Recall."

56. Hirschman, *The Rhetoric of Reaction.* I have benefitted from discussions with my colleague Geoff Dancy, who has also thought about the link between Hirschman's ideas and modern human rights pessimism.

57. Samantha Power, another human rights author, has found Hirschman's categories of perversity, futility, and jeopardy useful for thinking about modern human rights debates. Samantha Power, *"A Problem from Hell": America and the Age of Genocide* (New York: Basic Books, 2002).

58. Hirschman, *The Rhetoric of Reaction*, 7.

59. Hirschman, *The Rhetoric of Reaction*, 21.

60. Snyder and Vinjamuri, "Trials and Errors"; Geoff Dancy and Veronica Michel, "Human Rights Enforcement from Below: Private Actors and Prosecutorial Momentum in Latin America and Europe," *International Studies Quarterly* 60, no. 1 (2016): 176–88.

61. Kim and Sikkink, "Explaining the Deterrence Effect of Human Rights Prosecutions for Transitional Countries."

62. Hirschman, *The Rhetoric of Reaction*, 7.

63. Hirschman, *The Rhetoric of Reaction*, 65.

64. Posner, "Have Human Rights Treaties Failed?"

65. Moyn, "Human Rights and the Age of Inequality." Although this statement reflects a sense of the futility of human rights discourse, in general, Moyn is more of a perversity or jeopardy critic than a futility one.

66. Hirschman, *The Rhetoric of Reaction*, 7.

67. Hirschman, *The Rhetoric of Reaction*, 94.

68. Jack Goldsmith and Stephen D. Krasner, "The Limits of Idealism," *Daedalus* 132, no. 1 (2003): 47–64 at 51.

69. Hirschman, *The Rhetoric of Reaction*, 33.

70. Hirschman, *Journeys toward Progress.*

71. Adelman, *Worldly Philosopher.*

72. Adelman, *Worldly Philosopher*, 487.

73. Hirschman, *The Rhetoric of Reaction*, 36, 26, 54, 44.

74. Patrick Ball, conversation with author, at conference "How Do We Know What We Know? Charting the Future for Human Rights Documentation and Analysis" on Jan 23–24, 2015, Arizona State University in Tempe, AZ, January 2015.

75. Hirschman, *The Rhetoric of Reaction*, 36.

76. Hirschman, *The Rhetoric of Reaction*, 38.

77. Hirschman, *The Rhetoric of Reaction*, 151.

78. Joscelyne et al., "Mental Health Functioning in the Human Rights Field."

79. Joscelyne et al., "Mental Health Functioning in the Human Rights Field."

80. "Resilience," *Psychology Today*, accessed December 15, 2016, https://www.psychologytoday.com/basics/resilience.

81. No one knows who actually coined this phrase, but it was popularized by Eric Pooley, "Grins, Gore and Videotape: The Trouble with Local TV News," *New York Magazine* 22, no. 40 (October 9, 1989): 36–44 at 36.

82. While there has been a decline in the number of foreign correspondents, there has not been a decline in foreign news. Foreign news, however, is more likely to be drawn from the wire services than from foreign correspondents. In any case, there is no reason to believe that the level of violence in the foreign news coverage has declined.

83. I am indebted to Steven Pinker for this observation. Harvard Human Rights Colloquium, February 5, 2016.

84. Comment by Stephen Northfield at a workshop at the University of Toronto, Munk School of Global Affairs, "Community of Practice for Human Rights Education," December 5, 2016.

85. Christopher Fariss coined the phrase "a changing standard of accountability" for human rights, in his APSA article, Christopher J. Fariss, "New Takes on Human Rights Measurement," *Wrongs & Rights: The Newsletter for the APSA Human Rights Section*, May 31, 2012, http://cfariss.com/documents/human_rights_newsletter_may_2012.pdf. See also Christopher J. Fariss, "Respect for Human Rights Has Improved over Time: Modeling the Changing Standard of Accountability," *American Political Science Review* 108, no. 2 (2014): 297–318 at 297.

86. Others have made this argument. For example, Lynn Hunt wrote of a "logic of rights" and said that "rights questions thus revealed a tendency to cascade." Hunt, *Inventing Human Rights*, 147.

87. Fariss, "Respect for Human Rights Has Improved over Time."

88. Catholic Church, Archdiocese of São Paulo, *Torture in Brazil: A Report* (New York: Vintage Books, 1986), 79.

89. Clark and Sikkink, "Information Effects and Human Rights Data."

90. Over ninety articles in major political science and human rights journals from 1999 to 2011 used this data, often to reach negative conclusions about the effectiveness of human rights law or advocacy. I thank Brooke Coe for her research assistance in providing this fact. These are some of the studies that James Ron and Emilie Hafner-Burton refer to when they suggest that quantitative studies are more pessimistic about human rights progress. Hafner-Burton and Ron, "Seeing Double." This is also some of the data that Eric Posner refers to when he says there have been no improvements in human rights. Posner, *The Twilight of Human Rights Law*.

91. Todd Landman and Marco Larizza, "Inequality and Human Rights: Who Controls What, When, and How," *International Studies Quarterly* 53, no. 3 (2009): 715–736.

92. One reason human rights groups produce many reports is to get media attention for them, which raises the profile of the NGO and amplifies its message. As news

organizations have fewer resources to put foreign correspondents in the field, they may turn more often to NGO reports in their coverage of foreign events, thereby giving foreign news more of a focus on human rights violations.

93. Clark and Sikkink, "Information Effects and Human Rights Data."

94. This score begins in 1976 and thus excludes the worst years of repression in Brazil which were from 1968–1974.

95. A 2007 Brazilian government report makes clear that the worst period for deaths and disappearances was from 1971 to 1974, that the state rarely killed or disappeared its political opponents after 1979, and that there have not been any cases of disappearances after the 1985 transition to democracy. Secretaria Especial dos Direitos Humanos da Presidência da República, *Direito à memória e à verdade: Comissão Especial sobre Mortos e Desaparecidos Políticos*, Série Bibliográfica (Brasília: Comissão Especial Sobre Mortos e Desaparecidos Políticos, 2007).

96. *Brazil: Authorized Violence in Rural Areas*, Amnesty International (London, UK: Amnesty International Publications, 1988), 1.

97. See the website of Observatório das Violências Policiais-SP (Observatory of Police Violence in São Paulo), accessed March 1, 2017, http://www.ovp-sp.org/.

98. Posner, *The Twilight of Human Rights Law*, 1–2.

99. Comisión para el Esclarecimiento Histórico, *Guatemala: Memory of Silence = Tz'inil Na'tab'al.*

100. Sparrow, *The Character of Harms*, 192.

101. Fariss, "Respect for Human Rights Has Improved over Time."

102. Fariss, "Respect for Human Rights Has Improved over Time."

103. Ellen L. Lutz and Kathryn Sikkink, "International Human Rights Law and Practice in Latin America," *International Organization* 54, no. 3 (2000): 633–659; Simmons, *Mobilizing for Human Rights*, 160–61; Clark, "The Normative Context of Human Rights Criticism."

104. See Ball's work highlighted on the web page of a human rights data organization he founded, the Human Rights Data Analysis Group (DRDAG): https://hrdag.org/

105. I am indebted to Phuong Pham for this insight. See, e.g., Elliot R. Haut and Peter J. Pronovost, "Surveillance Bias in Outcome Reporting," *Journal of the American Medical Association* 305, no. 23 (2011): 2462–63.

106. On new tactics, see the New Tactics in Human Rights website at https://www.newtactics.org/

Chapter 6. What Does and Doesn't Work to Promote Human Rights?

1. Some of the work in this chapter draws on earlier work co-authored with Geoff Dancy and Hans Peter Schmitz. I thank them both for their permission to use (quite modified) versions of sections of our chapters. Geoff Dancy and Kathryn Sikkink, "Ratification And Human Rights Prosecutions: Toward A Transnational Theory Of Treaty Compliance," *New York University Journal of International Law and Politics* 44, no. 3 (2012): 751–790; Hans Peter Schmitz and Kathryn Sikkink, "International

Human Rights," in *Handbook of International Relations*, ed. Walter Carlsnaes, Thomas Risse, and Beth A. Simmons, 2nd ed. (London: SAGE, 2013): 827–854.

2. This narrative and all additional material about Nadia Murad Basee Taha and Murad Ismael in this chapter are based on two public presentations by Nadia Murad Basee Taha and Murad Ismael at the Harvard Kennedy School on March 28, 2016, "A Conversation with Nadia Murad Basee Taha" and a presentation to Human Security Class at Harvard Kennedy School on the Yazidi Genocide; where it draws on other sources, there are additional footnotes.

3. "ISIL May Have Committed Genocide, War Crimes in Iraq, Says UN Human Rights Report," *UN News Centre*, March 19, 2015, http://www.un.org/apps/news/story .asp?NewsID=50369#.V2VoqK4nKwn.

4. Throughout the book, I have used last names to refer to the people I interviewed. Nadia Murad Basee Taha, however, has launched an initiative and website called "I'm with Nadia," and it felt more reflective of that effort to use her first name in this narrative. To be consistent in this chapter, I also use Murad's first name. For more on the "I'm with Nadia" initiative, see http://www.nadiamurad.org/

5. Presentation, Human Security Class, Harvard Kennedy School, March 28, 2016.

6. Raya Jalabi, "Who Are the Yazidis and Why Is Isis Hunting Them?," *The Guardian*, August 11, 2014, https://www.theguardian.com/world/2014/aug/07/who-yazidi -isis-iraq-religion-ethnicity-mountains.

7. Presentation, Human Security Class, Harvard Kennedy School, March 28, 2016.

8. This section draws on a chapter co-authored with Hans Peter Schmitz. Schmitz and Sikkink, "International Human Rights." We discuss the political, economic, psychological, and ideological explanations for human rights violations, including war, authoritarianism, poverty, inequality, and dehumanizing ideologies, among other issues. There are some connections between our framework and work recently done by Emilie Hafner-Burton. She identifies six different "contexts" that contribute to human rights violations, including conflict, illiberal states, poverty and inequality, and dehumanization. She also usefully distinguishes between macro contexts that contribute to human rights violations, such as poverty, but which may be very difficult to change in the short term, and more proximate "rationales" that individuals engaged in repression tell themselves to justify their actions. Emilie M. Hafner-Burton, *Making Human Rights a Reality* (Princeton, NJ: Princeton University Press, 2013), chaps. 2–3.

9. Steven C. Poe, "The Decision to Repress: An Integrative Theoretical Approach to the Research on Human Rights and Repression," in *Understanding Human Rights Violations: New Systematic Studies*, ed. Sabine C. Carey and Steven C. Poe, Ethics and Global Politics (Aldershot: Ashgate, 2004): 16–42; Benjamin A. Valentino, *Final Solutions: Mass Killing and Genocide in the Twentieth Century*, Cornell Studies in Security Affairs (Ithaca, NY: Cornell University Press, 2004).

10. Daron Acemoglu and James A. Robinson, *Economic Origins of Dictatorship and Democracy* (Cambridge: Cambridge University Press, 2006).

11. Alison Liebhafsky Des Forges, *"Leave None to Tell the Story": Genocide in Rwanda* (New York: Human Rights Watch, International Federation of Human Rights, 1999); Scott Straus, "Second-Generation Comparative Research on Genocide,"

World Politics 59, no. 3 (2007): 476–501; Valentino, *Final Solutions*; J. Andrew Slack and Roy R. Doyon, "Population Dynamics and Susceptibility for Ethnic Conflict: The Case of Bosnia and Herzegovina," *Journal of Peace Research* 38, no. 2 (2001): 139–161.

12. Nyseth Brehm, "Conditions and Courses of Genocide"; James D. Fearon and David D. Laitin, "Ethnicity, Insurgency, and Civil War," *American Political Science Review* 97, no. 1 (2003): 75–90.

13. Des Forges, *Leave None to Tell the Story*; Scott Straus, *The Order of Genocide: Race, Power, and War in Rwanda* (Ithaca, NY: Cornell University Press, 2006); Valentino, *Final Solutions*.

14. There is a large literature on this topic. See, for example, Judith Green Kelley, *Ethnic Politics in Europe: The Power of Norms and Incentives* (Princeton, NJ: Princeton University Press, 2004).

15. Poe, "The Decision to Repress."

16. Steven C. Poe and C. Neal Tate, "Repression of Human Rights to Personal Integrity in the 1980s: A Global Analysis," *American Political Science Review* 88 (1994): 853–872; Steven C. Poe, C. Neal Tate, and Linda Camp Keith, "Repression of the Human Right to Personal Integrity Revisited: A Global Cross-National Study Covering the Years 1976–1993," *International Studies Quarterly* 43, no. 2 (1999): 291–313.

17. Nyseth Brehm, "Conditions and Courses of Genocide."

18. Christian Davenport, ed., *Paths to State Repression: Human Rights Violations and Contentious Politics* (Lanham, MD: Rowman & Littlefield Publishers, 2000); Poe and Tate, "Repression of Human Rights to Personal Integrity in the 1980s"; Poe, Tate, and Keith, "Repression of the Human Right to Personal Integrity Revisited"; James A. Piazza and James Igoe Walsh, "Transnational Terror and Human Rights," *International Studies Quarterly* 53, no. 1 (2009): 125–148.

19. E. Melander, T. Pettersson, and L. Themnér, "Organized Violence, 1989–2015," *Journal of Peace Research* 53, no. 5 (2016): 727–742. The data is from the UCDP/PRIO Armed Conflict Dataset, from Uppsala University and the Peace Research Institute of Oslo. See https://www.prio.org/Data/Armed-Conflict/UCDP-PRIO/.

20. For the newest data on battle-related deaths, see Melander, Pettersson, and Themnér, "Organized Violence, 1989–2015." Data also available on the Uppsala University, Department of Peace and Conflict website http://www.pcr.uu.se/research/ucdp/charts_and_graphs/#tocjump_9015420470103274_6

21. Tanisha M. Fazal, "Dead Wrong?: Battle Deaths, Military Medicine, and Exaggerated Reports of War's Demise," *International Security* 39, no. 1 (2014): 95–125. She refers to an argument by Stephen Pinker on the impact that the humanitarian revolution has had on the decline of war. See Pinker, *The Better Angels of Our Nature*.

22. For an introduction to R2P, see the website of the International Coalition for R2P, accessed March 1, 2017, http://www.responsibilitytoprotect.org/index.php/about-rtop/learn-about-rtop.

23. Stephen Hopgood, for example, seems to go out of his way to mention the ICC and R2P in the same sentence whenever possible, as if to underscore his belief that they are somehow one and the same. Hopgood, *The Endtimes of Human Rights*.

24. Walling, *All Necessary Measures*.

25. Power, *"A Problem from Hell"*; Michael Ignatieff, "Those Fighting Islamic State Are the Lesser Evil: An Interview with Michael Ignatieff," interview by Erich Follath, September 9, 2014, http://www.spiegel.de/international/world/interview-with-michael -ignatieff-on-islamic-state-and-mideast-turmoil-a-990667.html.

26. See, for example, Poe, Tate, and Keith, "Repression of the Human Right to Personal Integrity Revisited."

27. Robert Anthony Pape, *Dying to Win: The Strategic Logic of Suicide Terrorism* (New York: Random House, 2005).

28. Erica Chenoweth and Maria J. Stephan, *Why Civil Resistance Works: The Strategic Logic of Nonviolent Conflict*, Columbia Studies in Terrorism and Irregular Warfare (New York: Columbia University Press, 2011).

29. Presentation, Human Security Class, Harvard Kennedy School, March 28, 2016.

30. De Waal, "Writing Human Rights and Getting It Wrong."

31. Mark Peceny, *Democracy at the Point of Bayonets* (University Park: Pennsylvania State University Press, 1999).

32. Peksen, "Does Foreign Military Intervention Help Human Rights?"

33. Meernik, Poe, and Shaikh, "The Use of Military Force to Promote Human Rights"; Bruce Bueno de Mesquita and George W. Downs, "Intervention and Democracy," *International Organization* 60, no. 3 (2006): 627–49; Alexander B. Downes and Jonathan Monten, "Forced to Be Free?: Why Foreign-Imposed Regime Change Rarely Leads to Democratization," *International Security* 37, no. 4 (2013): 90–131.

34. Ignatieff, interview by Follath.

35. Julian Borger, *The Butcher's Trail: How the Search for Balkan War Criminals Became the World's Most Successful Manhunt* (New York: Other Press, 2016).

36. I am indebted to Derya Honça for this insight.

37. Poe and Tate, "Repression of Human Rights to Personal Integrity in the 1980s"; Poe, Tate, and Keith, "Repression of the Human Right to Personal Integrity Revisited."

38. Bruce Bueno de Mesquita et al., "Thinking Inside the Box: A Closer Look at Democracy and Human Rights," *International Studies Quarterly* 49, no. 3 (2005): 439–458; Christian Davenport, "The Promise of Democratic Pacification: An Empirical Assessment," *International Studies Quarterly* 48, no. 3 (2004): 539–560; David Cingranelli and Mikhail Filippov, "Electoral Rules and Incentives to Protect Human Rights," *The Journal of Politics* 72, no. 1 (2010): 243–257.

39. de Mesquita et al., "Thinking Inside the Box."

40. This understanding of democracy as multidimensional follows a long tradition in political science research on democracy, from Dahl to de Mesquita, et. al. Robert A. Dahl, *Polyarchy: Participation and Opposition* (New Haven: Yale University Press, 1971); de Mesquita et al., "Thinking Inside the Box."

41. Helen Fein, "'More Murder in the Middle': Life-Integrity Violations and Democracy in the 'World, 1987," *Human Rights Quarterly* 17, no. 1 (1995): 170–191 at 170. This relates to an argument by Edward Mansfield and Jack Snyder that democratizing

states are more likely to engage in war. Edward D. Mansfield, "Democratization and War," *Foreign Affairs* 74, no. 3 (1995): 79–97.

42. Nyseth Brehm, "Conditions and Courses of Genocide."

43. Steven Levitsky and Lucan Way, "The Myth of Democratic Recession," *Journal of Democracy* 26, no. 1 (2015): 45–58.

44. Joshua Kurlantzick, Robert Battison, as cited in Levitsky and Way, "The Myth of Democratic Recession," 45.

45. *Freedom House*, s.v. "Reports: Freedom in the World," accessed November 12, 2016, https://freedomhouse.org/report/freedom-world/freedom-world-2016.

46. Maxwell O. Chibundu, "Political Ideology as a Religion: The Idolatry of Democracy," *University of Maryland Law Journal of Race, Religion, Gender, and Class* 6, no. 1 (2006): 117–157.

47. Poe, Tate, and Keith, "Repression of the Human Right to Personal Integrity Revisited"; Risse, Ropp, and Sikkink, *The Power of Human Rights*; Todd Landman, *Protecting Human Rights: A Comparative Study*, Advancing Human Rights Series (Washington, DC: Georgetown University Press, 2005); Eric Neumayer, "Do International Human Rights Treaties Improve Respect for Human Rights?," *Conflict Resolution* 49, no. 6 (2005): 925–953.

48. de Mesquita et al., "Thinking Inside the Box."

49. Sen, "Freedoms and Needs"; Wesley Milner, "Economic Globalization and Rights: An Empirical Analysis," in *Globalization and Human Rights*, ed. Alison Brysk (Berkeley: University of California Press, 2002), 77–97; Han S. Park, "Correlates of Human Rights: Global Tendencies," *Human Rights Quarterly* 9, no. 3 (1987): 405–413.

50. Neil J. Mitchell and James M. McCormick, "Economic and Political Explanations of Human Rights Violations," *World Politics* 40, no. 4 (1988): 476–498; Poe and Tate, "Repression of Human Rights to Personal Integrity in the 1980s"; Poe, Tate, and Keith, "Repression of the Human Right to Personal Integrity Revisited"; Milner, "Economic Globalization and Rights."

51. Reinhard Heinisch, "The Economic Nature of Basic Human Rights: Economic Explanations of Cross-National Variations in Governmental Basic Human Rights Performance," *Peace & Change* 23, no. 3 (1998): 333–372.

52. Landman and Larizza, "Inequality and Human Rights."

53. Amartya Sen, "More than 100 Million Women Are Missing," *New York Review of Books* 37, no. 20 (December 20, 1990), http://www.nybooks.com/articles/1990/12/20/more-than-100-million-women-are-missing/.

54. See Max Roser, "Our World in Data," tables on trends in the UNDP Human Development Index (HDI), at https://ourworldindata.org/human-development-index/. Roser gets his data from "Table 2: Human Development Index Trends, 1980-2013," United Nations Development Programme, accessed March 18, 2017, http://hdr.undp.org/en/data.

55. On three different ways to measure income inequality, see Branko Milanović, *Worlds Apart: Measuring International and Global Inequality* (Princeton, NJ: Princeton University Press, 2005), chap. 1.

56. Branko Milanović, *Global Inequality: A New Approach for the Age of Globalization* (Cambridge, MA: The Belknap Press of Harvard University Press, 2016).

57. William H. Meyer, "Confirming, Infirming, and 'Falsifying' Theories of Human Rights: Reflections on Smith, Bolyard, and Ippolito Through the Lens of Lakatos," *Human Rights Quarterly* 21, no. 1 (1999): 220–228; Clair Apodaca, "Global Economic Patterns and Personal Integrity Rights After the Cold War," *International Studies Quarterly* 45, no. 4 (2001): 587–602; David L. Richards, Ronald D. Gelleny, and David H. Sacko, "Money with a Mean Streak? Foreign Economic Penetration and Government Respect for Human Rights in Developing Countries," *International Studies Quarterly* 45, no. 2 (2001): 219–239; Bruce London and Bruce A. Williams, "Multinational Corporate Penetration, Protest, and Basic Needs Provision in Non-Core Nations: A Cross-National Analysis," *Social Forces* 66 (March 1988): 747–773; Tony Evans, "Trading Human Rights," in *Global Trade and Global Social Issues*, ed. Annie Tayler and Caroline Thomas (London: Routledge, 1999): 31–52; Jackie G. Smith, Melissa Bolyard, and Anna Ippolito, "Human Rights and the Global Economy: A Response to Meyer," *Human Rights Quarterly* 21, no. 1 (1999): 207–219.

58. Emilie M. Hafner-Burton, "Right or Robust? The Sensitive Nature of Repression to Globalization," *Journal Of Peace Research* 42, no. 6 (November 2005): 679–98; Milner, "Economic Globalization and Rights."

59. M. Rodwan Abouharb and David L. Cingranelli, *Human Rights and Structural Adjustment* (Cambridge: Cambridge University Press, 2007).

60. See, for example, Piketty, *Capital in the Twenty-First Century*, especially "A Global Tax on Capital," 515–539; and Milanović, *Global Inequality*, especially "How Can Inequality in Rich Welfare States Be Reduced?" 217–222.

61. Kathryn Sikkink, *Ideas and Institutions: Developmentalism in Brazil and Argentina*, Cornell Studies in Political Economy (Ithaca: Cornell University Press, 1991).

62. Fernando Fajnzylber, *Industrialización en América Latina: De "la caja negra" al "casillero vacío": selección* (Santiago: United Nations, Economic Commission for Latin America and the Caribbean (CEPAL), 1990), http://repositorio.cepal.org /bitstream/11362/27955/1/S9000502_es.pdf.

63. Stephan Haggard, *Pathways from the Periphery: The Politics of Growth in the Newly Industrializing Countries*, Cornell Studies in Political Economy (Ithaca: Cornell University Press, 1990).

64. The World Bank, "Uruguay: Overview," accessed November 24, 2016, http:// www.worldbank.org/en/country/uruguay/overview.

65. Anna Heim, "Impact and Numbers from Uruguay's One Laptop per Child Program," *The Next Web (TNW)*, April 7, 2013, http://thenextweb.com/la/2013/04/07 /uruguays-one-laptop-per-child-program-impact-and-numbers/.

66. Jonathan Gilbert, "Uruguay's Most Unexpected Champion of Capitalism," *Fortune*, January 23, 2015, http://fortune.com/2015/01/23/uruguay-jose-mujica -economy-capitalism/.

67. Leo Kuper, *Genocide: Its Political Use in the Twentieth Century* (New Haven: Yale University Press, 1981); Fein, *Genocide*.

68. Fein, *Genocide*; Ervin Staub, *The Roots of Evil: The Origins of Genocide and*

Other Group Violence (Cambridge: Cambridge University Press, 1989); Weitz, *A Century of Genocide*; Nyseth Brehm, "Conditions and Courses of Genocide."

69. Presentation, Human Security Class, Harvard Kennedy School, March 28, 2016.

70. Nyseth Brehm, "Conditions and Courses of Genocide."

71. Weitz, *A Century of Genocide*.

72. Jeremy Diamond, "Donald Trump on Torture: 'We Have to Beat the Savages,'" *CNN*, March 6, 2016, http://www.cnn.com/2016/03/06/politics/donald-trump -torture/index.html.

73. John Hagan and Wenona Rymond-Richmond, "The Collective Dynamics of Racial Dehumanization and Genocidal Victimization in Darfur," *American Sociological Review* 73, no. 6 (2008): 875–902.

74. Stanley Milgram, "Some Conditions of Obedience and Disobedience to Authority," *Human Relations* 18, no. 1 (1965): 57–76.

75. Milgram, "Some Conditions of Obedience and Disobedience to Authority."

76. Amanda M. Murdie and David R. Davis, "Shaming and Blaming: Using Events Data to Assess the Impact of Human Rights INGOs," *International Studies Quarterly* 56, no. 1 (2012): 1–16.

77. Hathaway, "Do Human Rights Treaties Make a Difference?"; Emilie M. Hafner-Burton and Kiyoteru Tsutsui, "Human Rights in a Globalizing World: The Paradox of Empty Promises," *American Journal of Sociology* 110, no. 5 (2005): 1373–1411. For a more positive outlook from the first wave of studies, see Neumayer, "Do International Human Rights Treaties Improve Respect for Human Rights?"

78. Oona Hathaway, "The Promise and Limits of the International Law of Torture," in *Torture: Philosophical, Political and Legal Perspectives*, ed. Sanford Levinson (Oxford: Oxford University Press, 2004), 199–212; Emilie M. Hafner-Burton and Kiyoteru Tsutsui, "Justice Lost! The Failure of International Human Rights Law to Matter Where Needed Most," *Journal of Peace Research* 44, no. 4 (July 2007): 407–425 at 407.

79. Simmons, *Mobilizing for Human Rights*; Lupu, "The Informative Power of Treaty Commitment."

80. Simmons, *Mobilizing for Human Rights*.

81. Naomi Roht-Arriaza, *The Pinochet Effect*.

82. Hafner-Burton and Ron, "Seeing Double"; Hafner-Burton, *Making Human Rights a Reality*.

83. In our research, we count close to 110 transitions in over 80 countries. "Home," Transnational Justice Research Collaborative, last updated December 12, 2016, www .transitionaljusticedata.com.

84. Alfredo Romero, "The Rule of Law Façade: A Playbook for Regimes" (working paper, Carr Center for Human Rights Policy, Harvard Kennedy School, Cambridge, MA, 2016).

85. Levitsky and Way, "The Myth of Democratic Recession," 51.

86. Ryan Goodman and Derek Jinks, *Socializing States: Promoting Human Rights through International Law* (New York: Oxford University Press, 2013).

87. Hafner-Burton, *Making Human Rights a Reality*.

88. Clark, "The Normative Context of Human Rights Criticism."

89. Rodríguez-Garavito and de Sousa Santos, eds., *Law and Globalization from Below*; Balakrishnan Rajagopal, *International Law from Below: Development, Social Movements, and Third World Resistance* (Cambridge: Cambridge University Press, 2003).

90. My collaborators and co-authors on accountability work have included Carrie Booth Walling, Hun Joon Kim, Geoffrey Dancy, Bridget Marchesi, Leigh Payne, Tricia Olsen, Andrew Rieter, Francesca Lessa, and Gabriel Pereira.

91. Simon Zadek, "The Meaning of Accountability," in *Business and Human Rights: From Principles to Practice*, ed. Dorothée Baumann-Pauly and Justine Nolan (New York: Routledge, 2016), 240–43.

92. Zadek, "The Meaning of Accountability."

93. Ruth W. Grant and Robert O. Keohane, "Accountability and Abuses of Power in World Politics," *American Political Science Review* 99, no. 1 (2005): 29–43.

94. This database and the resulting research are based upon work supported by the National Science Foundation and the Arts and Humanities Research Council under two grants: the NSF (Grant No. 0961226) "Alternative Accountabilities for Human Rights Violations" and the Arts and Humanities Research Council (Grant No. 0AH/I500030/1) relating to the project titled "The impact of transitional justice on human rights and democracy." Any opinions, findings, and conclusions or recommendations expressed in this material are those of the authors and do not necessarily reflect the views of the National Science Foundation. I wish to thank our NSF/AHRC research teams for their assistance.

95. Kim and Sikkink, "Explaining the Deterrence Effect of Human Rights Prosecutions for Transitional Countries."

96. Snyder and Vinjamuri, "Trials and Errors."

97. Catalina Smulovitz, "The Discovery of Law: Political Consequences in the Argentine Case," in *Global Prescriptions: The Production, Exportation, and Importation of a New Legal Orthodoxy*, ed. Yves Dezalay and Bryant G. Garth (Ann Arbor: University of Michigan Press, 2002), 249–265.

98. Anne-Marie Slaughter, *A New World Order* (Princeton, NJ: Princeton University Press, 2004); Yonatan Lupu, "Best Evidence: The Role of Information in Domestic Judicial Enforcement of International Human Rights Agreements," *International Organization* 67, no. 3 (2013): 469–503 at 469; Courtenay Conrad, "Divergent Incentives for Dictators: Domestic Institutions and (International Promises Not to) Torture," *Journal of Conflict Resolution* 58, no. 1 (2014): 34–67.

99. Jeffrey K. Staton and Will H. Moore, "Judicial Power in Domestic and International Politics," *International Organization* 65, no. 3 (2011): 553–587.

100. Dancy and Sikkink, "Ratification and Human Rights Prosecutions."

101. Kim and Sikkink, "Explaining the Deterrence Effect of Human Rights Prosecutions for Transitional Countries"; Geoff Dancy et al., "Stopping State Agents of Violence or Promoting Political Compromise? The Powerful Role of Transitional Justice Mechanisms" (paper presented at the 2013 American Political Science Association Conference Annual Meeting, Chicago, IL, August 30, 2013), https://transitional

justicedata.com/files/Stopping%20Agents%20of%20Violence%20APSA%20 2013.10.24.pdf.

102. Sikkink, *The Justice Cascade*.

103. This work is based on two grants from the National Science Foundation (Nos. SES-0961226 and SES-1228519) and the Arts and Humanities Research Council (Grant Nos. AH/1500030/1 and AH/K502856/1). Any opinions, findings, and conclusions or recommendations expressed in this material are those of the authors and do not necessarily reflect the views of their Universities or those of the National Science Foundation or the Arts and Humanities Research Council.

104. On transnational advocacy networks, see Keck and Sikkink, *Activists beyond Borders*. On transnational legal processes, see Harold Koh, "Transnational Legal Process. (The 1994 Roscoe Pound Lecture)," *Nebraska Law Review* 75, no. 1 (1996): 181–207; Harold Koh, "Jefferson Memorial Lecture; Transnational Legal Process after September 11th," *Berkeley Journal of International Law* 22, no. 3 (2004): 337–54.

105. Keck and Sikkink, *Activists beyond Borders*; Risse, Ropp, and Sikkink, *The Power of Human Rights*.

106. Murdie and Davis, "Shaming and Blaming."

107. See, for example, Amanda Murdie, "The Impact of Human Rights NGO Activity on Human Right Practices," *International NGO Journal* 4, no. 10 (2009): 421–440; Amanda Murdie and Tavishi Bhasin, "Aiding and Abetting: Human Rights INGOs and Domestic Protest," *Journal of Conflict Resolution* 55, no. 2 (2011): 163–91; Murdie and Davis, "Shaming and Blaming"; David Davis, Amanda Murdie, and Coty Steinmetz, "'Makers and Shapers': Human Rights INGOs and Public Opinion," *Human Rights Quarterly* 34, no. 1 (2012): 199–224; Sam R. Bell, K. Chad Clay, and Amanda Murdie, "Neighborhood Watch: Spatial Effects of Human Rights INGOs," *The Journal of Politics* 74, no. 2 (2012): 354–368; Sam R. Bell et al., "Taking the Fight to Them: Neighborhood Human Rights Organizations and Domestic Protest" 44, no. 4 (2014): 853–75.

108. Keck and Sikkink, *Activists beyond Borders*.

109. Simmons, *Mobilizing for Human Rights*, 358.

110. This is the issue that the UN special representative on business and human rights John Ruggie has grappled with in his Guiding Principles on Business and Human Rights. Ruggie's Guiding Principles clarify that the state has the *duty to protect* against human rights abuses, including those by business enterprises, while corporations have a *responsibility to respect* human rights. "UN Guiding Principles on Business and Human Rights," United Nations Human Rights Council, June 2011, http:// www.ohchr.org/Documents/Publications/GuidingPrinciplesBusinessHR_EN.pdf.

111. Simmons, *Mobilizing for Human Rights*.

112. Kim and Sikkink, "Explaining the Deterrence Effect of Human Rights Prosecutions for Transitional Countries"; Sikkink, *The Justice Cascade*; Geoffrey Dancy, et al., "Behind Bars and Bargains: How Justice Policies Change Human Rights Practices in New Democracies" (unpublished manuscript, n.d.).

113. See Karisa Cloward, *When Norms Collide: Local Responses to Female Genital Mutilation and Early Marriage* (Oxford: Oxford University Press, 2016); Gerry

Mackie, "Ending Footbinding and Infibulation: A Convention Account," *American Sociological Review* 61, no. 6 (1996): 999–1017.

114. New Tactics in Human Rights, accessed June 18, 2016, https://www.newtactics .org/.

115. See Livingston, "Conference Report: Technology & Human Rights in the 21st Century."

116. Chenoweth and Stephan, *Why Civil Resistance Works*.

117. Hopgood, *The Endtimes of Human Rights*; James Ron, David Crow, and Shannon Golden, "The Struggle for a Truly Grassroots Human Rights Movement," *openDemocracy*, June 18, 2013, http://www.opendemocracy.net/openglobalrights/james -ron-david-crow-shannon-golden/struggle-for-truly-grassroots-human-rights-move; Ran Hirschl, *Towards Juristocracy: The Origins and Consequences of the New Constitutionalism* (Cambridge, MA: Harvard University Press, 2007).

118. Geoffrey Dancy, "The Impact of Human Rights Law in Time" (Ph.D. diss., University of Minnesota, 2013), http://search.proquest.com/docview/1447014720/.

119. See Hirschman, *The Rhetoric of Reaction*.

120. Sonia Cardenas, *Conflict and Compliance: State Responses to International Human Rights Pressure*, Pennsylvania Studies in Human Rights (Philadelphia: University of Pennsylvania Press, 2007); Clifford Bob, *The Global Right Wing and the Clash of World Politics*, Cambridge Studies in Contentious Politics (New York: Cambridge University Press, 2012).

121. Hirschman, *The Rhetoric of Reaction*.

122. Thanks to Jessica Tueller for suggesting this possibility.

123. James Ron, Archana Pandya, and David Crow, "Universal Values, Foreign Money: Funding Local Human Rights Organizations in the Global South," *Review of International Political Economy* 23, no. 1 (2016): 29–64.

124. We discuss this in detail in Keck and Sikkink, *Activists beyond Borders*, 97–102.

125. Dupuy, Ron, and Prakash, "Foreign Aid to Local NGOs."

126. Sergio Aguayo, interview by author, May 26, 2016, Cambridge, MA.

127. César Rodríguez-Garavito, "The Future of Human Rights: From Gatekeeping to Symbiosis," *Sur International Journal on Human Rights* 11, no. 20 (2014): 498–509 at 502.

128. César Rodríguez-Garavito, interview by author, April 20, 2016, Boston, MA.

129. Bahar Rumelili and Buke Bosnak, "Taking Stock of the Europeanization of Civil Society in Turkey: The Case of NGOs," in *The Europeanization of Turkey: Polity and Politics*, ed. Ali Tekin and Aylin Güney, Routledge Studies in Middle Eastern Politics 75 (London: Routledge, 2015), 127–144.

130. Murdie and Bhasin, "Aiding and Abetting"; Linnea Beatty, "Interrelation of Violent and Non-Violent Resistance in Burma," (Paper presented at APSA 2011 Annual Meeting, Seattle, WA, 2001), http://papers.ssrn.com/abstract=1900480.

131. Karina Ansolabehere, "Reforming and Transforming: A Multi-Directional Investigation of Human Rights," *openDemocracy*, December 4, 2013, http://www

.opendemocracy.net/openglobalrights/karina-ansolabehere/reforming-and-trans
forming-multi-directional-investigation-of-h.

132. Lucia Nader, "Solid Organisations in a Liquid World," *Sur International Journal on Human Rights* 11, no. 20 (2014): 482–489.

133. For corruption and professionalization, see V. Suresh, "Funds and Civil Liberties," *openDemocracy*, January 6, 2014, https://www.opendemocracy.net/openglobal
rights/v-suresh/funds-and-civil-liberties. For lack of an alternative, see James Ron's
clarifying comments to Dupuy, Ron, and Prakash, "Foreign Aid to Local NGOs."

134. Straus, *The Order of Genocide*.

135. Lepenies, "Possibilism," 449.

Chapter 7. Conclusions: Evidence for
Hope without Complacency

1. Jack Rendler, interview by author, November 13, 2016, Cambridge, MA.

2. "Zim Pastor's Arrest 'a Well Calculated Plan to Intimidate Activists,'" *News24*,
July 13, 2016, http://www.news24.com/Africa/Zimbabwe/zim-pastors-arrest-a-well
-calculated-plan-to-intimidate-activists-20160713.

3. Privilege Musvanhiri, "Zimbabwe Activist Evan Mawarire Is Freed," *DW*, June
14, 2016, http://www.dw.com/en/zimbabwe-activist-evan-mawarire-is-freed/a-1939
8879.

4. Jack Rendler, interview by author, November 13, 2016, Cambridge, MA.

5. "Resilience," *Psychology Today*, accessed December 15, 2016, https://www
.psychologytoday.com/basics/resilience.

6. Linz, *The Breakdown of Democratic Regimes*.

7. Sparrow, *The Character of Harms*.

8. Malcolm Sparrow, e-mail message to author, April 21, 2016. I thank Malcolm
for his permission to quote this.

9. See, for example, Fariss, "Respect for Human Rights Has Improved over Time";
Keith Schnakenberg and Christopher Fariss, "Dynamic Patterns of Human Rights
Practices," *Political Science Research and Methods* 2, no. 1 (2014): 1–31; Moore, "Quantitative Data in Human Rights." On the Human Rights Data Analysis Groups, see their
web site at https://hrdag.org/.

10. There are different ways to organize these debates. The Human Rights Lab at
the University of los Andes organizes the critiques into six categories: 1) lack of impact
and effectiveness; 2) lack of legitimacy; 3) problems from funding structures and resources dependence; 4) unintended effects of human rights advocacy; 5) over-
legalization; and 6) overloading. I believe that legitimacy critique is a broader umbrella
category and many of the issues raised in the Lab's categories 3–6 are related to legitimacy critiques. Rodríguez-Garavito and Luna, "A Human Rights Crisis?"

11. Moyn, "Human Rights in the Age of Inequality."

12. Samuel Moyn, *Christian Human Rights*, Intellectual History of the Modern
Age (Philadelphia: University of Pennsylvania Press, 2015); Moyn, *The Last Utopia*.

13. I thank Fernando Berdion Del Valle for his contributions to our work on individual rights and duties, from which these paragraphs are drawn: Kathryn Sikkink and Fernando Berdion Del Valle, "(Re)discovering Human Duties: Individual Responsibility in International Human Rights Law and Global Constitutions," *Minnesota Journal of International Law* 26, no. 1 (2017): 189–245.

14. On the importance for human rights of a more multipolar world, see Rodríguez-Garavito, "The Future of Human Rights."

15. James Ron and David Crow, "Who Trusts Local Human Rights Organizations? Evidence from Three World Regions," *Human Rights Quarterly* 37 (2015): 188–239.

16. Hopgood, *The Endtimes of Human Rights.*

17. William J. Dobson, *The Dictator's Learning Curve: Inside the Global Battle for Democracy* (New York: Anchor Books, 2013); Levitsky and Way, "The Myth of Democratic Recession."

18. Gerald Knaus, "Europe and Azerbaijan: The End of Shame," *Journal of Democracy* 26, no. 3 (2015): 5–18.

19. For an overview of the campaign, see the case "Protecting the Inter-American System of Human Rights," Human Rights & Governance: Case Studies, accessed December 16, 2016, http://hrcases.org/#/caso/4/1.

20. Moyn, "Human Rights and the Age of Inequality."

21. Charles Beitz also argues that human rights have broad normative reach and are not accurately described as minimal. See Beitz, "From Practice to Theory."

22. Cecilia L. Ridgeway, "Why Status Matters for Inequality," *American Sociological Review* 79, no. 1 (2014): 1–16.

23. Sen, "Freedoms and Needs," 31.

24. ESCR-Net, accessed April 10, 2017, https://www.escr-net.org/.

25. César Rodríguez-Garavito and Diana Rodríguez Franco, *Radical Deprivation on Trial: The Impact of Judicial Activism on Socioeconomic Rights in the Global South,* Comparative Constitutional Law and Policy (Cambridge: Cambridge University Press, 2015); César Rodríguez-Garavito, ed., *Business and Human Rights: Beyond the End of the Beginning* (Cambridge: Cambridge University Press, 2017); César Rodríguez-Garavito, "Beyond the Courtroom: The Impact of Judicial Activism on Socioeconomic Rights in Latin America," *Texas Law Review* 89, no. 7 (2011): 1669–98; Rodríguez-Garavito and de Sousa Santos, eds., *Law and Globalization from Below*; Rodríguez-Garavito, "The Future of Human Rights."

26. Heinz Klug, "Campaigning for Life: Building a New Transnational Solidarity in the Face of HIV/AIDS and TRIPS," in *Law and Globalization from Below: Towards a Cosmopolitan Legality,* ed. César Rodríguez-Garavito and Boaventura de Sousa Santos, Cambridge Studies in Law and Society (Cambridge: Cambridge University Press, 2005), 118–39.

27. For an overview of these issues and campaigns, see César Rodríguez-Garavito, ed., *Business and Human Rights: Beyond the End of the Beginning* (Cambridge: Cambridge University Press, 2017). Also see John Gerard Ruggie, *Just Business: Multinational Corporations and Human Rights* (New York: W. W. Norton & Co., 2013).

28. John Oliver, "*Last Week Tonight with John Oliver: Tobacco,*" YouTube video,

18:10, from a performance televised by HBO in 2015, posted by LastWeekTonight, February 15, https://www.youtube.com/watch?v=6UsHHOCH4q8.

29. We are indebted to Samuel Moyn for drawing our attention to this duty/rights issue.

30. Some efforts are already underway on these issues, such as the Financial Action Task Force and the Base Erosion and Profit Shifting (BEPS) projects at OECD.

31. Gabriel Zucman, *The Hidden Wealth of Nations: The Scourge of Tax Havens* (Chicago: University of Chicago Press, 2015).

32. "Human Rights in Tax Policy," Center for Economic and Social Rights, accessed December 18, 2016, http://www.cesr.org/section.php?id=229.

33. Raymond Offenheiser, conversation with author May 24, 2016, Boston, MA.

34. Sen, *The Idea of Justice*; Risse, *On Global Justice*.

35. Kennedy, "The International Human Rights Movement."

36. Rodríguez-Garavito, "The Future of Human Rights," 500.

37. Hafner-Burton, *Making Human Rights a Reality*.

38. See Maria Beatriz Bonna Nogueira, "The Promotion of LGBT Rights as International Human Rights Norms: Explaining Brazil's Diplomatic Leadership," *Global Governance* (unpublished manuscript, received November 12, 2016), Word file; Michelle Morais de Sa E Silva, "Conditional Cash Transfers and Improved Education Quality: A Political Search for the Policy Link," *International Journal of Educational Development* 45 (2015): 169–181.

39. Kathryn Sikkink et al., "Comprehensive Reparations Measures in Colombia: Accomplishments and Challenges" (unpublished report, submitted to Colombian government June 1, 2015), Word file).

40. On the Indian Supreme Court decision, see Jennifer Geist Rutledge, *Feeding the Future: School Lunch Programs as Global Social Policy* (New Brunswick, NJ: Rutgers University Press, 2016). On the contributions of economic and social rights campaigns in the Global South, see Rodríguez-Garavito and de Sousa Santos, eds., *Law and Globalization from Below*; César Rodríguez-Garavito, *Human Rights in Minefields: Extractive Economies, Environmental Conflicts, and Social Justice in the Global South* (Bogotá: Dejusticia, 2015), https://business-humanrights.org/en/new-book-human-rights-in-minefields-extractive-economies-environmental-conflicts-and-social-justice-in-the-global-south.

41. See Bonna Nogueira, "The Promotion of LGBT Rights as International Human Rights Norms."

42. This draws from a presentation by Yuen Foong Khong, roundtable at A Symposium on Soft Power and Manshel Lecture in Honor of Joseph S. Nye, Jr., Cambridge, MA, December 12, 2015.

43. Ideas from a response by Joseph Nye to the presentation by Yuen Foong Khong at "A Symposium on Soft Power."

44. Alastair Iain Johnston, "China and International Order. Which China? Which Order" (unpublished article, received January 6, 2017), Word file. I thank Johnston for permission to cite.

45. Harold Hongju Koh, "Foreword: On American Exceptionalism," *Stanford Law Review* 55, no. 5 (2003): 1479–1527.

46. See blog posting by Stephen Hopgood, "Fascism Rising," *openDemocracy* (blog), November 9, 2016, https://www.opendemocracy.net/openglobalrights/stephen -hopgood/fascism-rising.

47. Douglas Johnson, Alberto Mora, and Averell Schmidt, "The Strategic Costs of Torture: How 'Enhanced Interrogation' Hurt America," *Foreign Affairs* 95, no. 5 (2016): 121–132.

48. Peksen, "Does Foreign Military Intervention Help Human Rights"; Meernik, Poe, and Shaikhet, "The Use of Military Force to Promote Human Rights."

49. Andrew Stroehlein, Twitter post, November 30, 2016, 2:21am, https://twitter .com/astroehlein/status/803906671747694592. Stroehlein is the European Media Director for Human Rights Watch.

Introduction and Overview

For those whose interest is piqued by my claims about improvements in basic human well-being in the world, a number of websites feature excellent visual presentations of social, economic, and political data. In particular, see "Our World in Data," a web publication by Max Roser, an economist and media critic known for his research on global trends of living conditions and his visualizations of these trends. The brainchild of the late Hans Rosling, the website "Gapminder" presents innovative tools developed by his team and aimed at "unveiling the beauty of statistics for a fact-based world view." Rosling described the history of how this approach began in his famous Ted Talk, now found at https://www.ted.com/talks/hans _rosling_shows_the_best_stats_you_ve_ever_seen.

I'd also suggest you follow Max Roser or the Gapminder group on Twitter at @MaxCRoser and @gapminder for some rays of fact-based sunlight in a barrage of dismal news. Likewise, check out Nicholas Kristof's column, "Why 2017 May be the Best Year Ever," *New York Times*, January 21, 2017.

On conflict and war, see the Human Security Report Project website and data at http://www.hsrgroup.org/ as well as the websites for the Peace Research Institute of Oslo (PRIO) and the Department of Peace and Conflict Research at Uppsala University. These groups create a public good for the entire academic community by coding and compiling the most complete data on conflicts; see, for example, their map and chart of conflict fatalities over time at http://ucdp.uu.se/#/exploratory. Neil Halloran's animated, data-driven documentary, "The Fallen in World War II" on YouTube, found at https://www.youtube.com/results?search_query=the+fallen +of+world+war+ii+, provides a compelling visual display of the violence during World War II and the dramatic decline afterwards. For both an overview of broader trends in declining violence worldwide and a view of the psychology behind the numbers, another essential resource is Steven Pinker, *The Better Angels of Our Nature: Why Violence Has Declined* (Viking, 2011).

To further explore criticisms concerning the legitimacy and effectiveness of human rights law, institutions and movements, I suggest beginning with two publications by Amnesty International Netherlands. The first is Doutje Lettinga and Lars van Troost , eds., *Debating The Endtimes of Human Rights: Activism and Institutions in a Neo-Westphalian World* (2014), and the second Doutje Lettinga and Lars van Troost, eds., *Can Human Rights Bring Social Justice?: Twelve Essays* (2015); both available online at https://www.amnesty.nl/sites/default/files/public/can_human_rights _bring_social_justice.pdf and https://www.amnesty.nl/sites /default/files/public/debating_the_endtimes_of_human_rights .pdf. These two volumes provide an overview of critical approaches to the study of human rights as well as a commentary on those critiques by a range of academics and activists. For an exhaustive survey of critiques, see the forthcoming article by César Rodríguez-Garavito and Sean Luna, of the Human Rights Lab at the University of los Andes, "A Human Rights Crisis? Unpacking the Debate on the Future of the Human Rights Field," which can be viewed at https:// static1.squarespace.com/static/557f5fe4e4b0a17c309a0dcd /t/58a8908c29687f223ffbe21e/148744207549.

Finally, a lively way to follow debates among human rights activists and academics on a variety of issues is through the blog *Open Global Rights*, a multilingual online forum dedicated to facilitating discussion about the human rights law, institutions, and movements worldwide, at https://www.opendemocracy.net/openglobal rights. You can also follow *openDemocracy*'s blog on Twitter at @openRights_oD. Engaging in discussion and entertaining opposing viewpoints improves the quality of human rights work and I encourage interested readers to check out this community of scholars and activists.

To read more about Albert Hirschman and his idea of possibilism, I recommend any of the essays in my favorite book of his, *A Bias for Hope: Essays on Development and Latin America* (Yale University Press, 1971), which inspired the title of the book you are reading now. Jeremy Adelman's carefully researched biography of Hirschman's life and work, *Worldly Philosopher: The Odyssey of Albert O. Hirschman* (Princeton University Press, 2013) is also a joy to read. Although these works are not typically found in the canon of human rights literature, Hirschman's research provides a perspective on the world that can be enlightening to anyone trying to understand how and why change occurs, including those studying and working in the field of human rights.

The Legitimacy of Human Rights: Diverse Struggles

There is a wide selection of books and articles to choose from concerning the history of the international protection of human rights, some of which have been in print for many years, and others that are relatively new. On Latin American contributions to human rights, for example, see classics such as Johannes Morsink's *The Universal Declaration of Human Rights: Origins, Drafting, and Intent*, (University of Pennsylvania Press, 1999), especially chapters 4 and 5, as well as Mary Ann Glendon's article, "The Forgotten Crucible: The Latin American Influence on the Universal Human Rights Idea," *Harvard Human Rights Journal* 16 (2003). More recent work includes Patrick William Kelly's *Salvation in Small Steps: Latin America and the Making of Global Human Rights Politics* (Cambridge University Press, forthcoming). A discussion of a longer Latin American tradition of support for international law can be found in Arnulf Becker Lorca's *Mestizo International Law: A Global Intellectual History, 1842–1933* (Cambridge University Press, 2015), while Katherine Marino's *The Vanguard for Women's Rights: Pan-American Feminism and the Origins of Human Rights* (University of North Carolina Press, forthcoming) offers a meticulously researched discussion of Latin American contributions to women's rights as well as information on the lives of feminists like Bertha Lutz and Minerva Bernardino.

For a pure, gripping read on the origins of human rights in the immediate post-World War II period, with a subtext about the role of victims from the periphery of power, I recommend Philippe Sands, *East West Street: On the Origins of "Genocide" and "Crimes against Humanity"* (Alfred A. Knopf, 2016). For India's role in the post-World War II international order, see Manu Bhagavan, *India and the Quest for One World: The Peacemakers*, (Palgrave Macmillan, 2013).

The struggles for human rights during the Cold War have been the subject of a number of important books, including Roland

Burke's *Decolonization and the Evolution of International Human Rights* (University of Pennsylvania Press, 2010) and Steven L. B. Jensen's *The Making of International Human Rights: The 1960s, Decolonization, and the Reconstruction of Global Values* (Cambridge University Press, 2016). These carefully researched books document the myriad ways in which diplomats and activists from the Global South struggled to build the international human rights law and institutions that we often take for granted today.

The Effectiveness of Human Rights Laws, Institutions, and Movements

Unearthing the difficulties in measuring the effectiveness of international human rights law and activism required me to read from a wide range of different disciplines. A classic collection of essays edited by Daniel Kahneman, Paul Slovic, and Amos Tversky—*Judgment under Uncertainty: Heuristics and Biases* (Cambridge University Press, 1982)—sheds light on the cognitive heuristics that make it difficult for people to gauge accurately the likelihood of events. For a discussion of the unique characteristics of issues involving hidden harms, I suggest the work of my colleague Malcolm K. Sparrow, *The Character of Harms: Operational Challenges in Control* (Cambridge University Press, 2008). Ann Marie Clark and I also provide a more detailed explanation of the specific problems of human rights data in our article, "Information Effects and Human Rights Data: Is the Good News about Increased Human Rights Information Bad News for Human Rights Measures?" *Human Rights Quarterly* 35, no. 3 (2013), but for the true data mavens, the go-to article is Christopher J. Fariss, "Respect for Human Rights Has Improved over Time: Modeling the Changing Standard of Accountability," *American Political Science Review* 108, no. 2 (2014). Books on particular issues may also be of interest. On the decline of the child death penalty, for example, see Robyn Linde's *The Globalization of Childhood: The International Diffusion of Norms and Law against the Child Death Penalty* (Oxford University Press, 2016).

For those curious to know more about what works and what doesn't in the area of human rights promotion, four of my earlier books have taken up this issue. See *Activists beyond Borders: Advo-*

cacy Networks in International Politics (Cornell University Press, 1998), which I co-authored with Margaret Keck and in which we suggest a useful way of thinking about what we mean by effectiveness with respect to human rights movements. Next, in two different books from Cambridge University Press—*The Power of Human Rights: International Norms and Domestic Change* (1999) and *The Persistent Power of Human Rights: From Commitment to Compliance* (2013)—I worked with co-editors Thomas Risse and Stephen Ropp as well as with a group of talented scholars to examine human rights effectiveness around the world. Finally, in *The Justice Cascade: How Human Rights Prosecutions are Changing World Politics* (W. W. Norton & Co., 2011), I summarize research conducted with Hun Joon Kim about the effectiveness of human rights prosecutions in contributing to improvements in core physical integrity rights. I would also suggest Beth Simmons's 2009 book, *Mobilizing for Human Rights: International Law in Domestic Politics* (Cambridge University Press) as the definitive work on the effectiveness of international human rights law on state behavior, a must-read for anyone interested in this topic.

In the best new work about the perceptions of human rights work in the Global South, *Taking Root: Human Rights and Public Opinion in the Global South* (Oxford University Press, 2017), James Ron, Shannon Golden, David Crow, and Archana Pandya use extensive new survey research to demonstrate that public opinion about human rights movements and policies in the developing world is surprisingly positive. The New Tactics in Human Rights website (https://www.newtactics.org/) provides a survey of a wide range of tactics used by human rights movements worldwide and some discussion on the effectiveness of those tactics.

The classic and enduring work on causes of repression is Steven C. Poe, C. Neal Tate, and Linda Camp Keith, "Repression of the Human Right to Personal Integrity Revisited: A Global Cross-National Study Covering the Years 1976–1993," *International Studies Quarterly* (1999). Useful and updated summaries of this literature can be found in Emilie M. Hafner-Burton's *Making Human Rights a Reality* (Princeton University Press, 2013). Eric D. Weitz's *A Century of Genocide: Utopias of Race and Nation* (Princeton University Press, 2003), draws attention to the importance of particular ideologies in contributing to genocide and might be suitably paired with Sands' *East West Street*, mentioned in the second section of these suggestions.

Making Human Rights Work in the Twenty-First Century

My concern about the future of human rights is shared by many other scholars; recent work provides an urgent and compelling dialogue on the subject. Geoff Dancy and Christopher Fariss present a promising new approach in "Rescuing Human Rights Law from International Legalism and its Critics," *Human Rights Quarterly* 39, no. 1 (2017). *Human Rights Futures*, edited by Stephen Hopgood, Jack Snyder and Leslie Vinjamuri (Cambridge University Press, 2017), brings together a group of scholars from diverse theoretical traditions to address empirical and normative debates concerning the future of human rights. For a view incorporating a perspective from the Global South, see César Rodríguez-Garavito, "The Future of Human Rights: From Gatekeeping to Symbiosis," *Sur International Journal on Human Rights* 11, no. 20 (2014). Indeed, for anyone wishing to understand diverse human rights views, including many voices from the Global South, it is worth reading articles from any issue of the journal *Sur* and, in particular, a selection of interviews and articles in the tenth anniversary commemorative issue of the journal entitled "Human Rights in Motion." The collection can be found on the Conectas website in English, Spanish, and Portuguese. The English version is at http://www.conectas.org/Arquivos/edicao/pdfs/edicao-2015219104510-65051631.pdf. César Rodríguez-Garavito and Diana Rodríguez Franco also give an overview of recent campaigns in the Global South for economic and social rights in *Radical Deprivation on Trial: The Impact of Judicial Activism on Socioeconomic Rights in the Global South*, Comparative Constitutional Law and Policy (Cambridge University Press, 2015).

Finally, to read more about the strategic vision of community organizer Saul Alinksy, whose aphorism about the need for anger, hope, and the belief that you can make a difference provided a guiding metaphor for this book, see his *Rules for Radicals: A Practical Primer for Realistic Radicals* (Vintage Books, 1971).

Human Rights and Crimes against Humanity

ERIC D. WEITZ, *SERIES EDITOR*